GEORGE SEFERIS

COLLECTED POEMS (1924-1955)

GEORGE SEFERIS

COLLECTED POEMS

1924·1955

TRANSLATED, EDITED, AND INTRODUCED BY

EDMUND KEELEY

AND

PHILIP SHERRARD

PRINCETON, NEW JERSEY

PRINCETON UNIVERSITY PRESS · MCMLXVII

L.C. Card: 65-17142

Printed in the United States of America
By Princeton University Press,
Princeton, New Jersey

Publication of this book has been aided by
the Whitney Darrow Publication Reserve Fund
of Princeton University Press

The frontispiece by Yannis Moralis is part of a larger painting.
It appeared, along with nine other paintings by Mr. Moralis, in the
Greek edition of the collected poems of George Seferis, published
in Athens in 1965 by Icaros.

FOREWORD

THE poetry of George Seferis, whatever relation it may have to the literature of other countries, stems first of all from a tradition that is eminently Greek. This means that it not only shares in the modern revival which has produced, during the last hundred and fifty years or so, such distinguished Greek poets as Solomos, Kalvos, Palamas, Sikelianos, and Cavafy; it also proceeds, like most of the poetry that belongs to this revival, from earlier sources. One of these is the long tradition of Greek ballads and folk songs. Both the spirit of Greek folk literature and its dominant form, the "dekapentasyllavos,"[1] can be traced back directly at least to the Byzantine period, and both have been consistently influential since that time, though the form has naturally been modified in keeping with new needs. Seferis's early poem, "Erotikos Logos" (1930), is a major example of such modification: a successful attempt to adapt the dekapentasyllavos line to the expression of a contemporary sensibility. Another area of the post-medieval poetic tradition that has remained equally influential is the more complex and sophisticated literature which developed on the island of Crete during the sixteenth and seventeenth centuries. The dramatic literature of Crete includes plays such as *Abraham's Sacrifice*, a religious work, and the *Erophile*, a bloodthirsty tragedy in which all the main characters are killed or kill themselves; but the masterpiece of this more complex (and, in contrast with the folk ballads, more introspective) tradition is the epic romance, the *Erotokritos*, by Vitzentzos Kornaros, a work of 10,052 verses telling of the love of Aretousa, daughter of the king of Athens, and the valiant Erotokritos, son of one of the leading court families.

[1] A line of fifteen syllables, with a caesura after the eighth syllable and two main accents, one on the sixth or eighth syllable and one on the fourteenth.

This epic became immensely popular throughout the Greek world, great sections—and sometimes even the whole of it—being recited by heart as though an ordinary folk epic: the kind of recitation that haunts Seferis's persona in "Upon a Foreign Verse," where he speaks of

> . . . certain old sailors of my childhood who, leaning on their nets with winter coming on and the wind angering
> used to recite, with tears in their eyes, the song of Erotokritos;
> it was then I would shudder in my sleep at the unjust fate of Aretousa descending the marble stairs.

Seferis has written the best Greek critical commentary on the *Erotokritos*,[2] and its influence, as a monument to the poetic possibilities of the demotic Greek language,[3] is apparent from the use he makes of it in his "Erotikos Logos," where he introduces actual phrases from the epic into the text of his poem in order to establish an analogy between his diction and that of another vital, relevant moment in his nation's literary past.

Cretan literature of the sixteenth and seventeenth centuries and the folk tradition are, then, among the more important local sources of Seferis's art, particularly because of their creative exploitation of the Greek language; at the same time, however, the poetry of Seferis and that of his immediate predecessors differs in an important respect from the poetry of both these literatures: in the use made of images, characters, and myths that derive from ancient

[2] Included in Δοκιμές (see Bibliographical Note).

[3] Demotic Greek, as opposed to purist Greek (known as "katharevousa") is now the literary language of modern Greece, though it was not generally accepted as such until this century.

Greece. Whether it is Palamas contrasting the "people of relics"—who reign among the temples and olive groves of the Attic landscape—with the modern crowd crawling along sluggishly, like a caterpillar over a white flower (in *Life Immovable*); or Cavafy evoking—perhaps ironically, perhaps erotically—some scene out of his poetic world of Hellenistic Alexandria; or Sikelianos endeavoring to resurrect the whole pantheon of the ancient gods and to be a hierophant to their mysteries; or Seferis searching for the archaic king of Asine—the substantial man who fought with heroes—and finding only the unsubstantial void of contemporary existence; whichever it is, the ancient world in all its aspects preoccupies the imagination of these poets constantly. This preoccupation is only natural in a country which, like Greece, remains full of the physical remnants of antiquity; everywhere reminders of the ancient past leap to the eye and stimulate the mind:

> Scattered drums of a Doric column
> Razed to the ground
> By unexpected earthquakes

as Sikelianos puts it in *The Conscience of Personal Creativeness*, or to quote Seferis himself: "fragments of a life which was once complete, disturbing fragments, close to us, ours for one moment, and then mysterious and unapproachable as the lines of a stone licked smooth by the wave or of a shell in the sea's depths."[4] This means that the Greek poet who draws on classical mythology in shaping the drama of his verse enjoys a large advantage over his similarly disposed contemporaries in England or America: he can evoke characters and settings that have mythological overtones with less danger of being merely literary in doing so, with less

[4] From *Delphi* (see Bibliographical Note).

danger of arbitrarily imposing gods and heroes on an alien landscape—Tiresias on the Thames or Prometheus in Pennsylvania, for example—since his own natural landscape is that to which these gods and heroes themselves once belonged and in which they still confront the mind's eye plausibly.

Seferis, like most other poets of modern Greece, has fully exploited this advantage. His secret (in addition to his advantage) is that he always offers an appropriate setting—a poetically realistic setting—before he allows any legendary figures to appear on his stage; before he attempts to carry the reader to the level of myth, he earns his sympathy and belief by convincingly representing the present reality sustaining his myth—and it is a contemporary, Greek reality always. In this way the myth comes to life fully, the ancient and modern worlds meet in a metaphor without strain or contrivance as we find the legendary figures moving anachronistically onto the contemporary stage that the poet has set before our eyes. The anachronism is, of course, very much to the point: in one sense, what was then is now, but in another sense, what is now was then; the modern voyager, for instance, shares something of Odysseus's fate, while Odysseus finds a symbolic representation of his fate in the modern setting that the poet has him confront: the deserted, arid, repetitious land and the calm, embittering sea so frequently encountered in Seferis's poetry are symbolic of Odysseus's frustrating voyage, of his failure to realize the island paradise he longs for. And his fate is that of every wanderer seeking a final harbor, a spiritual fulfillment, that he can't seem to reach. The frustrations of the wanderer are perennial; as Seferis puts it in an illuminating commentary on the role of mythic characters in his verse:

". . . men of inconstancy, of wanderings and of wars, though they differ and may change in terms of greatness and value . . . always move among the same monsters and the same longings. So we keep the symbols and the names that the myth has brought down to us, realizing as we do so that the typical characters have changed in keeping with the passing of time and the different conditions of our world—which are none other than the conditions of everyone who seeks expression."[5]

The mythology of the ancient world thus plays a crucial role in Seferis, but it would be a mistake to regard this source in isolation, since all the various threads of the Greek tradition that we have mentioned here—folk, literary, and mythic—are tightly woven together in his work; one senses really the whole of the Greek past, as it is represented in poetry from the age of Homer down to the contemporary period, behind Seferis's maturest verse, giving it overtones and undertones sometimes too subtle for the non-Greek ear to catch (especially when they have to be caught in a language foreign to the text). But even as one does catch the sound of a richly traditional voice, a voice learned in the best poetry of previous ages, one is also aware that the voice is very much of the present age and that the poet's sensibility couldn't be farther from that of an antiquarian delving nostalgically into the past in order to escape from the bewilderments and afflictions of modern life: the past is always there to shape and illuminate an image of the present. And if this image seems inevitably to have its sorrow—that "*καημός της Ρωμιοσύνης*" which is so specifically Greek that Seferis rightly regards any translation of the phrase a distortion—one can take it simply for an index of the

[5] From "*"Ενα γράμμα γιὰ τὴν* ⟨Κίχλη⟩" [A Letter on "*Thrush*"], *'Αγγλο-ελληνικὴ 'Επιθεώρηση*, IV (July-August 1950), 501-506.

image's veracity, since a mature consciousness in the Greek world cannot but be aware of how much this world has achieved only to find everything suddenly ruined by the "war, destruction, exile" of constantly unpropitious times, as Seferis's persona puts it in "*Thrush*"—aware of how much and how little individual creative effort signifies in a world so vulnerable. It is the depth of this awareness, so often incomprehensible to nations with shorter and less tragic histories or with more superficial memories, that serves him for protection against those too-easily won positions, that too-readily assumed despair, from which much modern poetry issues.

If Seferis's sensibility has always been too specifically Greek to allow the easy sharing of what he himself has called "the 'Waste Land' feeling" that was common to Anglo-American and European poets after World War I,[6] his expression of this sensibility has been influenced by the example of several poets outside the Greek tradition. There is no doubt, for instance, that in the early phase of his career Seferis was keenly interested in the tonal and stylistic experiments of his French contemporaries, and, indeed, often seemed to be striving for a "pure" poetry in the manner of Valéry. With the appearance of *Mythistorema* in 1935, a distinct change in style became evident, in part the consequence of the poet's sympathetic reading of Eliot and Pound during the early thirties and in part the last phase of a personal stylistic catharsis that had already begun to show in *The Cistern* (1932). With *Mythistorema,* Seferis abandoned the relatively formal mode of his earlier volumes in favor of the much freer and more natural mode that is characteristic of all

6 In "Letter to a Foreign Friend" (included in Rex Warner's translation of Seferis's essays, *On the Greek Style*; see Bibliographical Note).

his mature poetry,[7] where we inevitably find a precisely controlled style, undecorated by embellishment, the coloring always primary and the imagery sparse. In this mature poetry Seferis also combines the modes of everyday speech with the forms and rhythms of traditional usage in a way that creates the effect of both density and economy—an effect almost impossible to reproduce in English, however carefully one may attempt to duplicate the particular character of the poet's style.

But if one discerns the influence of foreign sources in Seferis's stylistic development, one also discerns that the substance of his poetry has remained consistently individual since the start: in the finest poems of each of his volumes (often those least accessible to the Western reader because the least mythological or "classicist"), there is always that tragic sense of life which comes most forcefully out of a direct, personal experience of history—out of a poet *engagé* responding to what he has known and felt of human suffering, or at least what he has clearly seen of it at close quarters. This is not merely to repeat the frequently suggested relationship, for example, between Seferis's poetic representation of exile and his actual exile after the loss of his childhood home in the Asia Minor disaster of 1922 and during his many years away from Greece in his country's diplomatic service, valid though this relationship may be in some respects; more important, perhaps, than his capacity to make the personal poetic in this way is his capacity to capture the metaphoric significance of some event that has moved him, his capacity to transform a personal experience or insight into a metaphor that defines the

[7] We have chosen to open this collected edition with the poem in which Seferis's mature voice is first heard rather than with the poems of his less characteristic—and less translatable—early phase (see note to "Rhymed Poems," p. 487).

character of our times: for example, the metaphor of that "presentable and quiet" man who walks along weeping in "Narration," the "instrument of a boundless pain /that's finally lost all significance"; or the couple at the end of "The Last Day" who go home to turn on the light because they are sick of walking in the dusk; or the messengers in "Our Sun" who arrive, dirty and breathless, to die with only one intelligible sentence on their lips: "We don't have time" (all of these poems written, incidentally, either just before or just after the outbreak of World War II in Europe). These are the kind of metaphors that project Seferis's vision beyond any strictly local or strictly personal history and that bring to the mind's eye images as definitive, as universal, as any offered by the poetry of Seferis's contemporaries in Europe and America.

There are also moments when an event that would seem to be only of local or personal significance becomes the occasion for a simple statement of truth about the modern experience—a statement more direct, and sometimes more precise, than the poet's metaphoric mode allows: the second stanza of "The Last Stop" (p. 305), written on the eve of Seferis's return to Greece at the end of World War II, is an occasion of this kind, as is the conclusion of "Helen" (pp. 53ff.), written during the Cyprus conflict of the early 1950's. It is moments such as these, when the poet describes the corruption of war in a voice made wise and simple by the clearest vision, that raise his poems about specific historical events far above the level of political comment or propaganda and that show him to have sustained—through his poems about World War II and his volume dedicated to the people of Cyprus—the same universalizing sensibility that has shaped his image of contemporary history since *Mythistorema* and several earlier poems that anticipate it.

The distinguishing attribute of Seferis's genius—one that he shares with Yeats and Eliot—has always been his ability to make out of a local politics, out of a personal history or mythology, some sort of general statement or metaphor; his long Odyssean voyage on rotten timbers to those islands ever slightly out of reach has the same force of definitive, general insight that we find in Yeats's voyage to Byzantium or Eliot's journey over desert country to a fragmentary salvation. Seferis's politics are never simply the restricted politics of a nationalist—though he is very much a "national" poet in his choice of themes, and though his vision is often rendered in those terms that best characterize his nation: its landscape, its literature, its historical and mythic past. His politics are those of the poet with an especially acute sensitivity to the larger implications of contemporary history. Though he is preoccupied with his tradition as few other poets of the same generation are with theirs, and though he has long been engaged, directly and actively, in the immediate political aspirations of his nation, his value as a poet lies in what he has made of this preoccupation and this engagement in fashioning a broad poetic vision—in offering insights that carry with them the weight of universal truths and that thus serve to reveal the deeper meaning of our times. This collected edition will, it is hoped, both illustrate the full range of Seferis's vision and demonstrate how consistently penetrating his insights have remained throughout his mature years.

Katounia, Limni, Euboea, 1966

E. K.
P. S.

OTHER BOOKS BY THE TRANSLATORS:

EDMUND KEELEY

THE LIBATION

SIX POETS OF MODERN GREECE
(WITH PHILIP SHERRARD)

THE GOLD-HATTED LOVER

VASSILIS VASSILIKOS: THE PLANT, THE WELL, THE ANGEL
(WITH MARY KEELEY)

PHILIP SHERRARD

THE MARBLE THRESHING FLOOR

THE GREEK EAST AND THE LATIN WEST

ATHOS, THE MOUNTAIN OF SILENCE

SIX POETS OF MODERN GREECE
(WITH EDMUND KEELEY)

THE PURSUIT OF GREECE
(EDITOR)

CONSTANTINOPLE: ICONOGRAPHY OF A SACRED CITY

BYZANTIUM

ACKNOWLEDGMENTS

OUR work on this collected edition has been facilitated throughout by Mr. Seferis's generous interest and cooperation, for which we are most grateful. We would like to thank the firm of Ikaros, Athens, publishers of the Greek text of Seferis's poems, for allowing us to print their text *en face* and for allowing us to include the frontispiece by Yiannis Moralis, with the painter's permission. We are grateful to Thames and Hudson Ltd., London, and Alfred A. Knopf, Inc., New York, for granting us their permission to reproduce, in revised versions, those poems by Seferis which are included in our anthology *Six Poets of Modern Greece* and which are reprinted in the Penguin Ltd. (England) edition, *Four Greek Poets*. Translations from the present volume were originally published in *Poetry* (Chicago), *Shenandoah, Virginia Quarterly Review, The Times Literary Supplement, Encounter, The Charioteer*, and *Quarterly Review of Literature*. Parts of the Foreword first appeared in *The Kenyon Review, Book Week*, and *The Charioteer*.

CONTENTS

CONTENTS

CONTENTS

CONTENTS

ΜΥΘΙΣΤΟΡΗΜΑ

Si j'ai du goût, ce n'est guères
Que pour la terre et les pierres.

ARTHUR RIMBAUD

MYTHISTOREMA*

Si j'ai du goût, ce n'est guères
Que pour la terre et les pierres.

ARTHUR RIMBAUD*

Α΄

Τὸν ἄγγελο
τὸν περιμέναμε προσηλωμένοι τρία χρόνια
κοιτάζοντας πολὺ κοντὰ
τὰ πεῦκα τὸ γιαλὸ καὶ τ' ἄστρα.
Σμίγοντας τὴν κόψη τ' ἀλετριοῦ ἢ τοῦ καραβιοῦ τὴν καρένα
ψάχναμε νὰ βροῦμε πάλι τὸ πρῶτο σπέρμα
γιὰ νὰ ξαναρχίσει τὸ πανάρχαιο δρᾶμα.

Γυρίσαμε στὰ σπίτια μας τσακισμένοι
μ' ἀνήμπορα μέλη, μὲ τὸ στόμα ρημαγμένο
ἀπὸ τὴ γέψη τῆς σκουριᾶς καὶ τῆς ἁρμύρας.
Ὅταν ξυπνήσαμε ταξιδέψαμε κατὰ τὸ βοριά, ξένοι
βυθισμένοι μέσα σὲ καταχνιὲς ἀπὸ τ' ἄσπιλα φτερὰ τῶν
κύκνων ποὺ μᾶς πληγώναν.
Τὶς χειμωνιάτικες νύχτες μᾶς τρέλαινε ὁ δυνατὸς ἀγέρας
τῆς ἀνατολῆς
τὰ καλοκαίρια χανόμασταν μέσα στὴν ἀγωνία τῆς μέρας
ποὺ δὲ μποροῦσε νὰ ξεψυχήσει.

Φέραμε πίσω
αὐτὰ τ' ἀνάγλυφα μιᾶς τέχνης ταπεινῆς.

1

Three years
we waited intently for the herald
closely watching
the pines the shore and the stars.
One with the plough's blade or the keel of the ship,
we were searching to rediscover the first seed
so that the ancient drama could begin again.

We returned to our homes broken,
limbs incapable, mouths cracked
by the taste of rust and brine.
When we woke we travelled towards the north, strangers
plunged into mists by the spotless wings of swans that
 wounded us.
On winter nights the strong wind from the east maddened
 us,
in the summers we were lost in the agony of the day that
 couldn't die.

We brought back
these carved reliefs of a humble art.

B′

'Ακόμη ἕνα πηγάδι μέσα σὲ μιὰ σπηλιά.
Ἄλλοτε μᾶς εἴταν εὔκολο ν' ἀντλήσουμε εἴδωλα καὶ στο-
    λίδια
γιὰ νὰ χαροῦν οἱ φίλοι ποὺ μᾶς ἔμεναν ἀκόμη πιστοί.

Ἔσπασαν τὰ σκοινιά· μονάχα οἱ χαρακιὲς στοῦ πηγαδιοῦ
    τὸ στόμα
μᾶς θυμίζουν τὴν περασμένη μας εὐτυχία:
τὰ δάχτυλα στὸ φιλιατρό, καθὼς ἔλεγε ὁ ποιητής.
Τὰ δάχτυλα νοιώθουν τὴ δροσιὰ τῆς πέτρας λίγο
κι' ἡ θέρμη τοῦ κορμιοῦ τὴν κυριεύει
κι' ἡ σπηλιὰ παίζει τὴν ψυχή της καὶ τὴ χάνει
κάθε στιγμή, γεμάτη σιωπή, χωρὶς μιὰ στάλα.

2

Still another well inside a cave.
It used to be easy for us to draw up idols and ornaments
to please those friends who still remained loyal to us.

The ropes have broken; only the grooves on the well's lip
remind us of our past happiness:
the fingers on the rim, as the poet put it.*
The fingers feel the coolness of the stone a little,
then the body's fever prevails over it
and the cave stakes its soul and loses it
every moment, full of silence, without a drop of water.

* The asterisks refer to notes which appear on pages 479 to 488.

Γ′

Μέμνησο λουτρῶν οἷς ἐνοσφίσθης

Ξύπνησα μὲ τὸ μαρμάρινο τοῦτο κεφάλι στὰ χέρια
πού μοῦ ἐξαντλεῖ τοὺς ἀγκῶνες καὶ δὲν ξέρω ποῦ νὰ
τ' ἀκουμπήσω.
Ἔπεφτε στὸ ὄνειρο καθὼς ἔβγαινα ἀπὸ τὸ ὄνειρο
ἔτσι ἑνώθηκε ἡ ζωή μας καὶ θὰ εἶναι πολὺ δύσκολο νὰ
ξαναχωρίσει.

Κοιτάζω τὰ μάτια· μήτε ἀνοιχτὰ μήτε κλειστὰ
μιλῶ στὸ στόμα πού ὅλο γυρεύει νὰ μιλήσει
κρατῶ τὰ μάγουλα πού ξεπέρασαν τὸ δέρμα.
Δὲν ἔχω ἄλλη δύναμη·

τὰ χέρια μου χάνουνται καὶ μὲ πλησιάζουν
ἀκρωτηριασμένα.

3

Remember the baths where
*you were murdered**

I woke with this marble head in my hands;
it exhausts my elbows and I don't know where to put it
down.
It was falling into the dream as I was coming out of the
dream
so our life became one and it will be very difficult for it
to separate again.

I look at the eyes: neither open nor closed
I speak to the mouth which keeps trying to speak
I hold the cheeks which have broken through the skin
I haven't got any more strength.

My hands disappear and come toward me
mutilated.

Δ΄

Ἀργοναῦτες

Καὶ ψυχὴ
εἰ μέλλει γνώσεσθαι αὐτὴν
εἰς ψυχὴν
αὐτῇ βλεπτέον:
τὸν ξένο καὶ τὸν ἐχθρὸ τὸν εἴδαμε στὸν καθρέφτη.

Εἴτανε καλὰ παιδιὰ οἱ συντρόφοι, δὲ φωνάζαν
οὔτε ἀπὸ τὸν κάματο οὔτε ἀπὸ τὴ δίψα οὔτε ἀπὸ τὴν πα-
γωνιά,
εἴχανε τὸ φέρσιμο τῶν δέντρων καὶ τῶν κυμάτων
ποὺ δέχουνται τὸν ἄνεμο καὶ τὴ βροχὴ
δέχουνται τὴ νύχτα καὶ τὸν ἥλιο
χωρὶς ν' ἀλλάζουν μέσα στὴν ἀλλαγή.
Εἴτανε καλὰ παιδιά, μέρες ὁλόκληρες
ἵδρωναν στὸ κουπὶ μὲ χαμηλωμένα μάτια
ἀνασαίνοντας μὲ ρυθμὸ
καὶ τὸ αἷμα τους κοκκίνιζε ἕνα δέρμα ὑποταγμένο.
Κάποτε τραγούδησαν, μὲ χαμηλωμένα μάτια
ὅταν περάσαμε τὸ ἐρημόνησο μὲ τὶς ἀραποσυκιὲς
κατὰ τὴ δύση, πέρα ἀπὸ τὸν κάβο τῶν σκύλων
ποὺ γαυγίζουν.
Εἰ μέλλει γνώσεσθαι αὐτήν, ἔλεγαν
εἰς ψυχὴν βλεπτέον, ἔλεγαν
καὶ τὰ κουπιὰ χτυποῦσαν τὸ χρυσάφι τοῦ πελάγου

4

Argonauts

And if the soul
is to know itself
it must look
into a soul:*
the stranger and enemy, we've seen him in the mirror.

The companions were good men, they never complained
about the work or the thirst or the frost,
they had the bearing of trees and waves
that accept the wind and the rain
accept the night and the sun
without changing in the midst of change.
They were good men, whole days
they sweated at the oars with lowered eyes
breathing in rhythm
and their blood reddened a submissive skin.
Sometimes they sang, with lowered eyes
as we were passing the dry island with the Barbary figs
to the west, beyond the cape
of the barking dogs.
If it is to know itself, they said
it must look into a soul, they said
and the oars struck the sea's gold

μέσα στὸ ἡλιόγερμα.
Περάσαμε κάβους πολλοὺς πολλὰ νησιὰ τὴ θάλασσα
ποὺ φέρνει τὴν ἄλλη θάλασσα, γλάρους καὶ φῶκιες.
Δυστυχισμένες γυναῖκες κάποτε μὲ ὀλολυγμοὺς
κλαίγανε τὰ χαμένα τους παιδιὰ
κι᾽ ἄλλες ἀγριεμένες γύρευαν τὸ Μεγαλέξαντρο
καὶ δόξες βυθισμένες στὰ βάθη τῆς Ἀσίας.
Ἀράξαμε σ᾽ ἀκρογιαλιὲς γεμάτες ἀρώματα νυχτερινὰ
μὲ κελαϊδίσματα πουλιῶν, νερὰ ποὺ ἀφήνανε στὰ χέρια
τὴ μνήμη μιᾶς μεγάλης εὐτυχίας.
Μὰ δὲν τελειώναν τὰ ταξίδια.
Οἱ ψυχές τους ἔγιναν ἕνα μὲ τὰ κουπιὰ καὶ τοὺς σκαρμοὺς
μὲ τὸ σοβαρὸ πρόσωπο τῆς πλώρης
μὲ τ᾽ αὐλάκι τοῦ τιμονιοῦ
μὲ τὸ νερὸ ποὺ ἔσπαζε τὴ μορφή τους.
Οἱ σύντροφοι τέλειωσαν μὲ τὴ σειρά,
μὲ χαμηλωμένα μάτια. Τὰ κουπιά τους
δείχνουν τὸ μέρος ποὺ κοιμοῦνται στ᾽ ἀκρογιάλι.

Κανεὶς δὲν τοὺς θυμᾶται. Δικαιοσύνη.

in the sunset.
We passed many capes many islands the sea
leading to another sea, gulls and seals.
Sometimes unfortunate women wept
lamenting their lost children
and others raging sought Alexander the Great
and glories buried in the depths of Asia.
We moored on shores full of night-scents
with the singing of birds, waters that left on the hands
the memory of great happiness.
But the voyages did not end.
Their souls became one with the oars and the oarlocks
with the solemn face of the prow
with the rudder's wake
with the water that shattered their image.
The companions died in turn,
with lowered eyes. Their oars
mark the place where they sleep on the shore.*

No one remembers them. Justice.

Ε′

Δὲν τοὺς γνωρίσαμε

εἴταν ἡ ἐλπίδα στὸ βάθος ποὺ ἔλεγε
πὼς τοὺς εἴχαμε γνωρίσει ἀπὸ μικρὰ παιδιά.
Τοὺς εἴδαμε ἴσως δυὸ φορὲς κι᾿ ἔπειτα πήραν τὰ καράβια·
φορτία κάρβουνο, φορτία γεννήματα, κι᾿ οἱ φίλοι μας
χαμένοι πίσω ἀπὸ τὸν ὠκεανὸ παντοτινά.
Ἡ αὐγὴ μᾶς βρίσκει πλάι στὴν κουρασμένη λάμπα
νὰ γράφουμε ἀδέξια καὶ μὲ προσπάθεια στὸ χαρτὶ
πλεούμενα γοργόνες ἢ κοχύλια·
τὸ ἀπόβραδο κατεβαίνουμε στὸ ποτάμι
γιατὶ μᾶς δείχνει τὸ δρόμο πρὸς τὴ θάλασσα,
καὶ περνοῦμε τὶς νύχτες σὲ ὑπόγεια ποὺ μυρίζουν κατράμι.

Οἱ φίλοι μας ἔφυγαν

ἴσως νὰ μὴν τοὺς εἴδαμε ποτές, ἴσως
νὰ τοὺς συναπαντήσαμε ὅταν ἀκόμη ὁ ὕπνος
μᾶς ἔφερνε πολὺ κοντὰ στὸ κῦμα ποὺ ἀνασαίνει
ἴσως νὰ τοὺς γυρεύουμε γιατὶ γυρεύουμε τὴν ἄλλη ζωή,
πέρα ἀπὸ τ᾿ ἀγάλματα.

5

We didn't know them

it was hope deep down that said

we'd known them since early childhood.

We saw them perhaps twice and then they took to the ships;

cargoes of coal, cargoes of grain, and our friends

lost beyond the ocean forever.

Dawn finds us beside the tired lamp

drawing on paper, awkwardly, with effort,

ships mermaids or sea-shells;

at dusk we go down to the river

because it shows us the way to the sea;

and we spend the nights in cellars that smell of tar.

Our friends have left us

perhaps we never saw them, perhaps

we met them when sleep

still brought us close to the breathing wave

perhaps we search for them because we search for the other life

beyond the statues.

ϛ'

Μ. Ρ.

Τὸ περιβόλι μὲ τὰ συντριβάνια του στὴ βροχὴ
θὰ τὸ βλέπεις μόνο ἀπὸ τὸ χαμηλὸ παράθυρο
πίσω ἀπὸ τὸ θολὸ τζάμι. Ἡ κάμαρά σου
θὰ φωτίζεται μόνο ἀπὸ τὴ φλόγα τοῦ τζακιοῦ
καὶ κάποτε, στὶς μακρινὲς ἀστραπὲς θὰ φαίνουνται
οἱ ρυτίδες τοῦ μετώπου σου, παλιέ μου Φίλε.

Τὸ περιβόλι μὲ τὰ συντριβάνια ποὺ εἶταν στὸ χέρι σου
ρυθμὸς τῆς ἄλλης ζωῆς, ἔξω ἀπὸ τὰ σπασμένα
μάρμαρα καὶ τὶς κολόνες τὶς τραγικὲς
κι' ἕνας χορὸς μέσα στὶς πικροδάφνες
κοντὰ στὰ καινούργια λατομεῖα,
ἕνα γυαλὶ θαμπὸ θὰ τό 'χει κόψει ἀπὸ τὶς ὧρες σου.
Δὲ θ' ἀνασάνεις· τὸ χῶμα κι' ὁ χυμὸς τῶν δέντρων
θὰ ὁρμοῦν ἀπὸ τὴ μνήμη σου γιὰ νὰ χτυπήσουν
πάνω στὸ τζάμι αὐτὸ ποὺ τὸ χτυπᾶ ἡ βροχὴ
ἀπὸ τὸν ἔξω κόσμο.

6

*M. R.**

The garden with its fountains in the rain:
you will see it only from the low window
behind clouded glass. Your room
will be lit only by the flames from the fireplace
and sometimes the distant lightning will reveal
the wrinkles on your forehead, my old Friend.

The garden with the fountains that in your hands
was a rhythm of the other life, beyond the broken
statues and the tragic columns
and a dance among the oleanders
beside the new quarries,
misty glass will have cut off from your days.
You won't breathe; earth and the sap of the trees
will spring from your memory to strike
this window struck by the rain
from the outside world.

Z′

Νοτιὰς

Τὸ πέλαγο σμίγει κατὰ τὴ δύση μιὰ βουνοσειρά.
Ζερβά μας ὁ νοτιὰς φυσάει καὶ μᾶς τρελαίνει,
αὐτὸς ὁ ἀγέρας ποὺ γυμνώνει τὰ κόκκαλα ἀπ' τὴ σάρκα.
Τὸ σπίτι μας μέσα στὰ πεῦκα καὶ στὶς χαρουπιές.
Μεγάλα παράθυρα. Μεγάλα τραπέζια
γιὰ νὰ γράφουμε τὰ γράμματα ποὺ σοῦ γράφουμε
τόσους μῆνες καὶ τὰ ρίχνουμε
μέσα στὸν ἀποχωρισμὸ γιὰ νὰ γεμίσει.

Ἄστρο τῆς αὐγῆς, ὅταν χαμήλωνες τὰ μάτια
οἱ ὧρες μας εἶταν πιὸ γλυκειὲς ἀπὸ τὸ λάδι
πάνω στὴν πληγή, πιὸ πρόσχαρες ἀπὸ τὸ κρύο νερὸ
στὸν οὐρανίσκο, πιὸ γαλήνιες ἀπὸ τὰ φτερὰ τοῦ κύκνου.
Κρατοῦσες τὴ ζωή μας στὴν παλάμη σου.
Ὕστερα ἀπ' τὸ πικρὸ ψωμὶ τῆς ξενιτειᾶς
τὴ νύχτα ἂν μείνουμε μπροστὰ στὸν ἄσπρο τοῖχο
ἡ φωνή σου μᾶς πλησιάζει σὰν ἔλπιση φωτιᾶς
καὶ πάλι αὐτὸς ὁ ἀγέρας ἀκονίζει
πάνω στὰ νεῦρα μας ἕνα ξυράφι.

Σοῦ γράφουμε ὁ καθένας τὰ ἴδια πράματα
καὶ σωπαίνει ὁ καθένας μπρὸς στὸν ἄλλον
κοιτάζοντας, ὁ καθένας, τὸν ἴδιο κόσμο χωριστὰ
τὸ φῶς καὶ τὸ σκοτάδι στὴ βουνοσειρὰ

7

South Wind

Westward the sea merges with a mountain range.
On our left the south wind blows and drives us mad,
the kind of wind that strips bones of their flesh.
Our house among pines and carobs.
Large windows. Large tables
for writing you the letters we've been writing
so many months now, dropping them
into the gap of our separation to fill it up.

Star of dawn, when you lowered your eyes
our hours were sweeter than oil
on a wound, more joyful than cold water
to the palate, more peaceful than a swan's wings.
You held our life in the palm of your hand.
After the bitter bread of exile,
at night if we remain in front of the white wall,
your voice approaches us like the hope of fire;
and again this wind hones
a razor against our nerves.

Each of us writes you the same thing
and each falls silent in the other's presence,
watching, each of us, the same world separately
the light and darkness on the mountain range

κι' ἐσένα.
Ποιὸς θὰ σηκώσει τὴ θλίψη τούτη ἀπ' τὴν καρδιά μας;
Χτὲς βράδι μιὰ νεροποντὴ καὶ σήμερα
βαραίνει πάλι ὁ σκεπασμένος οὐρανός. Οἱ στοχασμοί μας
σὰν τὶς πευκοβελόνες τῆς χτεσινῆς νεροποντῆς
στὴν πόρτα τοῦ σπιτιοῦ μας μαζεμένοι κι' ἄχρηστοι
θέλουν νὰ χτίσουν ἕναν πύργο ποὺ γκρεμίζει.

Μέσα σὲ τοῦτα τὰ χωριὰ τ' ἀποδεκατισμένα
πάνω σ' αὐτὸ τὸν κάβο, ξέσκεπο στὸ νοτιὰ
μὲ τὴ βουνοσειρὰ μπροστά μας ποὺ σὲ κρύβει,
ποιὸς θὰ μᾶς λογαριάσει τὴν ἀπόφαση τῆς λησμονιᾶς;
Ποιὸς θὰ δεχτεῖ τὴν προσφορά μας, στὸ τέλος αὐτὸ τοῦ φθινοπώρου.

and you.
Who will lift this sorrow from our hearts?
Yesterday evening a heavy rain and again today
the covered sky burdens us. Our thoughts—
like the pine needles of yesterday's downpour
bunched up and useless in front of our doorway—
would build a collapsing tower.

Among these decimated villages
on this promontory, open to the south wind
with the mountain range in front of us hiding you,
who will calculate for us the cost of our decision to forget?
Who will accept our offering, at the end of this autumn?

Η΄

Μὰ τί γυρεύουν οἱ ψυχές μας ταξιδεύοντας
πάνω σὲ καταστρώματα κατελυμένων καραβιῶν
στριμωγμένες μὲ γυναῖκες κίτρινες καὶ μωρὰ ποὺ κλαῖνε
χωρὶς νὰ μποροῦν νὰ ξεχαστοῦν οὔτε μὲ τὰ χελιδονόψαρα
οὔτε μὲ τ' ἄστρα ποὺ δηλώνουν στὴν ἄκρη τὰ κατάρτια.
Τριμμένες ἀπὸ τοὺς δίσκους τῶν φωνογράφων
δεμένες ἄθελα μ' ἀνύπαρχτα προσκυνήματα
μουρμουρίζοντας σπασμένες σκέψεις ἀπὸ ξένες γλῶσσες.

Μὰ τί γυρεύουν οἱ ψυχές μας ταξιδεύοντας
πάνω στὰ σαπισμένα θαλάσσια ξύλα
ἀπὸ λιμάνι σὲ λιμάνι ;

Μετακινώντας τσακισμένες πέτρες, ἀνασαίνοντας
τὴ δροσιὰ τοῦ πεύκου πιὸ δύσκολα κάθε μέρα,
κολυμπώντας στὰ νερὰ τούτης τῆς θάλασσας
κι' ἐκείνης τῆς θάλασσας,
χωρὶς ἀφὴ
χωρὶς ἀνθρώπους
μέσα σὲ μιὰ πατρίδα ποὺ δὲν εἶναι πιὰ δική μας
οὔτε δική σας.

✧

8

What are they after, our souls, traveling
on the decks of decayed ships
crowded in with sallow women and crying babies
unable to forget themselves either with the flying fish
or with the stars that the masts point out at their tips
grated by gramophone records
committed to non-existent pilgrimages unwillingly,
murmuring broken thoughts from foreign languages?

What are they after, our souls, traveling
on rotten brine-soaked timbers
from harbor to harbor?

Shifting broken stones, breathing in
the pine's coolness with greater difficulty each day
swimming in the waters of this sea
and of that sea
without the sense of touch
without men
in a country that is no longer ours
nor yours.

✧

Τὸ ξέραμε πὼς εἶταν ὡραῖα τὰ νησιὰ
κάπου ἐδῶ τριγύρω ποὺ ψηλαφοῦμε
λίγο πιὸ χαμηλὰ ἢ λίγο πιὸ ψηλὰ
ἕνα ἐλάχιστο διάστημα.

We knew that the islands were beautiful
somewhere round about here where we're groping—
a little nearer or a little farther,
the slightest distance.

Θ΄

Εἶναι παλιὸ τὸ λιμάνι, δὲ μπορῶ πιὰ νὰ περιμένω
οὔτε τὸ φίλο ποὺ ἔφυγε στὸ νησὶ μὲ τὰ πεῦκα
οὔτε τὸ φίλο ποὺ ἔφυγε στὸ νησὶ μὲ τὰ πλατάνια
οὔτε τὸ φίλο ποὺ ἔφυγε γιὰ τ' ἀνοιχτά.
Χαϊδεύω τὰ σκουριασμένα κανόνια, χαϊδεύω τὰ κουπιὰ
νὰ ζωντανέψει τὸ κορμί μου καὶ ν' ἀποφασίσει.
Τὰ καραβόπανα δίνουν μόνο τὴ μυρωδιὰ
τοῦ ἁλατιοῦ τῆς ἄλλης τρικυμίας.

Ἂν τὸ θέλησα νὰ μείνω μόνος, γύρεψα
τὴ μοναξιά, δὲ γύρεψα μιὰ τέτοια ἀπαντοχή,
τὸ κομμάτιασμα τῆς ψυχῆς μου στὸν ὁρίζοντα,
αὐτὲς τὶς γραμμές, αὐτὰ τὰ χρώματα, αὐτὴ τὴ σιγή.

Τ' ἄστρα τῆς νύχτας μὲ γυρίζουν στὴν προσδοκία
τοῦ Ὀδυσσέα γιὰ τοὺς νεκροὺς μὲς στ' ἀσφοδίλια.
Μὲς στ' ἀσφοδίλια σὰν ἀράξαμε ἐδῶ πέρα θέλαμε νὰ βροῦμε
τὴ λαγκαδιὰ ποὺ εἶδε τὸν Ἄδωνι λαβωμένο.

9

The harbor is old, I can't wait any longer
for the friend who left for the island of pine-trees
or the friend who left for the island of plane-trees
or the friend who left for the open sea.
I stroke the rusted cannons, I stroke the oars
so that my body may revive and decide.
The sails give off only the smell
of salt from the other storm.

If I chose to remain alone, what I hoped for
was solitude, not this kind of waiting,
my soul shattered on the horizon,
these lines, these colors, this silence.

The stars of night take me back to the anticipation
of Odysseus waiting for the dead among the asphodels.*
When we moored here among the asphodels we hoped to find
the gorge that saw Adonis wounded.

Ι΄

Ὁ τόπος μας εἶναι κλειστός, ὅλο βουνὰ
ποὺ ἔχουν σκεπὴ τὸ χαμηλὸ οὐρανὸ μέρα καὶ νύχτα.
Δὲν ἔχουμε ποτάμια δὲν ἔχουμε πηγάδια δὲν ἔχουμε πηγές,
μονάχα λίγες στέρνες, ἄδειες κι᾿ αὐτές, ποὺ ἠχοῦν καὶ ποὺ
τὶς προσκυνοῦμε.
Ἦχος στεκάμενος κούφιος, ἴδιος μὲ τὴ μοναξιά μας
ἴδιος μὲ τὴν ἀγάπη μας, ἴδιος μὲ τὰ σώματά μας.
Μᾶς φαίνεται παράξενο ποὺ κάποτε μπορέσαμε νὰ χτίσουμε
τὰ σπίτια τὰ καλύβια καὶ τὶς στάνες μας.
Κι᾿ οἱ γάμοι μας, τὰ δροσερὰ στεφάνια καὶ τὰ δάχτυλα
γίνουνται αἰνίγματα ἀνεξήγητα γιὰ τὴν ψυχή μας.
Πῶς γεννηθήκαν πῶς δυναμώσανε τὰ παιδιά μας;

Ὁ τόπος μας εἶναι κλειστός. Τὸν κλείνουν
οἱ δυὸ μαῦρες Συμπληγάδες. Στὰ λιμάνια
τὴν Κυριακὴ σὰν κατεβοῦμε ν᾿ ἀνασάνουμε
βλέπουμε νὰ φωτίζουνται στὸ ἡλιόγερμα
σπασμένα ξύλα ἀπὸ ταξίδια ποὺ δὲν τέλειωσαν
σώματα ποὺ δὲν ξέρουν πιὰ πῶς ν᾿ ἀγαπήσουν.

10

Our country is closed in, all mountains
that have the low sky for a roof day and night.
We have no rivers, we have no wells, we have no springs,
only a few cisterns—and these empty—that echo, and we
worship them.
A stagnant hollow sound, the same as our loneliness
the same as our love, the same as our bodies.
We find it strange that once we were able to build
our houses, huts, and sheepfolds.
And our marriages, the cool coronals and the fingers,*
become enigmas inexplicable to our soul.
How were our children born, how did they grow strong?

Our country is closed in. The two black Symplegades*
close it in. When we go down
to the harbors on Sunday to breathe
we see, lit in the sunset,
the broken planks from voyages that never ended,
bodies that no longer know how to love.

ΙΑ΄

Τὸ αἷμα σου πάγωνε κάποτε σὰν τὸ φεγγάρι
μέσα στὴν ἀνεξάντλητη νύχτα τὸ αἷμα σου
ἅπλωνε τὶς ἄσπρες του φτεροῦγες πάνω
στοὺς μαύρους βράχους τὰ σχήματα τῶν δέντρων καὶ τὰ
σπίτια
μὲ λίγο φῶς ἀπὸ τὰ παιδικά μας χρόνια.

11

Sometimes your blood froze like the moon
in the limitless night your blood
spread its white wings over
the black rocks, the shapes of trees and houses,
with a little light from our childhood years.

IB′

Μποτίλια στὸ πέλαγο

Τρεῖς βράχοι λίγα καμένα πεῦκα κι᾽ ἕνα ρημοκλήσι
καὶ πάρα πάνω
τὸ ἴδιο τοπίο ἀντιγραμμένο ξαναρχίζει·
τρεῖς βράχοι σὲ σχῆμα πύλης, σκουριασμένοι
λίγα καμένα πεῦκα, μαῦρα καὶ κίτρινα
κι᾽ ἕνα τετράγωνο σπιτάκι θαμμένο στὸν ἀσβέστη·
καὶ πάρα πάνω ἀκόμη πολλὲς φορὲς
τὸ ἴδιο τοπίο ξαναρχίζει κλιμακωτὰ
ὣς τὸν ὁρίζοντα ὣς τὸν οὐρανὸ ποὺ βασιλεύει.

᾽Εδῶ ἀράξαμε τὸ καράβι νὰ ματίσουμε τὰ σπασμένα κουπιά,
νὰ πιοῦμε νερὸ καὶ νὰ κοιμηθοῦμε.
῾Η θάλασσα ποὺ μᾶς πίκρανε εἶναι βαθειὰ κι᾽ ἀνεξερεύνητη
καὶ ξεδιπλώνει μιὰν ἀπέραντη γαλήνη.
᾽Εδῶ μέσα στὰ βότσαλα βρήκαμε ἕνα νόμισμα
καὶ τὸ παίξαμε στὰ ζάρια.
Τὸ κέρδισε ὁ μικρότερος καὶ χάθηκε.

Ξαναμπαρκάραμε μὲ τὰ σπασμένα μας κουπιά.

12

Bottle in the Sea

Three rocks, a few burnt pines, a solitary chapel
and farther above
the same landscape repeated starts again:
three rocks in the shape of a gate-way, rusted,
a few burnt pines, black and yellow,
and a square hut buried in whitewash;
and still farther above, many times over,
the same landscape recurs level after level
to the horizon, to the twilight sky.

Here we moored the ship to splice the broken oars,
to drink water and to sleep.
The sea that embittered us is deep and unexplored
and unfolds a boundless calm.
Here among the pebbles we found a coin
and threw dice for it.
The youngest won it and disappeared.*

We set out again with our broken oars.

ΙΓ΄

Ὕδρα

Δελφίνια φλάμπουρα καὶ κανονιές.
Τὸ πέλαγο τόσο πικρὸ γιὰ τὴν ψυχή σου κάποτε
σήκωνε τὰ πολύχρωμα κι' ἀστραφτερὰ καράβια
λύγιζε, τὰ κλυδώνιζε κι' ὅλο μαβὶ μ' ἄσπρα φτερά,
τόσο πικρὸ γιὰ τὴν ψυχή σου κάποτε
τώρα γεμάτο χρώματα στὸν ἥλιο.

Ἄσπρα πανιὰ καὶ φῶς καὶ τὰ κουπιὰ τὰ ὑγρὰ
χτυπούσαν μὲ ρυθμὸ τυμπάνου ἕνα ἡμερωμένο κῦμα.

Θά εἶταν ὡραῖα τὰ μάτια σου νὰ κοίταζαν
θά εἶταν λαμπρὰ τὰ χέρια σου ν' ἁπλώνουνταν
θά εἶταν σὰν ἄλλοτε ζωηρὰ τὰ χείλια σου
μπρὸς σ' ἕνα τέτιο θᾶμα·
τὸ γύρευες
                    τί γύρευες μπροστὰ στὴ στάχτη
ἢ μέσα στὴ βροχὴ στὴν καταχνιὰ στὸν ἄνεμο,
τὴν ὥρα ἀκόμη ποὺ χαλάρωναν τὰ φῶτα
κι' ἡ πολιτεία βύθιζε κι' ἀπὸ τὶς πλάκες
σοῦ 'δειχνε τὴν καρδιά του ὁ Ναζωραῖος,
τί γύρευες ; γιατί δὲν ἔρχεσαι ; τί γύρευες ;

13

*Hydra**

Dolphins banners and the sound of cannons.
The sea once so bitter to your soul
bore the many-colored and glittering ships
it swayed, rolled and tossed them, all blue with white wings,
once so bitter to your soul
now full of colors in the sun.

White sails and sunlight and wet oars
struck with a rhythm of drums on stilled waves.

Your eyes would be lovely if they were to look,
your arms would be glowing if they were to stretch out,
your lips would come alive, as they used to,
at such a miracle;
you were looking for it
                    what were you looking for in front of ashes
or in the rain in the fog in the wind
even when the lights were growing dim
and the city was sinking and from the stone pavement
the Nazarene showed you his heart,
what were you looking for? why don't you come? what
      were you looking for?

ΙΔ΄

Τρία κόκκινα περιστέρια μέσα στὸ φῶς
χαράζοντας τὴ μοίρα μας μέσα στὸ φῶς
μὲ χρώματα καὶ χειρονομίες ἀνθρώπων
ποὺ ἀγαπήσαμε.

14

Three red pigeons in the light
inscribing our fate in the light
with colors and gestures of people
we have loved.

ΙΕ΄

Quid πλατανὼν opacissimus?

Ὁ ὕπνος σὲ τύλιξε, σὰν ἕνα δέντρο, μὲ πράσινα φύλλα
ἀνάσαινες, σὰν ἕνα δέντρο, μέσα στὸ ἥσυχο φῶς
μέσα στὴ διάφανη πηγὴ κοίταξα τὴ μορφή σου·
κλεισμένα βλέφαρα καὶ τὰ ματόκλαδα χάραζαν τὸ νερό.
Τὰ δάχτυλά μου στὸ μαλακὸ χορτάρι, βρῆκαν τὰ δάχτυλά σου
κράτησα τὸ σφυγμό σου μιὰ στιγμὴ
κι᾿ ἔνιωσα ἀλλοῦ τὸν πόνο τῆς καρδιᾶς σου.

Κάτω ἀπὸ τὸ πλατάνι, κοντὰ στὸ νερό, μέσα στὶς δάφνες
ὁ ὕπνος σὲ μετακινοῦσε καὶ σὲ κομμάτιαζε
γύρω μου, κοντά μου, χωρὶς νὰ μπορῶ νὰ σ᾿ ἀγγίξω ὁλόκληρη,
ἑνωμένη μὲ τὴ σιωπή σου·
βλέποντας τὸν ἴσκιο σου νὰ μεγαλώνει καὶ νὰ μικραίνει,
νὰ χάνεται στοὺς ἄλλους ἴσκιους, μέσα στὸν ἄλλο
κόσμο ποὺ σ᾿ ἄφηνε καὶ σὲ κρατοῦσε.

Τὴ ζωὴ ποὺ μᾶς ἔδωσαν νὰ ζήσουμε, τὴ ζήσαμε.
Λυπήσου ἐκείνους ποὺ περιμένουν μὲ τόση ὑπομονὴ
χαμένοι μέσα στὶς μαῦρες δάφνες κάτω ἀπὸ τὰ βαριὰ
πλατάνια
κι᾿ ὅσους μονάχοι τους μιλοῦν σὲ στέρνες καὶ σὲ πηγάδια
καὶ πνίγουνται μέσα στοὺς κύκλους τῆς φωνῆς.

15

*Quid πλατανῶν opacissimus?**

Sleep wrapped you in green leaves like a tree
you breathed like a tree in the quiet light
in the limpid spring I watched your face:
eyelids closed, eyelashes brushing the water.
In the soft grass my fingers found your fingers
I held your pulse a moment
and felt your heart's pain in another place.

Under the plane-tree, near the water, among laurel
sleep moved you and scattered you
around me, near me, without my being able to touch the
    whole of you—
one as you were with your silence;
seeing your shadow grow and diminish,
lose itself in the other shadows, in the other
world that let you go yet held you back.

The life that they gave us to live, we lived.
Pity those who wait with such patience
lost in the black laurel under the heavy plane-trees
and those, alone, who speak to cisterns and wells
and drown in the voice's circles.

Λυπήσου τὸ σύντροφο ποὺ μοιράστηκε τὴ στέρησή μας καὶ
τὸν ἱδρώτα
καὶ βύθισε μέσα στὸν ἥλιο σὰν κοράκι πέρα ἀπ' τὰ μάρμαρα,
χωρὶς ἐλπίδα νὰ χαρεῖ τὴν ἀμοιβή μας.

Δῶσε μας, ἔξω ἀπὸ τὸν ὕπνο, τὴ γαλήνη.

Pity the companion who shared our privation and our sweat
and plunged into the sun like a crow beyond the ruins
without hope of enjoying our reward.

Give us, outside sleep, serenity.

ΙϚ΄

ὄνομα δ' Ὀρέστης

Στὴ σφενδόνη, πάλι στὴ σφενδόνη, στὴ σφενδόνη,
πόσοι γύροι, πόσοι αἱμάτινοι κύκλοι, πόσες μαῦρες
σειρές· οἱ ἄνθρωποι ποὺ μὲ κοιτάζουν,
ποὺ μὲ κοιτάζαν ὅταν πάνω στὸ ἅρμα
σήκωσα τὸ χέρι λαμπρός, κι' ἀλάλαξαν.

Οἱ ἀφροὶ τῶν ἀλόγων μὲ χτυποῦν, τ' ἄλογα πότε θ' ἀπο-
στάσουν;
Τρίζει ὁ ἄξονας, πυρώνει ὁ ἄξονας, πότε ὁ ἄξονας θ' ἀ-
νάψει;
Πότε θὰ σπάσουν τὰ λουριά, πότε τὰ πέταλα
θὰ πατήσουν μ' ὅλο τὸ πλάτος πάνω στὸ χῶμα
πάνω στὸ μαλακὸ χορτάρι, μέσα στὶς παπαροῦνες ὅπου
τὴν ἄνοιξη μάζεψες μιὰ μαργαρίτα.
Εἴταν ὡραῖα τὰ μάτια σου μὰ δὲν ἤξερες ποῦ νὰ κοιτάξεις
δὲν ἤξερα ποῦ νὰ κοιτάξω μήτε κι' ἐγώ, χωρὶς πατρίδα
ἐγὼ ποὺ μάχομαι ἐδῶ-πέρα, πόσοι γύροι;
καὶ νιώθω τὰ γόνατα νὰ λυγίζουν πάνω στὸν ἄξονα
πάνω στὶς ρόδες πάνω στὸν ἄγριο στίβο
τὰ γόνατα λυγίζουν εὔκολα σὰν τὸ θέλουν οἱ θεοί,
κανεὶς δὲν μπορεῖ νὰ ξεφύγει, τί νὰ τὴν κάνεις τὴ δύναμη,
δὲν μπορεῖς

16

*The name is Orestes**

On the track, on the track again, on the track,
how many times around, how many bloodied laps, how many black
rows; the people who watch me,
who watched me when, in the chariot,
I raised my hand glorious, and they roared triumphantly.

The froth of the horses strikes me, when will the horses tire?
The axle creaks, the axle burns, when will the axle burst into flame?
When will the reins break, when will the hooves
tread flush on the ground
on the soft grass, among the poppies
where, in the spring, you picked a daisy.
They were lovely, your eyes, but you didn't know where to look
nor did I know where to look, I, without a country,
I who go on struggling here how many times around?
and I feel my knees give way over the axle
over the wheels, over the wild track
knees buckle easily when the gods so will it,
no one can escape, there's no point in being strong, you can't

νὰ ξεφύγεις τὴ θάλασσα ποὺ σὲ λίκνισε καὶ ποὺ γυρεύεις
τούτη τὴν ὥρα τῆς ἀμάχης, μέσα στὴν ἀλογίσια ἀνάσα
μὲ τὰ καλάμια ποὺ τραγουδοῦσαν τὸ φθινόπωρο σὲ τρόπο
λυδικὸ
τὴ θάλασσα ποὺ δὲν μπορεῖς νὰ βρεῖς ὅσο κι' ἂν τρέχεις
ὅσο κι' ἂν γυρίζεις μπροστὰ στὶς μαῦρες Εὐμενίδες ποὺ βαριοῦνται,
χωρὶς συχώρεση.

escape the sea that cradled you and that you search for
at this time of trial, with the horses panting,
with the reeds that used to sing in autumn to the Lydian
    mode
the sea you cannot find no matter how you run
no matter how you circle past the black, bored Eumenides,
unforgiven.

ΙΖ΄

Ἀστυάναξ

Τώρα πού θά φύγεις πάρε μαζί σου καί τό παιδί
πού εἶδε τό φῶς κάτω ἀπό ἐκεῖνο τό πλατάνι,
μιά μέρα πού ἀντηχούσαν σάλπιγγες κι' ἔλαμπαν ὅπλα
καί τ' ἄλογα ἱδρωμένα σκύβανε ν' ἀγγίξουν
τήν πράσινη ἐπιφάνεια τοῦ νεροῦ
στή γούρνα μέ τά ὑγρά τους τά ρουθούνια.

Οἱ ἐλιές μέ τίς ρυτίδες τῶν γονιῶν μας
τά βράχια μέ τή γνώση τῶν γονιῶν μας
καί τό αἷμα τοῦ ἀδερφοῦ μας ζωντανό στό χῶμα
εἴτανε μιά γερή χαρά μιά πλούσια τάξη
γιά τίς ψυχές πού γνώριζαν τήν προσευχή τους.

Τώρα πού θά φύγεις, τώρα πού ἡ μέρα τῆς πληρωμῆς
χαράζει, τώρα πού κανείς δέν ξέρει
ποιόν θά σκοτώσει καί πῶς θά τελειώσει,
πάρε μαζί σου τό παιδί πού εἶδε τό φῶς
κάτω ἀπ' τά φύλλα ἐκείνου τοῦ πλατάνου
καί μάθε του νά μελετᾶ τά δέντρα.

17

*Astyanax**

Now that you are leaving, take the boy with you also,
the boy who saw the light under that plane-tree,
one day when trumpets resounded and weapons shone
and the sweating horses, nostrils wet,
bent to the trough to touch
the green surface of the water.

The olive trees with the wrinkles of our fathers
the rocks with the wisdom of our fathers
and our brother's blood alive on the earth
were a vital joy, a rich pattern
for the souls who knew how to pray.

Now that you are leaving, now that the day of payment
dawns, now that no one knows
whom he will kill and how he will die,
take with you the boy who saw the light
under the leaves of that plane-tree
and teach him to study the trees.

ΙΗ΄

Λυποῦμαι γιατὶ ἄφησα νὰ περάσει ἕνα πλατὺ ποτάμι μέσα
 ἀπὸ τὰ δάχτυλά μου
χωρὶς νὰ πιῶ οὔτε μιὰ στάλα.
Τώρα βυθίζομαι στὴν πέτρα.
Ἕνα μικρὸ πεῦκο στὸ κόκκινο χῶμα,
δὲν ἔχω ἄλλη συντροφιά.
Ὅ,τι ἀγάπησα χάθηκε μαζὶ μὲ τὰ σπίτια
ποὺ εἴταν καινούργια τὸ περασμένο καλοκαίρι
καὶ γκρέμισαν μὲ τὸν ἀγέρα τοῦ φθινοπώρου.

18

I am sorry for having let a broad river pass through my fingers
without drinking a single drop.
Now I'm sinking into the stone.
A small pine-tree in the red soil
is all the company I have.
Whatever I loved vanished with the houses
that were new last summer
and collapsed in the autumn wind.

ΙΘ΄

Κι' ἂν ὁ ἀγέρας φυσᾶ δὲ μᾶς δροσίζει
κι' ὁ ἴσκιος μένει στενὸς κάτω ἀπ' τὰ κυπαρίσσια
κι' ὅλο τριγύρω ἀνήφοροι στὰ βουνά·

μᾶς βαραίνουν
οἱ φίλοι πού δὲν ξέρουν πιὰ πῶς νὰ πεθάνουν.

19

Even if the wind blows it doesn't cool us
and the shade under the cypress trees remains narrow
and all around it's uphill to the mountains;

they're a burden for us
the friends who no longer know how to die.

Κ΄

Στὸ στῆθος μου ἡ πληγὴ ἀνοίγει πάλι
ὅταν χαμηλώνουν τ' ἄστρα καὶ συγγενεύουν μὲ τὸ κορμί μου
ὅταν πέφτει σιγὴ κάτω ἀπὸ τὰ πέλματα τῶν ἀνθρώπων.

Αὐτὲς οἱ πέτρες ποὺ βουλιάζουν μέσα στὰ χρόνια ὡς ποῦ
θὰ μὲ παρασύρουν;
Τὴ θάλασσα τὴ θάλασσα, ποιὸς θὰ μπορέσει νὰ τὴν ἐξαντλήσει;
Βλέπω τὰ χέρια κάθε αὐγὴ νὰ γνέφουν στὸ γύπα καὶ στὸ
γεράκι
δεμένη πάνω στὸ βράχο ποὺ ἔγινε μὲ τὸν πόνο δικός μου,
βλέπω τὰ δέντρα ποὺ ἀνασαίνουν τὴ μαύρη γαλήνη τῶν πεθαμένων
κι' ἔπειτα τὰ χαμόγελα, ποὺ δὲν προχωροῦν, τῶν ἀγαλμάτων.

20

In my breast the wound opens again
when the stars descend and become kin to my body
when silence falls under the footsteps of men.

These stones sinking into time, how far will they drag me
    with them?
The sea, the sea, who will be able to drain it dry?*
I see the hands beckon each dawn to the vulture and the
    hawk
bound as I am to the rock that suffering has made mine,
I see the trees breathing the black serenity of the dead
and then the smiles—that don't develop—of the statues.

ΚΑ΄

Ἐμεῖς ποὺ ξεκινήσαμε γιὰ τὸ προσκύνημα τοῦτο
κοιτάξαμε τὰ σπασμένα ἀγάλματα
ξεχαστήκαμε καὶ εἴπαμε πὼς δὲ χάνεται ἡ ζωὴ τόσο εὔκολα
πὼς ἔχει ὁ θάνατος δρόμους ἀνεξερεύνητους
καὶ μιὰ δική του δικαιοσύνη·

πὼς ὅταν ἐμεῖς ὀρθοὶ στὰ πόδια μας πεθαίνουμε
μέσα στὴν πέτρα ἀδερφωμένοι
ἑνωμένοι μὲ τὴ σκληρότητα καὶ τὴν ἀδυναμία,
οἱ παλαιοὶ νεκροὶ ξεφύγαν ἀπ' τὸν κύκλο καὶ ἀναστήθηκαν
καὶ χαμογελᾶνε μέσα σὲ μιὰ παράξενη ἡσυχία.

21

We who set out on this pilgrimage
looked at the broken statues
we forgot ourselves and said that life is not so easily lost
that death has unexplored paths
and its own particular justice;

that while we, still upright on our feet, are dying,
become brothers in stone
united in hardness and weakness,
the ancient dead have escaped the circle and risen again
and smile in a strange silence.

ΚΒ′

Γιατὶ περάσαν τόσα καὶ τόσα μπροστὰ στὰ μάτια μας
ποὺ καὶ τὰ μάτια μας δὲν εἴδαν τίποτε, μὰ πάρα-πέρα
καὶ πίσω ἡ μνήμη σὰν τὸ ἄσπρο πανὶ μιὰ νύχτα σὲ μιὰ
    μάντρα
ποὺ εἴδαμε ὁράματα παράξενα, περισσότερο κι᾽ ἀπὸ σένα
νὰ περνοῦν καὶ νὰ χάνουνται μέσα στὸ ἀκίνητο φύλλωμα
    μιᾶς πιπεριᾶς·

γιατὶ γνωρίσαμε τόσο πολὺ τούτη τὴ μοίρα μας
στριφογυρίζοντας μέσα σὲ σπασμένες πέτρες, τρεῖς ἢ ἕξι
    χιλιάδες χρόνια
ψάχνοντας σὲ οἰκοδομὲς γκρεμισμένες ποὺ θά εἶταν ἴσως τὸ
    δικό μας σπίτι
προσπαθώντας νὰ θυμηθοῦμε χρονολογίες καὶ ἡρωικὲς
    πράξεις·
θὰ μπορέσουμε;

γιατὶ δεθήκαμε καὶ σκορπιστήκαμε
καὶ παλέψαμε μὲ δυσκολίες ἀνύπαρχτες ὅπως λέγαν
χαμένοι, ξαναβρίσκοντας ἕνα δρόμο γεμάτο τυφλὰ συντά-
    γματα
βουλιάζοντας μέσα σὲ βάλτους καὶ μέσα στὴ λίμνη τοῦ Μα-
    ραθώνα,
θὰ μπορέσουμε νὰ πεθάνουμε κανονικά;

22

So very much having passed before our eyes
that our eyes in the end saw nothing, but beyond
and behind was memory like the white sheet one night in
an enclosure
where we saw strange visions, even stranger than you,
pass by and vanish into the motionless foliage of a pepper-
tree;

having known this fate of ours so well
wandering around among broken stones, three or six
thousand years
searching in collapsed buildings that might have been
our homes
trying to remember dates and heroic deeds:
will we be able?

having been bound and scattered,
having struggled, as they said, with non-existent difficulties
lost, then finding again a road full of blind regiments
sinking in marshes and in the lake of Marathon,
will we be able to die properly?

ΚΓ΄

Λίγο ἀκόμα
θὰ ἰδοῦμε τὶς ἀμυγδαλιὲς ν᾿ ἀνθίζουν
τὰ μάρμαρα νὰ λάμπουν στὸν ἥλιο
τὴ θάλασσα νὰ κυματίζει

λίγο ἀκόμα,
νὰ σηκωθοῦμε λίγο ψηλότερα.

23

A little farther
we will see the almond trees blossoming
the marble gleaming in the sun
the sea breaking into waves

a little farther,
let us rise a little higher.

ΚΔ΄

’Εδῶ τελειώνουν τὰ ἔργα τῆς θάλασσας τὰ ἔργα τῆς ἀγάπης.
’Εκεῖνοι ποὺ κάποτε θὰ ζήσουν ἐδῶ ποὺ τελειώνουμε
ἂν τύχει καὶ μαυρίσει στὴ μνήμη τους τὸ αἷμα καὶ ξεχειλίσει
ἂς μὴ μᾶς ξεχάσουν, τὶς ἀδύναμες ψυχὲς μέσα στ’ ἀσφοδίλια,
ἂς γυρίσουν πρὸς τὸ ἔρεβος τὰ κεφάλια τῶν θυμάτων:

’Εμεῖς ποὺ τίποτε δὲν εἴχαμε θὰ τοὺς διδάξουμε τὴ γαλήνη.

Δεκέμβρης 1933 - Δεκέμβρης 1934

24

Here end the works of the sea, the works of love.
Those who will some day live here where we end—
should the blood happen to darken in their memory and
    overflow—
let them not forget us, the weak souls among the asphodels,
let them turn the heads of the victims towards Erebus:*

We who had nothing will teach them peace.

December 1933–December 1934

ΓΥΜΝΟΠΑΙΔΙΑ

Ἡ Θήρα γεωλογικῶς συνίσταται ἐξ ἐλαφρόπετρας καὶ πορσελάνης, ἐν τῷ κόλπῳ δ' αὐτῆς... ἐφάνησαν καὶ κατεβυθίσθησαν νῆσοι. Ὑπῆρξε κέντρον ἀρχαιοτάτης θρησκείας ἔνθα ἐτελοῦντο λυρικοὶ χοροὶ αὐστηροῦ καὶ βαρέος ρυθμοῦ καλούμενοι γυμνοπαιδίαι.

ΟΔΗΓΟΣ ΤΗΣ ΕΛΛΑΔΟΣ

GYMNOPAIDIA

Santorini is geologically composed of pumice stone and china clay; in her bay, islands have appeared and disappeared. This island was once the center of a very ancient religion. The lyrical dances, with a strict and heavy rhythm, performed here were called: Gymnopaidia.

GUIDE TO GREECE

Α'. ΣΑΝΤΟΡΙΝΗ

Σκύψε ἂν μπορεῖς στὴ θάλασσα τὴ σκοτεινὴ ξεχνώντας
τὸν ἦχο μιᾶς φλογέρας πάνω σὲ πόδια γυμνὰ
ποὺ πάτησαν τὸν ὕπνο σου στὴν ἄλλη ζωὴ τὴ βυθισμένη.

Γράψε ἂν μπορεῖς στὸ τελευταῖο σου ὄστρακο
τὴ μέρα τ' ὄνομα τὸν τόπο
καὶ ρίξε το στὴ θάλασσα γιὰ νὰ βουλιάξει.

Βρεθήκαμε γυμνοὶ πάνω στὴν ἀλαφρόπετρα
κοιτάζοντας τ' ἀναδυόμενα νησιὰ
κοιτάζοντας τὰ κόκκινα νησιὰ νὰ βυθίζουν
στὸν ὕπνο τους, στὸν ὕπνο μας.
Ἐδῶ βρεθήκαμε γυμνοὶ κρατώντας
τὴ ζυγαριὰ ποὺ βάραινε κατὰ τὸ μέρος
τῆς ἀδικίας.

Φτέρνα τῆς δύναμης θέληση ἀνίσκιωτη λογαριασμένη
ἀγάπη
στὸν ἥλιο τοῦ μεσημεριοῦ σχέδια ποὺ ὡριμάζουν,
δρόμος τῆς μοίρας μὲ τὸ χτύπημα τῆς νέας παλάμης
στὴν ὠμοπλάτη·
στὸν τόπο ποὺ σκορπίστηκε ποὺ δὲν ἀντέχει
στὸν τόπο ποὺ εἴταν κάποτε δικός μας
βουλιάζουν τὰ νησιὰ σκουριὰ καὶ στάχτη.

✧

I. SANTORINI

Bend if you can to the dark sea forgetting
the flute's sound on naked feet
that trod your sleep in the other, the sunken life.

Write if you can on your last shell
the day the name the place
and fling it into the sea so that it sinks.

We found ourselves naked on the pumice stone
watching the rising islands
watching the red islands sink
into their sleep, into our sleep.
Here we found ourselves naked, holding
the scales that tipped towards
injustice.

Instep of power, unshadowed will, considered love,
projects that ripen in the midday sun,
course of fate with a young hand
slapping the shoulder;
in the land that was scattered, that can't resist,
in the land that was once our land
the islands—rust and ash—are sinking.

✧

Βωμοὶ γκρεμισμένοι
κι' οἱ φίλοι ξεχασμένοι
φύλλα τῆς φοινικιᾶς στὴ λάσπη.

Ἄφησε τὰ χέρια σου ἂν μπορεῖς, νὰ ταξιδέψουν
ἐδῶ στὴν κόχη τοῦ καιροῦ μὲ τὸ καράβι
ποὺ ἄγγιξε τὸν ὁρίζοντα.
Ὅταν ὁ κύβος χτύπησε τὴν πλάκα
ὅταν ἡ λόγχη χτύπησε τὸ θώρακα
ὅταν τὸ μάτι γνώρισε τὸν ξένο
καὶ στέγνωσε ἡ ἀγάπη
μέσα σὲ τρύπιες ψυχές·
ὅταν κοιτάζεις γύρω σου καὶ βρίσκεις
κύκλο τὰ πόδια θερισμένα
κύκλο τὰ χέρια πεθαμένα
κύκλο τὰ μάτια σκοτεινά·
ὅταν δὲ μένει πιὰ οὔτε νὰ διαλέξεις
τὸ θάνατο ποὺ γύρευες δικό σου,
ἀκούγοντας μιὰ κραυγὴ
ἀκόμη καὶ τοῦ λύκου τὴν κραυγή,
τὸ δίκιο σου·
ἄφησε τὰ χέρια σου ἂν μπορεῖς νὰ ταξιδέψουν
ξεκόλλησε ἀπ' τὸν ἄπιστο καιρὸ
καὶ βούλιαξε,
βουλιάζει ὅποιος σηκώνει τὶς μεγάλες πέτρες.

Altars destroyed
and friends forgotten
leaves of the palm tree in mud.

Let your hands go traveling if you can
here on time's curve with the ship
that touched the horizon.
When the dice struck the flagstone
when the lance struck the breast-plate
when the eye recognized the stranger
and love went dry
in punctured souls;
when looking round you see
feet harvested everywhere
dead hands everywhere
eyes darkened everywhere;
when you can't any longer choose
even the death you wanted as your own—
hearing a cry,
even the wolf's cry,
your due:
let your hands go traveling if you can
free yourself from unfaithful time
and sink—
sinks whoever raises the great stones.

Β'. ΜΥΚΗΝΕΣ

Δός μου τὰ χέρια σου, δός μου τὰ χέρια σου, δός μου τὰ χέρια σου.

Εἶδα μέσα στὴ νύχτα
τὴ μυτερὴ κορυφὴ τοῦ βουνοῦ
εἶδα τὸν κάμπο πέρα πλημμυρισμένο
μὲ τὸ φῶς ἑνὸς ἀφανέρωτου φεγγαριοῦ
εἶδα, γυρίζοντας τὸ κεφάλι
τὶς μαῦρες πέτρες συσπειρωμένες
καὶ τὴ ζωή μου τεντωμένη σὰ χορδὴ
ἀρχὴ καὶ τέλος
ἡ τελευταία στιγμή·
τὰ χέρια μου.

Βουλιάζει ὅποιος σηκώνει τὶς μεγάλες πέτρες·
τοῦτες τὶς πέτρες τὶς ἐσήκωσα ὅσο βάσταξα
τοῦτες τὶς πέτρες τὶς ἀγάπησα ὅσο βάσταξα
τοῦτες τὶς πέτρες, τὴ μοίρα μου.
Πληγωμένος ἀπὸ τὸ δικό μου χῶμα
τυραννισμένος ἀπὸ τὸ δικό μου πουκάμισο
καταδικασμένος ἀπὸ τοὺς δικούς μου θεούς,
τοῦτες τὶς πέτρες.

Ξέρω πὼς δὲν ξέρουν, ἀλλὰ ἐγὼ

II. MYCENAE

Give me your hands, give me your hands, give me
your hands.

I have seen in the night
the sharp peak of the mountain,
seen the plain beyond flooded
with the light of an invisible moon,
seen, turning my head,
black stones huddled
and my life taut as a chord
beginning and end
the final moment:
my hands.

Sinks whoever raises the great stones;
I've raised these stones as long as I was able
I've loved these stones as long as I was able
these stones, my fate.
Wounded by my own soil
tortured by my own shirt
condemned by my own gods,
these stones.

I know that they don't know, but I

πού ἀκολούθησα τόσες φορὲς
τὸ δρόμο ἀπ' τὸ φονιὰ στὸ σκοτωμένο
ἀπὸ τὸ σκοτωμένο στὴν πληρωμὴ
κι' ἀπὸ τὴν πληρωμὴ στὸν ἄλλο φόνο,
ψηλαφώντας
τὴν ἀνεξάντλητη πορφύρα
τὸ βράδι ἐκεῖνο τοῦ γυρισμοῦ
πού ἄρχισαν νὰ σφυρίζουν οἱ Σεμνὲς
στὸ λιγοστὸ χορτάρι —
εἶδα τὰ φίδια σταυρωτὰ μὲ τὶς ὀχιὲς
πλεγμένα πάνω στὴν κακὴ γενιὰ
τὴ μοίρα μας.

Φωνὲς ἀπὸ τὴν πέτρα ἀπὸ τὸν ὕπνο
βαθύτερες ἐδῶ πού ὁ κόσμος σκοτεινιάζει,
μνήμη τοῦ μόχθου ριζωμένη στὸ ρυθμὸ
πού χτύπησε τὴ γῆς μὲ πόδια
λησμονημένα.
Σώματα βυθισμένα στὰ θεμέλια
τοῦ ἄλλου καιροῦ, γυμνά. Μάτια
προσηλωμένα προσηλωμένα, σ' ἕνα σημάδι
πού ὅσο κι' ἂν θέλεις δὲν τὸ ξεχωρίζεις·
ἡ ψυχὴ
πού μάχεται γιὰ νὰ γίνει ψυχή σου.

Μήτε κι' ἡ σιωπὴ εἶναι πιὰ δική σου
ἐδῶ πού σταματήσαν οἱ μυλόπετρες.

Ὀχτώβρης 1935

who've followed so many times
the path from killer to victim
from victim to punishment
from punishment to the next murder,
groping
the inexhaustible purple
that night of the return
when the Furies began whistling
in the meager grass—
I've seen snakes crossed with vipers
knotted over the evil generation
our fate.

Voices out of the stone out of sleep
deeper here where the world darkens,
memory of toil rooted in the rhythm
beaten upon the earth by feet
forgotten.
Bodies sunk into the foundations
of the other time, naked. Eyes
fixed, fixed on a point
that you can't make out, much as you want to:
the soul
struggling to become your own soul.

Not even the silence is now yours
here where the mill stones have stopped turning.

October 1935

ΤΕΤΡΑΔΙΟ ΓΥΜΝΑΣΜΑΤΩΝ

BOOK OF EXERCISES*

ΔΟΣΜΕΝΑ

POEMS GIVEN

ΓΡΑΜΜΑ ΤΟΥ ΜΑΘΙΟΥ ΠΑΣΚΑΛΗ

Οἱ οὐρανοξύστες τῆς Νέας Ὑόρκης δὲ θὰ γνωρίσουν ποτὲ
τὴ δροσούλα ποὺ κατεβαίνει στὴν Κηφισιὰ
μὰ οἱ δυὸ καμινάδες ποὺ μ' ἄρεσαν στὴν ξενιτειὰ πίσω ἀπ'
τὰ κέδρα, γυρίζουν πάλι
σὰ βλέπω τὰ δυὸ κυπαρίσσια πάνω ἀπὸ τὴ γνώριμή σου
τὴν ἐκκλησιὰ
ποὺ ἔχει τοὺς κολασμένους ζωγραφιστοὺς νὰ τυραννιοῦνται
μὲς στὴ φωτιὰ καὶ στὴν ἀθάλη.

Ὅλο τὸ Μάρτη τὰ λαγόνια σου τὰ ὡραῖα τὰ ρήμαξαν οἱ
ρεματισμοὶ καὶ τὸ καλοκαίρι πῆγες στὴν Αἰδηψό.
Θεοί! πῶς ἀγωνίζεται ἡ ζωὴ γιὰ νὰ περάσει, θά 'λεγες
φουσκωμένο ποτάμι ἀπὸ τὴν τρύπα βελόνας.
Κάνει ζέστη βαθιὰ ὣς τὴ νύχτα, τ' ἄστρα πετᾶνε σκνίπες,
πίνω ἄγουρες γκαζόζες καὶ διψῶ·
φεγγάρι καὶ κινηματογράφος, φαντάσματα καὶ πνιγερὸς
ἀνήμπορος λιμιώνας.

Βερίνα, μᾶς ἐρήμωσε ἡ ζωὴ κι' οἱ ἀττικοὶ οὐρανοὶ κι' οἱ
διανοούμενοι ποὺ σκαρφαλώνουν στὸ ἴδιο τους κεφάλι
καὶ τὰ τοπία ποὺ κατάντησαν νὰ παίρνουν πόζες ἀπὸ τὴν
ξεραΐλα κι' ἀπὸ τὴν πείνα
σὰν τοὺς νέους ποὺ ξόδεψαν ὅλη τους τὴν ψυχὴ γιὰ νὰ φο-
ρέσουν ἕνα μονογυάλι

LETTER OF MATHIOS PASKALIS

The skyscrapers of New York will never know the coolness
that comes down on Kifisia*
but when I see the two cypresses above your familiar church
with the paintings of the damned being tortured in fire and
brimstone
then I recall the two chimneys behind the cedars I used to
like so much when I was abroad.

All March rheumatism wracked your lovely loins and in
summer you went to Aedipsos.*
God! what a struggle it is for life to keep going, as though
it were a swollen river passing through the eye of a
needle.
Heavy heat till nightfall, the stars discharging midges, I
myself drinking bitter lemonades and still remaining
thirsty;
Moon and cinema, phantoms and the suffocating pestiferous
marshes.

Verina, life has ruined us, along with the Attic skies and the
intellectuals clambering up their own heads
and the landscapes reduced by drought and hunger to
posing
like young men selling their souls in order to wear a
monocle

σὰν τὶς κοπέλες ἡλιοτρόπια ρουφώντας τὴν κορφή τους γιὰ
νὰ γίνουν κρίνα.

Ἀργοῦν οἱ μέρες· οἱ μέρες οἱ δικές μου τριγυρίζουν μέσα
στὰ ρολόγια καὶ ρυμουλκοῦνε τὸ λεπτοδείχτη.
Γιὰ θυμήσου σὰ στρίβαμε λαχανιασμένοι τὰ σοκάκια γιὰ
νὰ μὴ μᾶς ξεκοιλιάσουν οἱ φάροι τῶν αὐτοκινήτων.
Ἡ σκέψη τοῦ ξένου κόσμου μᾶς κύκλωνε καὶ μᾶς στένευε
σὰν ἕνα δίχτυ
καὶ φεύγαμε μ' ἕνα λεπίδι κρυμμένο μέσα μας κι' ἔλεγες
«ὁ Ἁρμόδιος κι' ὁ Ἀριστογείτων».

Βερίνα, σκύψε τὸ κεφάλι νὰ σὲ ἰδῶ, μὰ κι' ἂ σ' ἔβλεπα θὰ
γύρευα νὰ κοιτάξω πιὸ πέρα.
Τί ἀξίζει ἕνας ἄνθρωπος τί θέλει καὶ πῶς θὰ δικαιολογήσει
τὴν ὕπαρξή του στὴ δευτέρα παρουσία;
Ἄ! νὰ βρισκόμουνα ξυλάρμενος χαμένος στὸν Εἰρηνι-
κὸν Ὠκεανὸ μόνος μὲ τὴ θάλασσα καὶ τὸν ἀγέρα
μόνος καὶ χωρὶς ἀσύρματο οὔτε δύναμη γιὰ νὰ παλέψω μὲ
τὰ στοιχεῖα.

Κοκκιναράς, 5 Αὐγούστου 1928

like young girls sucking a sunflower to make its head lily-
like.

The days pass slowly; my own days circulate among the
clocks dragging the second hand in tow.
Remember how we used to twist breathlessly through the
alleys so as not to be gutted by the headlights of cars.
The idea of the world abroad enveloped us and gathered
us in like a net
and we left with a sharp knife hidden within us and you
said "Harmodios and Aristogeiton."

Verina, lower your head so that I can see you, though even
if I were to see you I'd want to look beyond.
What's a man's value? What does he want and how will he
justify his existence at the Second Coming?
Ah, to find myself on a derelict ship lost in the Pacific Ocean
alone with the sea and the wind
alone and without a wireless or strength to fight the
elements.

Kokkinaras, 5 August 1928

ΛΕΩΦΟΡΟΣ ΣΥΓΓΡΟΥ, 1930

Στὸ Γιῶργο Θεοτοκᾶ ποὺ τὴν ἀνακάλυψε

Ὅταν σὲ νικήσει
τὸ χαμογέλιο ποὺ ἀνασαίνει πλάι σου, πάει νὰ σκύψει καὶ δὲ συγκατανεύει

ὅταν ἡ ζάλη ποὺ σοῦ ἀπόμεινε ἀρμενίζοντας στὰ βιβλία ξεκολλήσει ἀπὸ τὸ μυαλό σου στὶς πιπεριὲς δεξιὰ κι᾿ ἀριστερὰ

ὅταν ἀφήσεις τὸ πετρωμένο καράβι ποὺ ταξιδεύει πρὸς τὸ βυθὸ μ᾿ ἄρμενα συντριμμένα
τὴν καμάρα μὲ τὰ χρυσαφικά της
τὶς κολόνες μὲ τὴν ἔνια τους ποὺ τὶς στενεύει

ὅταν ἀφήσεις τὰ κορμιὰ τὰ πελεκημένα ἐπίτηδες γιὰ νὰ μετροῦν καὶ γιὰ νὰ θησαυρίζουν
τὴν ψυχὴ ποὺ δὲν ἐξισώνεται, ὅ,τι καὶ νὰ κάνεις, μὲ τὴν ψυχή σου
τὸ χέρι τοῦ φόρου
τὸ γυναίκειο ἐκεῖνο προσωπάκι στὸ λίκνο ποὺ λάμπει στὸν ἥλιο

ὅταν ἀφήσεις τὴν καρδιά σου καὶ τὴ σκέψη σου νὰ γίνουν ἕνα

SYNGROU AVENUE, 1930

To George Theotokas, who discovered it*

When the smile
breathing beside you conquers you, tries to submit and
doesn't consent

when the dizziness that remains from your wandering
among books moves from your mind to the pepper-
trees on either side

when you leave the petrified ship traveling with broken
rigging towards the depths
the arch with gold decoration
the columns with their care making them more narrow

when you leave behind you the bodies deliberately carved
for counting and for hoarding riches
the soul that, whatever you do, doesn't match your own soul
the hand of the impost
that small feminine face in the cradle shining in the sun

when you let your heart and your thought become one

μὲ τὸ μαυριδερὸ ποτάμι ποὺ τεντώνει ξυλιάζει καὶ φεύγει:

Σπάσε τὸ νῆμα τῆς 'Αριάδνης καὶ νά!
Τὸ γαλάζιο κορμὶ τῆς γοργόνας.

with the blackish river that stretches, stiffens and leaves:

Break Ariadne's thread and look!
The blue body of the mermaid.

ΠΑΝΩ Σ' ΕΝΑΝ ΞΕΝΟ ΣΤΙΧΟ

Στὴν Ἕλλη, Χριστούγεννα 1931

Εὐτυχισμένος ποὺ ἔκανε τὸ ταξίδι τοῦ Ὀδυσσέα.
Εὐτυχισμένος ἂν στὸ ξεκίνημα, ἔνιωθε γερὴ τὴν ἀρματωσιὰ
μιᾶς ἀγάπης, ἁπλωμένη μέσα στὸ κορμί του, σὰν τὶς
φλέβες ὅπου βουίζει τὸ αἷμα.

Μιᾶς ἀγάπης μὲ ἀκατέλυτο ρυθμό, ἀκατανίκητης σὰν τὴ
μουσικὴ καὶ παντοτινῆς
γιατὶ γεννήθηκε ὅταν γεννηθήκαμε καὶ σὰν πεθαίνουμε, ἂν
πεθαίνει, δὲν τὸ ξέρουμε οὔτε ἐμεῖς οὔτε ἄλλος κανείς.

Παρακαλῶ τὸ θεὸ νὰ μὲ συντρέξει νὰ πῶ, σὲ μιὰ στιγμὴ
μεγάλης εὐδαιμονίας, ποιὰ εἶναι αὐτὴ ἡ ἀγάπη·
κάθομαι κάποτε τριγυρισμένος ἀπὸ τὴν ξενιτειά, κι' ἀκούω
τὸ μακρινὸ βούισμά της, σὰν τὸν ἀχὸ τῆς θάλασσας
ποὺ ἔσμιξε μὲ τὸ ἀνεξήγητο δρολάπι.

Καὶ παρουσιάζεται μπροστά μου, πάλι καὶ πάλι, τὸ φάντασμα τοῦ Ὀδυσσέα, μὲ μάτια κοκκινισμένα ἀπὸ τοῦ
κυμάτου τὴν ἁρμύρα
κι' ἀπὸ τὸ μεστωμένο πόθο νὰ ξαναδεῖ τὸν καπνὸ ποὺ βγαίνει ἀπὸ τὴ ζεστασιὰ τοῦ σπιτιοῦ του καὶ τὸ σκυλί του
ποὺ γέρασε προσμένοντας στὴ θύρα.

UPON A FOREIGN VERSE

For Elli, Christmas 1931

Fortunate he who's made the voyage of Odysseus.*
Fortunate if on setting out he's felt the rigging of a love
strong in his body, spreading there like veins where
the blood throbs.

A love of indissoluble rhythm, unconquerable like music
and endless
because it was born when we were born and when it dies,
if it does die, neither we know nor does anyone else.

I ask God to help me say, at some moment of great happiness, what that love is;
sometimes when I sit surrounded by exile I hear its distant
murmur like the sound of sea struck by an inexplicable
hurricane.

And again and again the shade of Odysseus appears before
me, his eyes red from the waves' salt,
from his ripe longing to see once more the smoke ascending from his warm hearth and the dog grown old
waiting by the door.

Στέκεται μεγάλος, ψιθυρίζοντας ἀνάμεσα στ' ἀσπρισμένα
του γένεια, λόγια τῆς γλώσσας μας, ὅπως τὴ μιλούσαν
πρὶν τρεῖς χιλιάδες χρόνια.
Ἁπλώνει μιὰ παλάμη ροζιασμένη ἀπὸ τὰ σκοινιὰ καὶ τὸ
δοιάκι, μὲ δέρμα δουλεμένο ἀπὸ τὸ ξεροβόρι ἀπὸ τὴν
κάψα κι' ἀπὸ τὰ χιόνια.

Θά 'λεγες πὼς θέλει νὰ διώξει τὸν ὑπεράνθρωπο Κύκλωπα
ποὺ βλέπει μ' ἕνα μάτι, τὶς Σειρῆνες ποὺ σὰν τὶς ἀ-
κούσεις ξεχνᾶς, τὴ Σκύλλα καὶ τὴ Χάρυβδη ἀπ' ἀνάμεσό μας·
τόσα περίπλοκα τέρατα, ποὺ δὲ μᾶς ἀφήνουν νὰ στοχαστοῦ-
με, πὼς εἴταν κι' αὐτὸς ἕνας ἄνθρωπος ποὺ πάλεψε μέσα στὸν κόσμο, μὲ τὴν ψυχὴ καὶ μὲ τὸ σῶμα.

Εἶναι ὁ μεγάλος 'Οδυσσέας· ἐκεῖνος ποὺ εἶπε νὰ γίνει τὸ
ξύλινο ἄλογο καὶ οἱ 'Αχαιοὶ κερδίσανε τὴν Τροία.
Φαντάζομαι πὼς ἔρχεται νὰ μ' ἁρμηνέψει πῶς νὰ φτιάξω
κι' ἐγὼ ἕνα ξύλινο ἄλογο γιὰ νὰ κερδίσω τὴ δική μου
Τροία.

Γιατὶ μιλᾶ ταπεινὰ καὶ μὲ γαλήνη, χωρὶς προσπάθεια, λὲς
μὲ γνωρίζει σὰν πατέρας
εἴτε σὰν κάτι γέρους θαλασσινούς, ποὺ ἀκουμπισμένοι στὰ
δίχτυα τους, τὴν ὥρα ποὺ χειμώνιαζε καὶ θύμωνε ὁ
ἀγέρας,

μοῦ λέγανε, στὰ παιδικά μου χρόνια, τὸ τραγούδι τοῦ 'Ε-
ρωτόκριτου μὲ τὰ δάκρυα στὰ μάτια·

A large man, whispering through his whitened beard words in our language spoken as it was three thousand years ago.
He extends a palm calloused by the ropes and the tiller, his skin weathered by the dry north wind, by heat and snow.

It's as if he wants to expel from among us the superhuman one-eyed Cyclops, the Sirens who make you forget with their song, Scylla and Charybdis:
so many complex monsters that prevent us from remembering that he too was a man struggling in the world with soul and body.

He is the mighty Odysseus: he who proposed the wooden horse with which the Achaeans captured Troy.
I imagine he's coming to tell me how I too may build a wooden horse to capture my own Troy.

Because he speaks humbly and calmly, without effort, as though he were my father
or certain old sailors of my childhood who, leaning on their nets with winter coming on and the wind angering,

used to recite, with tears in their eyes, the song of Erotocritos;*

τότες πού τρόμαζα μέσα στόν ὕπνο μου ἀκούγοντας τήν ἀντίδικη μοίρα τῆς Ἀρετῆς νά κατεβαίνει τά μαρμαρένια σκαλοπάτια.

Μοῦ λέει τό δύσκολο πόνο νά νιώθεις τά πανιά τοῦ καραβιοῦ σου φουσκωμένα ἀπό τή θύμηση καί τήν ψυχή σου νά γίνεται τιμόνι.
Καί νά 'σαι μόνος, σκοτεινός μέσα στή νύχτα καί ἀκυβέρνητος σάν τ' ἄχερο στ' ἁλώνι.

Τήν πίκρα νά βλέπεις τούς συντρόφους σου καταποντισμένους μέσα στά στοιχεῖα, σκορπισμένους: ἕναν-ἕναν.
Καί πόσο παράξενα ἀντρειεύεσαι μιλώντας μέ τούς πεθαμένους, ὅταν δέ φτάνουν πιά οἱ ζωντανοί πού σοῦ ἀπομέναν.

Μιλᾶ... βλέπω ἀκόμη τά χέρια του πού ξέραν νά δοκιμάσουν ἂν εἶταν καλά σκαλισμένη στήν πλώρη ἡ γοργόνα
νά μοῦ χαρίζουν τήν ἀκύμαντη γαλάζια θάλασσα μέσα στήν καρδιά τοῦ χειμώνα.

it was then I would shudder in my sleep at the unjust fate
of Aretousa descending the marble steps.

He tells me of the harsh pain you feel when the ship's sails
swell with memory and your soul becomes a rudder;
of being alone, dark in the night, and helpless as chaff on
the threshing floor;

of the bitterness of seeing your companions one by one
pulled down into the elements and scattered;
and of how strangely you gain strength conversing with the
dead when the living who remain are no longer
enough.

He speaks . . . I still see his hands that knew how to judge
the carving of the mermaid at the prow
presenting me the waveless blue sea in the heart of winter.

ΔΕΚΑΕΞΙ ΧΑ·Ι·-ΚΑ·Ι·

Τοῦτο τὸ ἀκαριαῖον...
ΜΑΡΚΟΣ ΑΥΡΗΛΙΟΣ

Α΄

Στάξε στὴ λίμνη
μόνο μιὰ στάλα κρασὶ
καὶ σβήνει ὁ ἥλιος.

Β΄

Στὸν κάμπο οὔτ᾿ ἕνα
τετράφυλλο τριφύλλι·
ποιὸς φταίει ἀπ᾿ τοὺς τρεῖς;

Γ΄

Στὸν κῆπο τοῦ Μουσείου

Ἄδειες καρέκλες
τ᾿ ἀγάλματα γυρίσαν
στ᾿ ἄλλο μουσεῖο.

Δ΄

Νά ᾿ναι ἡ φωνὴ
πεθαμένων φίλων μας
ἢ φωνογράφος;

SIXTEEN HAIKU

Τοῦτο τὸ ἀκαριαῖον . . .
MARCUS AURELIUS*

1

Spill into the lake
but a drop of wine
and the sun vanishes.

2

In the field not one
fourleaf clover:
which of the three's to blame?

3

In the Museum garden

Empty chairs:
the statues have gone back
to the other museum.

4

Is it the voice
of our dead friends or
the gramophone?

Ε΄

Τὰ δάχτυλά της
στὸ θαλασσὶ μαντήλι
κοίτα: κοράλλια.

Ϛ΄

Συλλογισμένο
τὸ στῆθος της βαρὺ
μὲς στὸν καθρέφτη.

Ζ΄

Φόρεσα πάλι
τὴ φυλλωσιὰ τοῦ δέντρου
κι' ἐσὺ βελάζεις.

Η΄

Νύχτα, ὁ ἀγέρας
ὁ χωρισμὸς ἁπλώνει
καὶ κυματίζει.

5

Her fingers
against the blue scarf—
look: corals.

6

Meditative
her breasts heavy
in the looking-glass.

7

Again I put on
the tree's foliage
and you—you bleat.

8

Night, the wind
separation
spreads and undulates.

Θ΄

Νέα Μοίρα

Γυμνὴ γυναίκα
τὸ ρόδι ποὺ ἔσπασε εἴταν
γεμάτο ἀστέρια.

Ι΄

Τώρα σηκώνω
μιὰ νεκρὴ πεταλούδα
χωρὶς φτιασίδι.

ΙΑ΄

Ποῦ νὰ μαζεύεις
τὰ χίλια κομματάκια
τοῦ κάθε ἀνθρώπου.

ΙΒ΄

Ἄγονος γραμμὴ

Τὸ δοιάκι τί ἔχει ;
Ἡ βάρκα γράφει κύκλους
κι᾽ οὔτε ἕνας γλάρος.

9

Young Fate

Naked woman
the pomegranate that broke
was full of stars.

10

Now I raise
a dead butterfly
without make-up.

11

How can you gather together
the thousand fragments
of each person?

12

Unprofitable line

What's wrong with the rudder?
The boat inscribes circles
and there's not a single gull.

ΙΓ′

Ἄρρωστη Ἐρινὺς

Δὲν ἔχει μάτια
τὰ φίδια ποὺ κρατοῦσε
τῆς τρῶν τὰ χέρια.

ΙΔ′

Τούτη ἡ κολόνα
ἔχει μιὰ τρύπα, βλέπεις
τὴν Περσεφόνη;

ΙΕ′

Βουλιάζει ὁ κόσμος
κρατήσου, θὰ σ' ἀφήσει
μόνο στὸν ἥλιο.

ΙϚ′

Γράφεις·
τὸ μελάνι λιγόστεψε
ἡ θάλασσα πληθαίνει.

13

Sick Fury

She has no eyes,
the snakes she held
devour her hands.

14

This column has a hole:
can you see
Persephone?

15

The world sinks:
hang on, it'll leave you
alone in the sun.

16

You write:
the ink grew less,
the sea increases.

Τοῦτο τὸ σῶμα πού ἔλπιζε σὰν τὸ κλωνὶ ν' ἀνθίσει
καὶ νὰ καρπίσει καὶ στὴν παγωνιὰ νὰ γίνει αὐλὸς
ἡ φαντασία τὸ βύθισε σ' ἕνα βουερὸ μελίσσι
γιὰ νὰ περνᾶ καὶ νὰ τὸ βασανίζει ὁ μουσικὸς καιρός.

This body that hoped to flower like a branch,
to bear fruit, to become a flute in the frost—
imagination has thrust it into a noisy bee-hive
so that musical time may come and torture it.

ΦΥΓΗ

Δὲν εἴταν ἄλλη ἡ ἀγάπη μας
ἔφευγε ξαναγύριζε καὶ μᾶς ἔφερνε
ἕνα χαμηλωμένο βλέφαρο πολὺ μακρινὸ
ἕνα χαμόγελο μαρμαρωμένο, χαμένο
μέσα στὸ πρωινὸ χορτάρι
ἕνα παράξενο κοχύλι ποὺ δοκίμαζε
νὰ τὸ ἐξηγήσει ἐπίμονα ἡ ψυχή μας.

Ἡ ἀγάπη μας δὲν εἴταν ἄλλη ψηλαφοῦσε
σιγὰ μέσα στὰ πράγματα ποὺ μᾶς τριγύριζαν
νὰ ἐξηγήσει γιατί δὲ θέλουμε νὰ πεθάνουμε
μὲ τόσο πάθος.

Κι᾿ ἂν κρατηθήκαμε ἀπὸ λαγόνια κι᾿ ἂν ἀγκαλιάσαμε
μ᾿ ὅλη τὴ δύναμή μας ἄλλους αὐχένες
κι᾿ ἂν σμίξαμε τὴν ἀνάσα μας μὲ τὴν ἀνάσα
ἐκείνου τοῦ ἀνθρώπου
κι᾿ ἂν κλείσαμε τὰ μάτια μας, δὲν εἴταν ἄλλη
μονάχα αὐτὸς ὁ βαθύτερος καημὸς νὰ κρατηθοῦμε
μέσα στὴ φυγή.

FLIGHT

Our love was not other than this:
it left came back and brought us
a distant eyelid lowered far away
a stony smile, lost
in the dawn grass
a strange shell our soul
insistently tried to explain.

Our love was not other than this: it groped
silently among the things around us
to explain why we don't want to die
so passionately.

And if we've held on by the loins, clasped
other necks as tightly as we could,
mingled our breath with the breath
of that person
if we've closed our eyes, it was not other than this:
simply that deep longing to hang on
in our flight.

ΠΕΡΙΓΡΑΦΗ

Πλησιάζει μὲ τὰ θολά της μάτια ἐκεῖνο τὸ ἀνάγλυφο χέρι
τὸ χέρι ποὺ κράτησε τὸ δοιάκι
τὸ χέρι ποὺ κράτησε τὴν πένα
τὸ χέρι ποὺ ἁπλώθηκε στὸν ἄνεμο,
ὅλα τὴν ἀπειλοῦν τὴ σιωπή της.

Ἀπὸ τὰ πεῦκα μιὰ κίνηση τρέχει πρὸς τὴ θάλασσα
παίζει μὲ τὴν ταπεινὴ πνοὴ τοῦ ἀγέρα
καὶ τὴν ἀναχαιτίζουν οἱ δυὸ μαῦρες Συμπληγάδες.
Ἄνοιξα τὴν καρδιά μου κι᾽ ἀνάσανα!
Στὸ πέλαγο ἀνατρίχιαζε τὸ χρυσὸ δέρας.
Δικό της τὸ χρῶμα τὸ ρίγος καὶ τὸ δέρμα
δικές της οἱ κορυφογραμμὲς στὸν ὁρίζοντα στὴν παλάμη
μου.
Ἄνοιξα τὴν καρδιά μου
γεμάτη εἰκόνες ποὺ ἔσβησαν κιόλας, τὸ σπέρμα τοῦ
Πρωτέα.

Ἐδῶ κοίταξα τὸ φεγγάρι
βαμμένο στὸ αἷμα
τῆς νέας λύκαινας.

Σπέτσες, Αὔγουστος 1934

DESCRIPTION

She draws near with her clouded eyes, that sculptured hand
the hand that held the tiller
the hand that held the pen
the hand that opened in the wind,
everything threatens her silence.

A ripple runs from the pine-trees towards the sea
plays with the breeze's humble breath
and is checked by the two black Symplegades.*
I opened my heart and breathed deeply!
The golden fleece shivered on the sea.
Hers the color the shudder and the skin
hers the mountain-ridges on the horizon of my palm.
I opened my heart
full of images that vanished at once, the seed of Proteus.

Here I gazed at the moon
dyed in the blood
of a young she-wolf.

Spetses, August 1934

ΣΙΡΟΚΟ 7 ΛΕΒΑΝΤΕ

Στὸν Δ. Ι. Ἀντωνίου

Πράγματα ποὺ ἀλλάξαν τὴ μορφή μας
βαθύτερα ἀπ' τὴ σκέψη καὶ περισσότερο
δικά μας ὅπως τὸ αἷμα καὶ περισσότερο
βυθίσανε στὴν κάψα τοῦ μεσημεριοῦ
πίσω ἀπὸ τὰ κατάρτια.

Μέσα στὶς ἁλυσίδες καὶ στὶς προσταγὲς
κανεὶς δὲ θυμᾶται.

Οἱ ἄλλες μέρες οἱ ἄλλες νύχτες
σώματα, πόνος καὶ ἡδονὴ
ἡ πίκρα τῆς ἀνθρώπινης γύμνιας κομματιασμένη
πιὸ χαμηλὴ κι' ἀπὸ τὶς πιπεριὲς σὲ σκονισμένους δρόμους
καὶ τόσες γοητεῖες καὶ τόσα σύμβολα
στὸ τελευταῖο κλωνάρι·
στὸν ἴσκιο τοῦ μεγάλου καραβιοῦ
ἴσκιος ἡ μνήμη.

Τὰ χέρια ποὺ μᾶς ἄγγιξαν δὲ μᾶς ἀνήκουν, μόνο
βαθύτερα, ὅταν σκοτεινιάζουν τὰ τριαντάφυλλα
ἕνας ρυθμὸς στὸν ἴσκιο τοῦ βουνοῦ, τριζόνια
νοτίζει τὴ σιωπή μας μὲς στὴ νύχτα

SIROCCO 7 LEVANTE

For D. I. Antoniou*

Things that changed our shape
deeper than thought and more so
our own like blood and more so
sank into the midday heat
behind the masts.

Among chains and commands
no one remembers.

Other days other nights
bodies, pain and pleasure
the bitterness of human nakedness shattered
lower even than the pepper-trees along dusty roads
and so many charms and so many symbols
on the final branch;
in the shade of the big ship
memory's a shade.

The hands that touched us don't belong to us, only
deeper, when the roses darken,
a rhythm in the mountain's shadow—crickets—
moistens our silence in the night

γυρεύοντας τὸν ὕπνο τοῦ πελάγου
γλιστρώντας πρὸς τὸν ὕπνο τοῦ πελάγου.

Στὸν ἴσκιο τοῦ μεγάλου καραβιοῦ
τὴν ὥρα ποὺ σφύριξε ὁ ἐργάτης
ἄφησα τὴ στοργὴ στοὺς ἀργυραμοιβούς.

Πήλιο, 19 Αὐγούστου 1935

seeking the sea's sleep
slipping towards the sea's sleep.

In the shade of the big ship
as the capstan whistled
I abandoned tenderness to the money-changers.

Pelion, 19 August 1935

ΜΕ ΤΟΝ ΤΡΟΠΟ ΤΟΥ Γ. Σ.

Ὅπου καὶ νὰ ταξιδέψω ἡ Ἑλλάδα μὲ πληγώνει.

Στὸ Πήλιο μέσα στὶς καστανιὲς τὸ πουκάμισο τοῦ Κενταύρου
γλιστροῦσε μέσα στὰ φύλλα γιὰ νὰ τυλιχτεῖ στὸ κορμί μου
καθὼς ἀνέβαινα τὴν ἀνηφόρα κι᾽ ἡ θάλασσα μ᾽ ἀκολουθοῦσε
ἀνεβαίνοντας κι᾽ αὐτὴ σὰν τὸν ὑδράργυρο θερμομέτρου
ὣς ποὺ νὰ βροῦμε τὰ νερὰ τοῦ βουνοῦ.
Στὴ Σαντορίνη ἀγγίζοντας νησιὰ ποὺ βουλιάζαν
ἀκούγοντας νὰ παίζει ἕνα σουραύλι κάπου στὶς ἀλαφρόπετρες
μοῦ κάρφωσε τὸ χέρι στὴν κουπαστὴ
μιὰ σαΐτα τιναγμένη ξαφνικὰ
ἀπὸ τὰ πέρατά μιᾶς νιότης βασιλεμένης.
Στὶς Μυκῆνες σήκωσα τὶς μεγάλες πέτρες καὶ τοὺς θησαυροὺς τῶν Ἀτρειδῶν
καὶ πλάγιασα μαζί τους στὸ ξενοδοχεῖο τῆς «Ὡραίας Ἑλένης τοῦ Μενελάου»·
χάθηκαν μόνο τὴν αὐγὴ ποὺ λάλησε ἡ Κασσάντρα
μ᾽ ἕναν κόκορα κρεμασμένο στὸ μαῦρο λαιμό της.
Στὶς Σπέτσες στὸν Πόρο καὶ στὴ Μύκονο
μὲ χτίκιασαν οἱ βαρκαρόλες.

⁘

IN THE MANNER OF G. S.

Wherever I travel Greece wounds me.

On Pelion among the chestnut trees the Centaur's shirt*
slipped through the leaves to fold around my body
as I climbed the slope and the sea came after me
climbing too like mercury in a thermometer
till we found the mountain waters.
On Santorini touching islands that were sinking*
hearing a pipe play somewhere on the pumice stone
my hand was nailed to the gunwale
by an arrow shot suddenly
from the confines of a vanished youth.
At Mycenae I raised the great stones and the treasures of
the house of Atreus
and slept with them at the hotel "Belle Helène";
they disappeared only at dawn when Cassandra crowed,
a cock hanging from her black throat.
On Spetses, Poros, and Mykonos*
the barcaroles sickened me.

✧

Τί θέλουν ὅλοι αὐτοὶ ποὺ λένε
πὼς βρίσκουνται στὴν Ἀθήνα ἢ στὸν Πειραιᾶ;
Ὁ ἕνας ἔρχεται ἀπὸ τὴ Σαλαμίνα καὶ ρωτάει τὸν ἄλλο μήπως «ἔρχεται ἐξ Ὁμονοίας»
«Ὄχι ἔρχομαι ἐκ Συντάγματος» ἀπαντᾶ κι' εἶν' εὐχαριστημένος
«βρῆκα τὸ Γιάννη καὶ μὲ κέρασε ἕνα παγωτό».
Στὸ μεταξὺ ἡ Ἑλλάδα ταξιδεύει
δὲν ξέρουμε τίποτε δὲν ξέρουμε πὼς εἴμαστε ξέμπαρκοι ὅλοι ἐμεῖς
δὲν ξέρουμε τὴν πίκρα τοῦ λιμανιοῦ σὰν ταξιδεύουν ὅλα τὰ καράβια·
περιγελᾶμε ἐκείνους ποὺ τὴ νιώθουν.

Παράξενος κόσμος ποὺ λέει πὼς βρίσκεται στὴν Ἀττικὴ καὶ δὲ βρίσκεται πουθενά·
ἀγοράζουν κουφέτα γιὰ νὰ παντρευτοῦνε
κρατοῦν «σωσίτριχα» φωτογραφίζουνται
ὁ ἄνθρωπος ποὺ εἶδα σήμερα καθισμένος σ' ἕνα φόντο μὲ πιτσούνια καὶ μὲ λουλούδια
δέχουνταν τὸ χέρι τοῦ γέρο φωτογράφου νὰ τοῦ στρώνει τὶς ρυτίδες
ποὺ εἶχαν ἀφήσει στὸ πρόσωπό του
ὅλα τὰ πετεινὰ τ' οὐρανοῦ.

Στὸ μεταξὺ ἡ Ἑλλάδα ταξιδεύει ὁλοένα ταξιδεύει
κι' ἂν «ὁρῶμεν ἀνθοῦν πέλαγος Αἰγαῖον νεκροῖς»

What do they want, all those who believe
they're in Athens or Piraeus?
Someone comes from Salamis and asks someone else whether
he comes "from Omonia Square?"
"No, from Syntagma," replies the other, pleased;*
"I met Yianni and he treated me to an ice cream."
In the meantime Greece is traveling
and we don't know anything, we don't know we're all sailors
out of work,
we don't know how bitter the port becomes when all the
ships have gone;
we mock those who do know.

Strange people! they say they're in Attica but they're really
nowhere;
they buy sugared almonds to get married
they carry hair tonic, have their photographs taken
the man I saw today sitting against a background of pigeons
and flowers
let the hands of the old photographer smoothe away the
wrinkles
left on his face
by all the birds in the sky.

Meanwhile Greece goes on traveling, always traveling
and if we see "the Aegean flower with corpses"*

εἶναι ἐκεῖνοι ποὺ θέλησαν νὰ πιάσουν τὸ μεγάλο καράβι μὲ
τὸ κολύμπι
ἐκεῖνοι ποὺ βαρέθηκαν νὰ περιμένουν τὰ καράβια ποὺ δὲν
μποροῦν νὰ κινήσουν
τὴν ΕΛΣΗ τὴ ΣΑΜΟΘΡΑΚΗ τὸν ΑΜΒΡΑΚΙΚΟ.
Σφυρίζουν τὰ καράβια τώρα ποὺ βραδιάζει στὸν Πειραιᾶ
σφυρίζουν ὁλοένα σφυρίζουν μὰ δὲν κουνιέται κανένας ἀρ-
γάτης
καμμιὰ ἁλυσίδα δὲν ἔλαμψε βρεμένη στὸ στερνὸ φῶς ποὺ
βασιλεύει
ὁ καπετάνιος μένει μαρμαρωμένος μὲς στ' ἄσπρα καὶ στὰ
χρυσά.

Ὅπου καὶ νὰ ταξιδέψω ἡ Ἑλλάδα μὲ πληγώνει·
παραπετάσματα βουνῶν ἀρχιπέλαγα γυμνοὶ γρανίτες...
Τὸ καράβι ποὺ ταξιδεύει τὸ λένε ΑΓ ΩΝΙΑ 937.

Ἀ/π *Αὐλίς*, περιμένοντας νὰ ξεκινήσει.
Καλοκαίρι 1936

it will be with those who tried to catch the big ship by
    swimming after it
those who got tired waiting for the ships that cannot move
the ELSI, the SAMOTHRAKI, the AMVRAKIKOS.
The ships hoot now that dusk falls on Piraeus,
hoot and hoot, but no capstan moves,
no chain gleams wet in the vanishing light,
the captain stands like a stone in white and gold.

Wherever I travel Greece wounds me,
curtains of mountains, archipelagos, naked granite.
They call the one ship that sails AG ONIA 937.

M/S *Aulis,* waiting to sail. Summer 1936

Ο ΓΕΡΟΣ

Πέρασαν τόσα κοπάδια τόσοι φτωχοὶ
καὶ πλούσιοι καβαλάρηδες, ἄλλοι
ἀπὸ τὰ μακρινὰ χωριὰ εἴχαν μείνει
τὴ νύχτα στὰ χαντάκια τῆς δημοσιᾶς
ἄναψαν φωτιὲς γιὰ τοὺς λύκους, βλέπεις
τὴ στάχτη ; Μαυριδεροὶ κύκλοι ἐπουλωμένοι.
Εἶναι γεμάτος σημάδια σὰν τὸ δρόμο.
Στὸ ξεροπήγαδο πιὸ πάνω ρίχναν τὰ λυσσασμένα
σκυλιά, δὲν ἔχει μάτια εἶναι γεμάτος
σημάδια κι' ἀλαφρύς· φυσᾶ ὁ ἀγέρας·
δὲν ξεχωρίζει τίποτε ξέρει τὰ πάντα,
ἄδειο θηκάρι τζίτζικα σὲ κούφιο δέντρο
δὲν ἔχει μάτια μήτε στὰ χέρια, ξέρει
τὴν αὐγὴ καὶ τὸ δείλι ξέρει τ' ἀστέρια
τὸ αἷμα τους δὲν τὸν θρέφει, μήτε νεκρὸς
δὲν εἶναι, δὲν ἔχει φυλὴ δὲ θὰ πεθάνει
θὰ τὸν ξεχάσουν ἔτσι, μήτε πρόγονος.
Τὰ κουρασμένα νύχια στὰ δάχτυλά του
γράφουν σταυροὺς πάνω σὲ σάπιες θύμησες
καθὼς φυσᾶ ὁ ἀγέρας θολός. Χιονίζει.

Εἴδα τὴν πάχνη γύρω στὰ πρόσωπα
εἴδα τὰ χείλια ὑγρὰ τὰ δάκρυα παγωμένα
στὴν κόχη τοῦ ματιοῦ, εἴδα τὴ γραμμὴ

THE OLD MAN

So many flocks have passed so many poor
and rich riders, some
from distant villages had spent
the night in road-side ditches
lighting fires against the wolves: do you see
the ashes? Blackish circles cicatrized.
He's full of marks like the road.
In the dry well above they'd thrown the rabid
dogs. He's got no eyes, he's full
of marks, he's light; the wind blows;
he distinguishes nothing, knows everything,
empty sheath of a cicada on a hollow tree.
He's got no eyes, not even in his hands, he knows
dawn and dusk, knows the stars,
their blood doesn't nourish him, nor is
he dead, he has no race, he won't die,
they'll simply forget him, he has no ancestors.
His tired fingernails
inscribe crosses on decayed memories
while the wind blows darkly. It snows.

I saw the hoarfrost around the faces
I saw the lips wet, tears frozen
in the corner of the eye, I saw the line

τοῦ πόνου πλάι στὰ ρουθούνια καὶ τὴν προσπάθεια
στὶς ρίζες τοῦ χεριοῦ, εἶδα τὸ σῶμα νὰ τελειώνει.
Δὲν εἶναι μόνος ὁ ἴσκιος αὐτὸς δεμένος
σ' ἕνα στεγνὸ ραβδὶ ποὺ δὲ λυγίζει
δὲ σκύβει νὰ πλαγιάσει, δὲν μπορεῖ·
ὁ ὕπνος θὰ σκόρπιζε τὶς κλείδωσές του
στὰ χέρια τῶν παιδιῶν νὰ παίξουν.
Προστάζει σὰν τοὺς πεθαμένους κλώνους
ποὺ σπᾶνε ὅταν νυχτώνει καὶ ξυπνᾶ
ὁ ἀγέρας μὲς στὶς λαγκαδιὲς
προστάζει τοὺς ἴσκιους τῶν ἀνθρώπων
ὄχι τὸν ἄνθρωπο μέσα στὸν ἴσκιο
ποὺ δὲν ἀκούει παρὰ τὴ χαμηλὴ φωνὴ
τῆς γῆς καὶ τοῦ πελάγου ἐκεῖ ποὺ σμίγουν
τῆς μοίρας τὴ φωνή. Στέκεται ὁλόρθος
στὴν ὄχθη, μέσα σὲ κουβάρια κόκκαλα
μέσα σὲ στίβες κίτρινα φύλλα:
ἄδειο κλουβὶ προσμένοντας
τὴν ὥρα τῆς φωτιᾶς.

Ντρένοβο, Φλεβάρης 1937

of pain by the nostrils and the effort
at the roots of the hand, I saw the body come to an end.
He isn't alone, this shadow
bound to a dry inflexible stick
he doesn't bend to lie down, he can't:
sleep will have scattered his joints
as playthings into the hands of children.
He commands like dead branches
that break when night comes and the wind
wakes in the ravines
he commands the shades of men
not the man in the shadow
who hears nothing but the low voices
of earth and sea there where they mix
with the voice of destiny. He stands upright
on the bank, among piles of bones
among heaps of yellow leaves:
empty cage that waits
for the hour of fire.

Drenovo, February 1937

Ο κ. ΣΤΡΑΤΗΣ ΘΑΛΑΣΣΙΝΟΣ

Κι' ἑτοιμαζότουνα νὰ φωνάξει δυνατὰ γιὰ νὰ δείξει πὼς δὲν πέθανε.

ΣΟΛΩΜΟΣ, *Η ΓΥΝΑΙΚΑ ΤΗΣ ΖΑΚΥΘΟΣ*

MR. STRATIS THALASSINOS*

And he was preparing to cry out to show that he wasn't dead.

SOLOMOS, *THE WOMAN OF ZAKYNTHOS*

ΠΕΝΤΕ ΠΟΙΗΜΑΤΑ ΤΟΥ κ. Σ. ΘΑΛΑΣΣΙΝΟΥ

Α'. HAMPSTEAD

Σὰν ἕνα πουλὶ μὲ σπασμένη φτερούγα
ποὺ θά 'χε χρόνια μέσα στὸν ἀγέρα ταξιδέψει
σὰν ἕνα πουλὶ ποὺ δὲν μπόρεσε νὰ βαστάξει
τὸν ἀγέρα καὶ τὴ φουρτούνα
πέφτει τὸ βράδι.
Πάνω στὸ πράσινο χορτάρι
εἶχαν χορέψει ὅλη τὴ μέρα τρεῖς χιλιάδες ἀγγέλοι
γυμνοὶ σὰν ἀτσάλι
πέφτει τὸ βράδι χλομό·
οἱ τρεῖς χιλιάδες ἀγγέλοι
μαζέψαν τὰ φτερά τους καὶ γενήκαν
ἕνα σκυλὶ
ξεχασμένο
ποὺ γαυγίζει
μοναχὸ
καὶ γυρεύει τὸν ἀφέντη του
ἢ τὴ δευτέρα παρουσία
ἢ ἕνα κόκκαλο.
Τώρα γυρεύω λίγη ἡσυχία
θὰ μοῦ 'φτανε μιὰ καλύβα σ' ἕνα λόφο
ἢ σὲ μιὰ ἀκρογιαλιὰ
θὰ μοῦ 'φτανε μπροστὰ στὸ παράθυρό μου

FIVE POEMS BY MR. S. THALASSINOS

I. HAMPSTEAD

Like a bird with broken wing
that had traveled through wind for years
like a bird unable to endure
tempest and wind
the evening falls.
On the green grass
three thousand angels had danced the day long
naked as steel
the pale evening falls;
the three thousand angels
gathered in their wings, became
a dog
forgotten
that barks
alone
and searches for its master
or the Second Coming
or a bone.
Now I long for a little quiet
all I want is a hut on a hill
or near a seashore
all I want in front of my window

ἕνα σεντόνι βουτημένο στὸ λουλάκι
ἁπλωμένο σὰν τὴ θάλασσα
θὰ μοῦ 'φτανε στὴ γλάστρα μου
ἔστω κι' ἕνα ψεύτικο γαρούφαλο
ἕνα κόκκινο χαρτὶ σ' ἕνα τέλι
ἔτσι ποὺ νὰ μπορεῖ ὁ ἀγέρας
ὁ ἀγέρας νὰ τὸ κυβερνᾶ χωρὶς προσπάθεια
ὅσο θέλει.
Θά 'πεφτε τὸ βράδι
τὰ κοπάδια θ' ἀντιλαλούσαν κατεβαίνοντας στὸ μαντρί τους
σὰ μιὰ πολὺ ἁπλὴ κι' εὐτυχισμένη σκέψη
καὶ θά 'πεφτα νὰ κοιμηθῶ
γιατὶ δὲ θά 'χα
οὔτε ἕνα κερὶ ν' ἀνάψω,
φῶς,
νὰ διαβάσω.

1931

is a sheet immersed in bluing
spread there like the sea
all I want in my vase
is even a false carnation
red paper wound on wire
so that the wind
the wind can control it easily
as much as it wants to.
The evening would fall
the flocks would echo descending to their fold
like some quite simple happy thought
and I would lie down to sleep
because I wouldn't have
even a candle to light,
light,
to read.

1931

Β'. ΨΥΧΟΛΟΓΙΑ

Ὁ κύριος αὐτὸς
κάθε πρωὶ κάνει τὸ λουτρό του
μέσα στὰ νερὰ τῆς νεκρῆς θάλασσας
ἔπειτα φορεῖ ἕνα πικρὸ χαμόγελο
γιὰ τὴ δουλειὰ καὶ γιὰ τοὺς πελάτες.

II. PSYCHOLOGY

This gentleman
takes his bath each morning
in the waters of the Dead Sea
then dons a bitter smile
for business and clients.

Γ'. ΟΛΑ ΠΕΡΝΟΥΝ

Ξεχάσαμε τὸν ἡρωικό μας ἀντίλογο μὲ τὶς Εὐμενίδες
μᾶς πῆρε ὁ ὕπνος μᾶς πήραν γιὰ πεθαμένους κι' ἔφυγαν
φωνάζοντας
«Γιού! Γιού! Πούουου... πάξ!»
βρίζοντας τοὺς θεοὺς ποὺ μᾶς προστατεύουν.

III. ALL THINGS PASS AWAY

We forgot our heroic dispute with the Eumenides
we fell asleep, they thought we were dead and they fled
shouting
"Yiou! Yiou! Pouououou . . . pax!"*
cursing the gods that protect us.

Δ΄. ΦΩΤΙΕΣ ΤΟΥ ΑΗ ΓΙΑΝΝΗ

Ἡ μοίρα μας χυμένο μολύβι δὲν μπορεῖ ν' ἀλλάξει
δὲν μπορεῖ νὰ γίνει τίποτε.
Ἔχυσαν τὸ μολύβι μέσα στὸ νερὸ κάτω ἀπὸ τ' ἀστέρια κι'
ἂς ἀνάβουν οἱ φωτιές.

Ἂν μείνεις γυμνὴ μπροστὰ στὸν καθρέφτη τὰ μεσάνυχτα
βλέπεις
βλέπεις τὸν ἄνθρωπο νὰ περνᾶ στὸ βάθος τοῦ καθρέφτη
τὸν ἄνθρωπο μέσα στὴ μοίρα σου ποὺ κυβερνᾶ τὸ κορμί σου
μέσα στὴ μοναξιὰ καὶ στὴ σιωπή, τὸν ἄνθρωπο
τῆς μοναξιᾶς καὶ τῆς σιωπῆς
κι' ἂς ἀνάβουν οἱ φωτιές.

Τὴν ὥρα ποὺ τέλειωσε ἡ μέρα καὶ δὲν ἄρχισε ἡ ἄλλη
τὴν ὥρα ποὺ κόπηκε ὁ καιρὸς
ἐκεῖνον ποὺ ἀπὸ τώρα καὶ πρὶν ἀπὸ τὴν ἀρχὴ κυβερνοῦσε
τὸ κορμί σου
πρέπει νὰ τὸν εὕρεις
πρέπει νὰ τὸν ζητήσεις γιὰ νὰ τὸν εὕρει τουλάχιστο
κάποιος ἄλλος, ὅταν θά 'χεις πεθάνει.

Εἶναι τὰ παιδιὰ ποὺ ἀνάβουν τὶς φωτιὲς καὶ φωνάζουν
μπροστὰ στὶς φλόγες μέσα στὴ ζεστὴ νύχτα (Μήπως

IV. FIRES OF ST. JOHN*

Our fate: spilled lead; our fate can't change—
nothing's to be done.
They spilled the lead in water under the stars, and may the
fires burn.

If you stand naked before a mirror at midnight you see,
you see a man moving through the mirror's depths
the man destined to rule your body
in loneliness and silence, the man
of loneliness and silence
and may the fires burn.

At the hour when one day ends and the next has not begun
at the hour when time is suspended
you must find the man who then and now, from the very
beginning, ruled your body
you must look for him so that someone else at least
will find him, after you are dead.

It is the children who light the fires and cry out before the
flames in the hot night

ἔγινε ποτὲς φωτιὰ ποὺ νὰ μὴν τὴν ἄναψε κάποιο παιδί, ὦ Ἡρόστρατε)
καὶ ρίχνουν ἁλάτι μέσα στὶς φλόγες γιὰ νὰ πλαταγίζουν
(Πόσο παράξενα μᾶς κοιτάζουν ξαφνικὰ τὰ σπίτια, τὰ
χωνευτήρια τῶν ἀνθρώπων, σὰν τὰ χαϊδέψει κάποια
ἀνταύγεια).

Μὰ ἐσὺ ποὺ γνώρισες τὴ χάρη τῆς πέτρας πάνω στὸ θαλασ-
σόδαρτο βράχο
τὸ βράδι ποὺ ἔπεσε ἡ γαλήνη
ἄκουσες ἀπὸ μακριὰ τὴν ἀνθρώπινη φωνὴ τῆς μοναξιᾶς καὶ
τῆς σιωπῆς
μέσα στὸ κορμί σου
τὴ νύχτα ἐκείνη τοῦ Ἅη Γιάννη
ὅταν ἔσβησαν ὅλες οἱ φωτιὲς
καὶ μελέτησες τὴ στάχτη κάτω ἀπὸ τ᾽ ἀστέρια.

(Was there ever a fire that some child did not light,
O Herostratus)*
and throw salt on the flames to make them crackle
(How strangely the houses—crucibles for men—suddenly
stare at us when the flame's reflection caresses them).

But you who knew the stone's grace on the sea-whipped rock
the evening when stillness fell
heard from far off the human voice of loneliness and silence
inside your body
that night of St. John
when all the fires went out
and you studied the ashes under the stars.

Ε'. ΝΙΖΙΝΣΚΙ

Παρουσιάστηκε καθὼς κοίταζα στὸ τζάκι μου τ' ἀναμμένα κάρβουνα. Κρατοῦσε στὰ χέρια ἕνα μεγάλο κουτὶ κόκκινα σπίρτα. Μοῦ τό 'δειξε σὰν τοὺς ταχυδακτυλουργοὺς ποὺ βγάζουν ἀπὸ τὴ μύτη τοῦ διπλανοῦ μας ἕνα ἀβγό. Τράβηξε ἕνα σπίρτο, ἔβαλε φωτιὰ στὸ κουτί, χάθηκε πίσω ἀπὸ μιὰ πελώρια φλόγα, κι' ὕστερα στάθηκε μπροστά μου. Θυμᾶμαι τὸ βυσσινί του χαμόγελο καὶ τὰ γυαλένια του μάτια. Ἕνα ὀργανέτο στὸ δρόμο χτυποῦσε ὁλοένα τὴν ἴδια νότα. Δὲν ξέρω νὰ πῶ τί φοροῦσε. Μ' ἔκανε νὰ συλλογίζομαι ἐπίμονα ἕνα πορφυρὸ κυπαρίσσι. Σιγὰ - σιγὰ τὰ χέρια του ἄρχισαν νὰ ξεχωρίζουν ἀπὸ τὸ τεντωμένο του κορμὶ σὲ σταυρό. Ἀπὸ ποῦ μαζεύτηκαν τόσα πουλιά; Θά 'λεγες πὼς τὰ εἶχε κρυμμένα κάτω ἀπὸ τὶς φτεροῦγες του. Πετούσαν ἀδέξια, παλαβά, μὲ ὁρμή· χτυπούσαν πάνω στοὺς τοίχους τῆς στενῆς κάμαρας, πάνω στὰ τζάμια, καὶ στρώνανε τὸ πάτωμα σὰ χτυπημένα. Ἔνιωθα στὰ πόδια ἕνα ζεστὸ στρῶμα ἀπὸ πούπουλα καὶ σφυγμοὺς νὰ φουσκώνει. Τὸν κοίταζα μὲ μιὰ παράξενη θέρμη ποὺ κυρίευε τὸ κορμί μου σὰν κυκλοφορία. Ὅταν τελείωσε νὰ ὑψώνει τὰ χέρια, ὅταν οἱ παλάμες του ἄγγιξαν ἡ μιὰ τὴν ἄλλη, ἔκανε ἕνα ξαφνικὸ πήδημα, σὰ νὰ εἶχε σπάσει τὸ ἐλατήριο τοῦ ρολογιοῦ μπροστά μου. Χτύπησε στὸ ταβάνι ποὺ ἤχησε μονοκόμματα μ' ἕναν ἦχο κυμβάλου, τέντωσε τὸ δεξί του χέρι, ἔπιασε τὸ σύρμα τῆς λάμπας, κουνήθηκε λιγάκι, ἀφέθηκε, κι' ἄρχισε νὰ γράφει μέσα

V. NIJINSKI*

He appeared as I was staring at the lighted coals in my fireplace. He held in his hands a large box of red matches which he displayed to me like a conjuror taking an egg out of the nose of the person in the next seat. He struck a match, set fire to the box, disappeared behind an enormous flame, and then stood before me. I recall his crimson smile and his vitreous eyes. A hurdy-gurdy in the street went on repeating the same note. I don't know how to describe what he was wearing, but he kept making me think of a purple cypress. Gradually his arms began to separate from his taut body and to form a cross. Where did so many birds come from? It was as if he'd had them hidden under his wings. They flew clumsily, madly, violently, knocking against the walls of the narrow room, against the window panes, then covered the floor as though wounded. I felt a warm layer of down and pulsations growing at my feet. I gazed at him, a strange fever possessed my body like a current coursing through it. When he'd finished raising his arms and his palms were together, he gave a sudden leap, as if the spring of a watch had broken in front of me. He knocked against the ceiling, making it echo with the sound of a cymbal, extended his right arm, seized the wire of the lamp, moved slightly, relaxed, then began to describe with his body a figure of eight against the darkness. The sight made me

στὸ σκοτεινὸ φῶς, μὲ τὸ κορμί του, τὸν ἀριθμὸ 8. Τὸ θέαμα αὐτὸ μὲ ζάλισε καὶ σκέπασα μὲ τὰ δυό μου χέρια τὸ πρόσωπό μου. Ἔσφιγγα τὸ σκοτάδι πάνω στὰ βλέφαρά μου, ἀκούγοντας τὸ ὀργανέτο ποὺ ἐξακολουθοῦσε ἀκόμη στὴν ἴδια νότα κι᾿ ἔπειτα σταμάτησε ἀπότομα. Ἕνας ξαφνικὸς ἀέρας μὲ χτύπησε, παγωμένος. Ἔνιωσα τὰ πόδια μου ξυλιασμένα. Ἄκουσα ἀκόμη ἕνα χαμηλὸ καὶ βελουδένιο ἦχο φλογέρας, κι᾿ ἀμέσως ἔπειτα, ἕνα στρωτὸ καὶ παχὺ πλατάγισμα. Ἄνοιξα τὰ μάτια. Τὸν εἶδα πάλι νὰ πατᾶ μὲ τὰ νύχια σὲ μιὰ κρουσταλλένια σφαίρα, στὴ μέση τῆς κάμαρας, κρατώντας στὸ στόμα ἕνα ἀλλόκοτο πράσινο σουραύλι, ποὺ τὸ κυβερνούσαν τὰ δάχτυλά του, σὰ νὰ εἴταν ἑφτὰ χιλιάδες. Τὰ πουλιὰ τώρα ξαναζωντάνευαν μὲ μιὰ ἐξωφρενικὴ τάξη, ὑψωνόντουσαν, σμίγανε, σχηματίζανε μιὰ χοντρὴ συνοδεία ποὺ θὰ μποροῦσες νὰ τὴν ἀγκαλιάσεις, καὶ βγαίναν πρὸς τὴ νύχτα, ἀπὸ τὸ παράθυρο, ποὺ δὲν ξέρω πῶς, βρέθηκε ἀνοιχτό. Ὅταν δὲν ἀπόμεινε πιὰ οὔτε μισὴ φτερούγα, ἐκτὸς ἀπὸ μιὰ πνιγερὴ μυρωδιὰ κυνηγιοῦ, ἀποφάσισα νὰ τὸν κοιτάξω κατὰ πρόσωπο. Πρόσωπο δὲν ὑπῆρχε˙ πάνω ἀπὸ τὸ πορφυρὸ κορμί, θά ᾿λεγες ἀκέφαλο, καμάρωνε μιὰ μαλαματένια προσωπίδα, ἀπὸ ἐκεῖνες ποὺ βρέθηκαν στοὺς μυκηναϊκοὺς τάφους, μ᾿ ἕνα μυτερὸ γένι ποὺ ἄγγιζε τὴν τραχηλιά. Προσπάθησα νὰ σηκωθῶ. Δὲν εἶχα κάνει τὴν πρώτη κίνηση, κι᾿ ἕνας κατακλυσμιαῖος ἦχος, σὰ νὰ εἶχαν σωριαστεῖ μιὰ στίβα τάσια σὲ νεκρώσιμο ἐμβατήριο, μὲ κάρφωσε στὴ θέση μου. Εἴταν ἡ προσωπίδα. Τὸ πρόσωπό του φανερώθηκε πάλι, ὅπως τὸ εἶδα στὴν ἀρχή, τὰ μάτια, τὸ χαμόγελο καὶ κάτι ποὺ τώρα παρατηρούσα γιὰ πρώτη φορά: τὸ λευκὸ δέρμα τεντωμένο ἀπὸ δυὸ κατάμαυρα τσουλούφια ποὺ τὸ δάγκωναν μπροστὰ

dizzy and I covered my face with both hands, crushing the darkness against my eyelids, while the hurdy-gurdy went on repeating the same note and then stopped abruptly. A sudden icy wind struck me; I felt my legs go numb. Now I also heard the low velvety sound of a flute, followed immediately by a heavy and regular beating. I opened my eyes and again saw him, standing tiptoe on a crystal sphere in the middle of the room, in his mouth a strange green flute over which he was running his fingers as though there were thousands of them. The birds now came back to life in an extraordinary order, rose up, mingled, formed into a cortege as wide as my outspread arms, and went out into the night through the window that was somehow open. When the last flutter had died away and only a suffocating smell of hunting was left, I decided to look him in the face. There was no face: above the purple body, seemingly headless, he sported a golden mask, of the kind found in Mycenaean tombs, with a pointed beard reaching down to the throat. I tried to get up, but I'd hardly made the first movement when a cataclysmic sound, like a pile of kettledrums collapsing in a funeral march, rooted me to the spot. It was the mask. His face appeared again as I'd originally seen it—the eyes, the smile, and something which I now remarked for the first time: the white skin suspended from two black curls that pinned it into place at the temples. He tried to leap but no

στ' αὐτιά. Δοκίμασε νὰ πηδήξει, μὰ δὲν εἶχε πιὰ τὴν εὐκινησία του τὴν πρώτη. Θαρῶ μάλιστα πὼς σκόνταψε σ' ἕνα βιβλίο πεσμένο κατὰ τύχη καὶ γονάτισε μὲ τὸ ἕνα γόνατο. Μπορούσα τώρα νὰ τὸν κοιτάξω μὲ προσοχή. Ἔβλεπα τοὺς πόρους στὸ δέρμα του νὰ βγάζουν ψιλὲς στάλες ἱδρώτα. Κάτι σὰ λαχάνιασμα μὲ βάραινε. Προσπάθησα νὰ ἐξηγήσω γιατί τὰ μάτια του μοῦ εἶχαν φανεῖ τόσο περίεργα. Τά 'κλεισε. Ἔκανε νὰ σηκωθεῖ, μὰ θὰ εἶταν τρομερὰ δύσκολο, γιατὶ φαινόταν ν' ἀγωνίζεται νὰ μαζέψει ὅλη του τὴ δύναμη, χωρὶς νὰ μπορεῖ νὰ καταφέρει τίποτε. Ἀπεναντίας γονάτισε καὶ μὲ τὸ ἄλλο γόνατο. Ἔβλεπα τὸ ἄσπρο δέρμα τρομερὰ χλομό, πρὸς ἕνα κίτρινο φιλντισί, καὶ τὰ μαῦρα μαλλιὰ σὰν πεθαμένα. Μολονότι βρισκόμουνα μπροστὰ σὲ μιὰν ἀγωνία, εἶχα τὸ συναίσθημα πὼς εἴμουνα καλύτερα, πὼς εἶχα κάτι νικήσει.

Δὲν πρόφταξα νὰ ἀνασάνω καὶ τὸν εἶδα, ὁλότελα πεσμένο χάμω, νὰ βυθίζεται μέσα σὲ μιὰ πράσινη παγόδα ποὺ εἶναι ζωγραφισμένη πάνω στὸ χαλί μου.

longer possessed his initial agility. I think he even stumbled against a book fallen there by accident, and he knelt down on one knee. Now I could observe him carefully. I saw the pores of his skin oozing fine beads of sweat. Something like breathlessness came over me. I tried to discover why his eyes had seemed so strange. He closed them and began to get up; but it must have been terribly difficult, for he seemed to concentrate all his strength without being able to do anything. He even knelt now on the other knee as well. The white skin seemed terribly pale, like yellow ivory, and his black hair was lifeless. Though I was witnessing an agonizing struggle, I had the feeling that I was better, that I'd triumphed over something.

Before I could draw breath I saw him, fallen full length now, plunge into a green pagoda portrayed on my carpet.

Ο κ. ΣΤΡΑΤΗΣ ΘΑΛΑΣΣΙΝΟΣ ΠΕΡΙΓΡΑΦΕΙ ΕΝΑΝ ΑΝΘΡΩΠΟ

1

Μὰ τί ἔχει αὐτὸς ὁ ἄνθρωπος;
Ὅλο τὸ ἀπόγεμα (χτὲς προχτὲς καὶ σήμερα) κάθεται μὲ
τὰ μάτια καρφωμένα σὲ μιὰ φλόγα
σκόνταψε πάνω μου τὸ βράδι καθὼς κατέβαινε τὴ σκάλα
μοῦ εἶπε:
«Τὸ κορμὶ πεθαίνει τὸ νερὸ θολώνει ἡ ψυχὴ
διστάζει
κι' ὁ ἀγέρας ξεχνάει ὅλο ξεχνάει
μὰ ἡ φλόγα δὲν ἀλλάζει».
Μοῦ εἶπε ἀκόμη:
«Ξέρετε ἀγαπῶ μιὰ γυναίκα ποὺ ἔφυγε ἴσως στὸν κάτω
κόσμο· δὲν εἶναι γι' αὐτὸ ποὺ φαίνομαι τόσο ἐρημω-
μένος
προσπαθῶ νὰ κρατηθῶ ἀπὸ μιὰ φλόγα
γιατὶ δὲν ἀλλάζει».
Ὕστερα μοῦ διηγήθηκε τὴν ἱστορία του.

2. ΠΑΙΔΙ

Ὅταν ἄρχισα νὰ μεγαλώνω μὲ βασάνιζαν τὰ δέντρα
γιατί χαμογελᾶτε; πῆγε ὁ νοῦς σας στὴν ἄνοιξη ποὺ εἶναι
σκληρὴ γιὰ τὰ μικρὰ παιδιά;

MR. STRATIS THALASSINOS DESCRIBES A MAN

1

But what's wrong with that man?
All afternoon (yesterday the day before yesterday and
today) he's been sitting there staring at a flame
he bumped into me at evening as he went downstairs
he said to me:
"The body dies the water clouds the soul
hesitates
and the wind forgets always forgets
but the flame doesn't change."
He also said to me:
"You know I love a woman who's gone away perhaps to the
nether world; that's not why I seem so deserted
I try to keep myself going with a flame
because it doesn't change."
Then he told me the story of his life.

2. CHILD

When I began to grow up the trees tormented me—
why do you smile? Were you thinking of spring, so harsh for
children?

μ' ἄρεσαν πολὺ τὰ πράσινα φύλλα
νομίζω πὼς ἔμαθα λίγα γράμματα γιατὶ τὸ στουπόχαρτο
πάνω στὸ θρανίο μου εἴταν κι' ἐκεῖνο πράσινο
μὲ βασάνιζαν οἱ ρίζες τῶν δέντρων ὅταν μέσα στὴ ζεστασιὰ
τοῦ χειμώνα ἐρχόντανε νὰ τυλιχτοῦν γύρω στὸ κορμί μου
δὲν ἔβλεπα ἄλλα ὄνειρα σὰν εἴμουν παιδί·
ἔτσι γνώρισα τὸ κορμί μου.

3. *ΕΦΗΒΟΣ*

Τὸ καλοκαίρι στὰ δεκαέξι μου χρόνια τραγούδησε μιὰ ξένη
φωνὴ μέσα στ' αὐτιά μου
εἴταν θυμοῦμαι στὴν ἀκροθαλασσιά, ἀνάμεσα στὰ κόκκινα
δίχτυα καὶ μιὰ βάρκα ξεχασμένη στὴν ἄμμο, σκελετὸς
δοκίμασα νὰ τὴν πλησιάσω τὴ φωνὴ ἐκείνη βάζοντας τὴν
ἀκοή μου πάνω στὴν ἄμμο
ἡ φωνὴ χάθηκε
μὰ ἕνα πεφταστέρι
σὰ νά 'βλεπα γιὰ πρώτη φορὰ ἕνα πεφταστέρι
καὶ στὰ χείλια ἡ ἁρμύρα τοῦ κυμάτου.
Τὴ νύχτα ἐκείνη δὲν ἦρθαν πιὰ οἱ ρίζες τῶν δέντρων.
Τὴν ἄλλη μέρα ἕνα ταξίδι ἀνοίχτηκε μέσα στὸ νοῦ μου κι'
ἔκλεισε πάλι σὰ ζωγραφισμένο βιβλίο·
συλλογίστηκα νὰ πηγαίνω κάθε βράδι στ' ἀκρογιάλι
νὰ μάθω πρῶτα τ' ἀκρογιάλι κι' ἔπειτα νὰ πάρω τὸ πέλαγο·
τὴν τρίτη μέρα ἀγάπησα μιὰ κοπέλα πάνω σὲ μιὰ κορφὴ

I was very fond of the green leaves
I think I learned a little at school simply because the blotting paper on my desk was also green.
It was the roots of the trees that tormented me when in the warmth of winter they'd come and wind themselves around my body.
I had no other dreams as a child.
That's how I got to know my body.

3. ADOLESCENT

In the summer of my sixteenth year a strange voice sang in my ears;
it was, I remember, at the sea's edge, among the red nets and a boat abandoned on the sand, a skeleton
I tried to get closer to that voice by laying my ear to the sand
the voice disappeared
but there was a shooting star
as though I were seeing a shooting star for the first time
and on my lips the salt taste of waves.
From that night the roots of the trees no longer came to me.
The next day a journey opened in my mind and closed again, like a picture book;
I thought of going down to the shore every evening
first to learn about the shore and then to go to sea;
the third day I fell in love with a girl on a hill;

εἶχε ἕνα ἄσπρο σπιτάκι σὰ ρημοκλήσι
μιὰ γριὰ μάνα στὸ παραθύρι μὲ σκυμμένα γυαλιὰ πάνω σὲ
βελόνες, πάντα σιωπηλὴ
μιὰ γλάστρα βασιλικὸ μιὰ γλάστρα γαρούφαλα
τὴν ἔλεγαν νομίζω Βάσω Φρόσω ἢ Μπίλιω·
ἔτσι ξέχασα τὴ θάλασσα.
Μιὰ δευτέρα τοῦ 'Οχτώβρη
βρῆκα μιὰ σπασμένη στάμνα μπροστὰ στὸ ἄσπρο σπιτάκι
ἡ Βάσω (γιὰ συντομία) φάνηκε μ' ἕνα μαῦρο φουστάνι
ἀχτένιστα μαλλιὰ καὶ κόκκινα μάτια
ὅταν τὴ ρώτησα:
«Πέθανε, ὁ γιατρὸς λέει πέθανε γιατὶ δὲ σφάξαμε τὸ μαῦρο
κόκορα στὰ θεμέλια... ποῦ νὰ βρεθεῖ μαῦρος κόκορας
ἐδῶ-πέρα... μονάχα ἄσπρα κοπάδια... καὶ τὰ πουλιὰ
τὰ πουλοῦν μαδημένα στὴν ἀγορά».
Δὲν φανταζόμουνα ἔτσι τὴ θλίψη καὶ τὸ θάνατο
ἔφυγα καὶ ξαναγύρισα στὴ θάλασσα.
Τὴ νύχτα πάνω στὴν κουβέρτα τοῦ «Ἅη Νικόλα» ὀνειρεύ-
τηκα μιὰ παμπάλαιη ἐλιὰ νὰ δακρύζει.

4. *ΠΑΛΙΚΑΡΙ*

Ταξίδεψα ἕνα χρόνο μὲ τὸν Καπετὰν Δυσσέα
εἴμουν καλὰ
στὴν καλοκαιριὰ βολευόμουνα στὴν πλώρη πλάι στὴ γοργόνα

she had a small white cottage like a country chapel
an old mother at the window, glasses bent low over her knitting, always silent
a pot of basil a pot of carnations—
I think she was called Vasso, Frosso, or Billio;
so I forgot the sea.
One Monday in October
I found a broken pitcher in front of the white cottage
Vasso (for short) appeared in a black dress, her hair uncombed, her eyes red.
When I questioned her she said:
"She died, the doctor said she died because we didn't kill the black cock when we dug the foundations . . . Where could we find a black cock around here . . . ? Only white flocks . . . and in the market the chickens are sold already plucked."
I hadn't imagined grief and death would be like that;
I left and went back to sea.
That night, on the deck of the "St. Nicholas," I dreamt of a very old olive tree weeping.

4. YOUNG MAN

I sailed for a year with Captain Odysseus
I was fine
in fair weather I made myself comfortable in the prow beside the mermaid

τραγουδούσα τὰ κόκκινα χείλια της κοιτάζοντας τὰ χελιδονόψαρα,
στὴ φουρτούνα τρύπωνα σὲ μιὰ γωνιὰ στ' ἀμπάρι μαζὶ μὲ τὸ καραβόσκυλο ποὺ μὲ ζέσταινε.
Σὰ βγῆκε ὁ χρόνος εἶδα ἕνα πρωὶ μιναρέδες
ὁ ναύκληρος μοῦ εἶπε:
«Εἶναι ἡ Ἁγιὰ Σοφιά, θὰ σὲ πάω τὸ βράδι στὶς γυναῖκες».
Ἔτσι γνώρισα τὶς γυναῖκες ποὺ φοροῦν μονάχα κάλτσες
ἐκεῖνες ποὺ διαλέγουμε, μάλιστα.
Εἴταν ἕνας περίεργος τόπος
ἕνα περιβόλι μὲ δυὸ καρυδιὲς μιὰ δράνα ἕνα πηγάδι
τριγύρω ὁ τοῖχος μὲ σπασμένα γυαλιὰ στὴν ἄκρη
ἕνα αὐλάκι τραγουδοῦσε «Εἰς τὸ ρεῦμα τῆς ζωῆς μου».
Τότες εἶδα γιὰ πρώτη μου φορὰ μιὰ καρδιὰ
τρυπημένη μὲ τὴ γνωστὴ σαΐτα
ζωγραφισμένη στὸν τοῖχο μὲ κάρβουνο.
Εἶδα τὰ φύλλα τῆς κληματαριᾶς κίτρινα
πεσμένα χάμω
κολλημένα στὶς πλάκες στὴ φτωχὴ λάσπη
κι' ἔκανα ἕνα βῆμα νὰ πάω πίσω στὸ καράβι.
Τότες ὁ ναύκληρος μ' ἅρπαξε ἀπὸ τὸ γιακὰ καὶ μὲ πέταξε μέσα στὸ πηγάδι·
τὸ ζεστὸ νερὸ καὶ τόση ζωὴ τριγύρω στὸ δέρμα...
Ἔπειτα τὸ κορίτσι μοῦ εἶπε παίζοντας ἀπρόσεχτα μὲ τὸ δεξί του στῆθος:
«Εἶμαι ἀπὸ τὴ Ρόδο, μὲ ἀρρεβώνιασαν 13 χρονῶ γιὰ 100 παράδες».
Καὶ τ' αὐλάκι τραγουδοῦσε «Εἰς τὸ ρεῦμα τῆς ζωῆς μου».

I sang of her red lips as I gazed at the flying-fish,
in storms I took refuge in a corner of the hold with the
ship's dog who kept me warm.
One morning at the end of the year I saw minarets
the mate told me:
"That's Saint Sophia, tonight I'll take you to the women."
So I got to know those women who wear only stockings—
those we select, in fact.
It was a strange place
a garden with two walnut trees a trellis a well
a wall with broken glass along the top surrounding it
a gutter singing: "On the stream of my life."
Then for the first time I saw a heart
pierced by the familiar arrow
drawn in charcoal on the wall.
I saw the leaves of the vine yellow
fallen to the ground
stuck to the flagstones to the humble mud
and I started to go back to the ship.
Then the mate seized me by the collar and threw me into
the well:
warm water and so much life around the skin . . .
Afterwards the girl, playing idly with her right breast, told
me:
"I'm from Rhodes, at 13 they got me engaged for a hundred
paras."
And the gutter sang: "On the stream of my life . . ."

Θυμήθηκα τὴ σπασμένη στάμνα μέσα στὸ δροσερὸ ἀπομεσήμερο καὶ συλλογίστηκα·
« Θὰ πεθάνει κι' αὐτή, πῶς θὰ πεθάνει ; »
Τῆς εἶπα μονάχα
« Πρόσεξε θὰ τὸ χαλάσεις εἶναι ἡ ζωή σου ».
Τὸ βράδι στὸ καράβι δὲ βάσταξα νὰ σιμώσω τὴ γοργόνα, τὴ ντρεπόμουνα.

5. *ΑΝΤΡΑΣ*

Ἀπὸ τότες εἶδα πολλὰ καινούργια τοπία· πράσινους κάμπους ποὺ σμίγουν τὸ χῶμα μὲ τὸν οὐρανό, τὸν ἄνθρωπο μὲ τὸ σπόρο, μέσα σὲ μιὰν ἀκαταμάχητη ὑγρασία· πλατάνια καὶ ἔλατα· λίμνες μὲ τσαλακωμένες ὀπτασίες καὶ κύκνους ἀθάνατους γιατὶ ἔχασαν τὴ φωνή τους — σκηνικὰ ποὺ ξετύλιγε ὁ θεληματικὸς σύντροφός μου, ὁ πλανόδιος ἐκεῖνος θεατρίνος, καθὼς ἔπαιζε τὸ μακρὺ βούκινο ποὺ τοῦ εἶχε ρημάξει τὰ χείλια, καὶ γκρέμιζε μὲ μιὰ στριγγιὰ φωνή, ὅ,τι πρόφταινα νὰ χτίσω, σὰν τὴ σάλπιγγα στὴν Ἱεριχώ. Εἶδα καὶ μιὰ παλιὰ εἰκόνα σὲ κάποια χαμηλοτάβανη αἴθουσα· τὴ θαύμαζε πολὺς λαός. Παράσταινε τὴν ἀνάσταση τοῦ Λαζάρου. Δὲ θυμᾶμαι οὔτε τὸ Χριστὸ οὔτε τὸ Λάζαρο. Μόνο, σὲ μιὰ γωνιά, τὴν ἀηδία ζωγραφισμένη σ' ἕνα πρόσωπο ποὺ κοίταζε τὸ θαῦμα σὰ νὰ τὸ μύριζε. Ἀγωνιζότανε νὰ προστατέψει τὴν ἀνάσα του μ' ἕνα πελώριο πανὶ ποὺ τοῦ κρεμότανε ἀπὸ τὸ κεφάλι. Αὐτὸς ὁ κύριος τῆς «Ἀναγέννησης» μ' ἔμαθε νὰ μὴν περιμένω πολλὰ πράματα ἀπὸ τὴ δευτέρα παρουσία...

✧

I recalled the broken pitcher in the cool afternoon and I thought:
"She'll die too, how will she die?"
All I said to her was:
"Careful, you'll ruin it, it's your livelihood."
That evening on the ship I couldn't bear to go near the mermaid, I was ashamed of facing her.

5. *MAN*

Since then I've seen many new landscapes: green plains intermingling soil and sky, man and seed, in an irresistible dampness; plane-trees and fir-trees; lakes with wrinkled visions and swans immortal because they'd lost their voices —scenery unfolded by my willing companion, that strolling player, as he sounded the long horn that had ruined his lips and that destroyed with its shrill note whatever I managed to build, like the trumpet at Jericho. I saw an old picture in some low-ceilinged room; a lot of people were admiring it. It showed the raising of Lazarus. I don't recall either the Christ in it or the Lazarus. Only, in one corner, the disgust portrayed on someone's face as he gazed at the miracle as if he were smelling it. He was trying to protect his breathing with the huge cloth draped around his head. This "Renaissance" gentleman taught me not to expect much from the Second Coming . . .

✧

Μᾶς ἔλεγαν θὰ νικήσετε ὅταν ὑποταχτεῖτε.
Ὑποταχτήκαμε καὶ βρήκαμε τὴ στάχτη.
Μᾶς ἔλεγαν θὰ νικήσετε ὅταν ἀγαπήσετε.
Ἀγαπήσαμε καὶ βρήκαμε τὴ στάχτη.
Μᾶς ἔλεγαν θὰ νικήσετε ὅταν ἐγκαταλείψετε τὴ ζωή σας.
Ἐγκαταλείψαμε τὴ ζωή μας καὶ βρήκαμε τὴ στάχτη...

Βρήκαμε τὴ στάχτη. Μένει νὰ ξαναβροῦμε τὴ ζωή μας, τώρα ποὺ δὲν ἔχουμε πιὰ τίποτα. Φαντάζομαι, ἐκεῖνος ποὺ θὰ ξανάβρει τὴ ζωή, ἔξω ἀπὸ τόσα χαρτιά, τόσα συναισθήματα, τόσες διαμάχες καὶ τόσες διδασκαλίες, θὰ εἶναι κάποιος σὰν ἐμᾶς, μόνο λιγάκι πιὸ σκληρὸς στὴ μνήμη. Ἐμεῖς, δὲ μπορεῖ, θυμόμαστε ἀκόμη τί δώσαμε. Ἐκεῖνος θὰ θυμᾶται μονάχα τί κέρδισε ἀπὸ τὴν κάθε του προσφορά. Τί μπορεῖ νὰ θυμᾶται μιὰ φλόγα; Ἂ θυμηθεῖ λίγο λιγότερο ἀπ᾽ ὅ,τι χρειάζεται, σβήνει· ἂ θυμηθεῖ λίγο περισσότερο ἀπ᾽ ὅ,τι χρειάζεται, σβήνει. Νὰ μποροῦσε νὰ μᾶς διδάξει, ὅσο ἀνάβει, νὰ θυμόμαστε σωστά. Ἐγὼ τελείωσα· νὰ γινότανε τουλάχιστο νὰ ἀρχίσει κάποιος ἄλλος ἀπὸ κεῖ ποὺ τελείωσα ἐγώ. Εἶναι ὧρες ποὺ ἔχω τὴν ἐντύπωση πὼς ἔφτασα στὸ τέρμα, πὼς ὅλα εἶναι στὴ θέση τους, ἕτοιμα νὰ τραγουδήσουν συνταιριασμένα. Ἡ μηχανὴ στὸ σημεῖο νὰ ξεκινήσει. Μπορῶ μάλιστα νὰ τὴ φανταστῶ σὲ κίνηση, ζωντανή, σὰν κάτι ἀνυποψίαστα καινούργιο. Ἀλλὰ ὑπάρχει κάτι ἀκόμα· ἕνα ἀπειροελάχιστο ἐμπόδιο, ἕνα σπυρὶ τῆς ἄμμου, ποὺ μικραίνει, μικραίνει χωρὶς νὰ εἶναι δυνατὸ νὰ ἐκμηδενιστεῖ. Δὲν ξέρω τί πρέπει νὰ πῶ ἢ τί πρέπει νὰ κάνω. Τὸ ἐμπόδιο αὐτὸ

They told us you'll conquer when you submit.
We submitted and found ashes.
They told us you'll conquer when you love.
We loved and found ashes.
They told us you'll conquer when you abandon your life.
We abandoned our life and found ashes.

We found ashes. It remains to rediscover our life, now that we've nothing left. I imagine that he who'll rediscover life, in spite of so much paper, so many emotions, so many debates and so much teaching, will be someone like us, only with a slightly tougher memory. We ourselves can't help still remembering what we've given. He'll remember only what he's gained from each of his offerings. What can a flame remember? If it remembers a little less than is necessary, it goes out; if it remembers a little more than is necessary, it goes out. If only it could teach us, while it burns, to remember correctly. I've come to an end: if only someone else could begin at the point where I've ended. There are times when I have the impression that I've reached the limit, that everything's in its place, ready to sing together in harmony. The machine on the point of starting. I can even imagine it in motion, alive, like something unsuspectedly new. But there's still something: an infinitesimal obstacle, a grain of sand, shrinking and shrinking yet unable to disappear completely. I don't know what I ought to say or what I ought to do. Sometimes that obstacle seems

μοῦ παρουσιάζεται κάποτε σὰν ἕνας κόμπος δάκρυ χωμένος σὲ κάποια κλείδωση τῆς ὀρχήστρας ποὺ θὰ τὴν κρατᾶ βουβὴ ὥς ποὺ νὰ διαλυθεῖ. Κι' ἔχω τὸ ἀσήκωτο συναίσθημα πὼς ὁλόκληρη ἡ ζωὴ ποὺ μοῦ ἀπομένει δὲ θά 'ναι ἀρκετὴ γιὰ νὰ καταλύσει αὐτὴ τὴ στάλα μέσα στὴν ψυχή μου. Καὶ μὲ καταδιώκει ἡ σκέψη πὼς ἂν μ' ἔκαιγαν ζωντανὸ αὐτὴ ἡ ἐπίμονη στιγμὴ θὰ παραδινότανε τελευταία.

Ποιὸς θὰ μᾶς βοηθοῦσε; Κάποτε, ὅταν εἴμουν ἀκόμη στὰ καράβια, ἕνα μεσημέρι τὸν 'Ιούλιο, βρέθηκα μόνος σὲ κάποιο νησί, σακάτης μέσα στὸν ἥλιο. Ἕνα καλὸ μελτέμι μοῦ ἔφερνε στοργικοὺς στοχασμούς, ὅταν ἦρθαν καὶ κάθησαν λίγο πάρα πέρα, μιὰ νέα γυναίκα μὲ διάφανο φουστάνι, ποὺ ἄφηνε νὰ ζωγραφίζεται τὸ κορμί της, λιγνὸ καὶ θεληματικὸ σὰ ζαρκαδιοῦ, κι' ἕνας σιωπηλὸς ἄντρας ποὺ μιὰ ὀργιὰ μακριά της, τὴν κοίταζε στὰ μάτια. Μιλούσαν μιὰ γλώσσα ποὺ δὲν καταλάβαινα. Τὸν ἐφώναζε Τζίμ. Τὰ λόγια τους ὅμως δὲν εἶχαν κανένα βάρος καὶ οἱ ματιές τους σωφιλιασμένες καὶ ἀκίνητες ἄφηναν τὰ μάτια τους τυφλά. Τοὺς συλλογίζομαι πάντα γιατὶ εἶναι οἱ μόνοι ἄνθρωποι, ποὺ εἶδα στὴ ζωή μου νὰ μὴν ἔχουν τὸ ἁρπαχτικὸ ἢ τὸ κυνηγημένο ὕφος ποὺ γνώρισα σ' ὅλους τοὺς ἄλλους. Τὸ ὕφος ἐκεῖνο ποὺ τοὺς κάνει ν' ἀνήκουν στὸ κοπάδι τῶν λύκων ἢ στὸ κοπάδι τῶν ἀρνιῶν. Τοὺς συναπάντησα πάλι τὴν ἴδια μέρα σ' ἕνα ἀπὸ τὰ νησιώτικα κλησάκια ποὺ βρίσκει κανεὶς ὅπως παραπατᾶ καὶ τὰ χάνει μόλις βγεῖ. Κρατούσαν πάντα τὴν ἴδια ἀπόσταση κι' ἔπειτα πλησίασαν καὶ φιληθήκανε. Ἡ γυναίκα ἔγινε μιὰ θαμπὴ εἰκόνα καὶ χάθηκε, μικρὴ καθὼς εἶταν. Ρωτιόμουν ἂν ἤξεραν πῶς εἶχαν βγεῖ ἀπὸ τὰ δίχτυα τοῦ κόσμου...

to me like a teardrop wedged into some articulation of the orchestra, keeping it silent until it's been dissolved. And I have an unbearable feeling that all the rest of my life won't be sufficient to dissolve this drop within my soul. And I'm haunted by the thought that, if they were to burn me alive, this obstinate moment would be the last to surrender.

Who will help us? Once, while I was still a seaman, one June afternoon, I found myself alone on some island, crippled in the sun. A fair Etesian wind brought tender thoughts to my mind; and it was then that a young woman, her transparent dress showing the lines of her body, slender and positive like a gazelle's, and a man, silent as he gazed into her eyes across the few feet that separated them, came and sat down not far from where I was. They spoke in a language I didn't understand. But their words had no weight and their glances, mingled and motionless, left their eyes blind. I always think of them because they're the only people I've ever seen who didn't have the grasping or hunted look that I've seen in everyone else. That look that classes them either with a pack of wolves or a flock of sheep. I met them again the same day in one of those island chapels one stumbles upon only to lose again as soon as one gets out. They were still keeping the same distance from each other; but then they came together and kissed. The woman became a cloudy image and vanished, small as she was. I wondered whether they knew how they'd escaped from the world's nets . . .

Εἶναι καιρὸς νὰ πηγαίνω. Ξέρω ἕνα πεῦκο ποὺ σκύβει κοντὰ σὲ μιὰ θάλασσα. Τὸ μεσημέρι, χαρίζει στὸ κουρασμένο κορμὶ ἕναν ἴσκιο μετρημένο σὰν τὴ ζωή μας, καὶ τὸ βράδι, ὁ ἀγέρας περνώντας μέσα ἀπὸ τὰ βελόνια του, πιάνει ἕνα περίεργο τραγούδι, σὰν ψυχὲς ποὺ κατάργησαν τὸ θάνατο, τὴ στιγμὴ ποὺ ξαναρχίζουν νὰ γίνουνται δέρμα καὶ χείλια. Κάποτε ξενύχτησα κάτω ἀπὸ αὐτὸ τὸ δέντρο. Τὴν αὐγὴ εἴμουνα καινούργιος σὰ νὰ μὲ εἴχαν κόψει τὴν ὥρα ἐκείνη ἀπὸ τὸ λατομεῖο.

Ἄ! νὰ ζήσει κανεὶς τουλάχιστο ἔτσι, ἀδιάφορο.

Λονδίνο, 5 Ἰουνίου 1932

It's time for me to go. I know a pine-tree that overhangs the sea. At noon it provides the tired body with a shade as measured as our life, and at evening the wind passing through its needles strikes up a strange song, like souls that have abolished death the moment they again start becoming skin and lips. Once I spent the night awake under that tree. At daybreak I was as fresh as if they'd just cut me out of the quarry.

Ah, if one could at least live like that—but it doesn't really matter.

London, 5 June 1932

ΣΗΜΕΙΩΣΕΙΣ ΓΙΑ ΜΙΑ «ΕΒΔΟΜΑΔΑ»

British grown daffodils

ΔΕΥΤΕΡΑ

Μέσα στὰ σκυφτὰ ἀσφοδίλια οἱ τυφλοὶ κοιμοῦνται
ἕνας λαὸς τυφλῶν καὶ τ' ἀσφοδίλια σκύβουν
μαυρισμένα ἀπὸ τὴν πάχνη τῆς αὐγῆς.
(Θυμοῦμαι τὰ παφιοπέδιλα τὸν ἄλλο χειμώνα
κλεισμένα στὴ ζέστη.
Ἀρκείτω βίος).
Προσκέφαλά τους ὄργανα ἐξοντωμένα
ραχιτικοὶ φωνογράφοι
τρύπιες φυσαρμόνικες
ἁρμόνια γονατισμένα·
νά 'χουν πεθάνει;
Ἕνας ἀκίνητος τυφλὸς δὲν ξεχωρίζει εὔκολα
κάποτε ζωντανεύουν τὰ ὄνειρά τους γι' αὐτὸ λέω πὼς κοιμοῦνται.
Τριγύρω στὰ σπίτια, φορέματα ἀγγέλων μοῦ γνέφουν μαρμαρωμένα
τὸ ποτάμι δὲν κυλᾶ ἔχει ξεχάσει τὴ θάλασσα
κι' ὅμως ὑπάρχει ἡ θάλασσα καὶ ποιὸς θὰ τὴν ἐξαντλήσει;
οἱ τυφλοὶ κοιμοῦνται,
οἱ ἄγγελοι γυμνοὶ τρέχουν μέσα στὶς φλέβες τους
τοὺς πίνουν τὸ αἷμα καὶ τοὺς δίνουν φρόνηση

NOTES FOR A "WEEK"

British grown daffodils

MONDAY

Among the bending asphodels the blind are sleeping
a crowd of blind people and the asphodels bend
blackened by the hoarfrost of dawn.
(I remember the paphiopedilums of another winter
enclosed in the hothouse heat.
Enough of life).*
Their pillows, demolished instruments
rickety phonographs
harmonicas full of holes
organs fallen to their knees;
are they dead?
You can't make out a motionless blind man easily.
Sometimes their dreams come alive, that's why I say they're
    sleeping.
All around on the houses, marble robes of angels beckon me
the river doesn't roll, it has forgotten the sea
and yet there is the sea and who will drain it dry?*
The blind are sleeping,
angels run naked in their veins
they drink their blood and they make them prudent

κι' ἡ καρδιὰ μὲ τὰ φριχτά της μάτια λογαριάζει
πότε θὰ στερέψει.
Κοιτάζω τὸ ποτάμι
ἀνάλαφρες σπιλιάδες περνοῦν κάτω ἀπὸ τὸν ἀνήμπορο ἥλιο
τίποτε ἄλλο, τὸ ποτάμι περιμένει·
λυπήσου ἐκείνους ποὺ περιμένουν.
Τίποτε ἄλλο· φτάνει γιὰ σήμερα.

. . . .
. . . .
. . . .
. . . .

ΠΕΜΠΤΗ

Τὴν εἴδα νὰ πεθαίνει πολλὲς φορὲς
κάποτε κλαίγοντας στὴν ἀγκαλιά μου
κάποτε στὴν ἀγκαλιὰ ἑνὸς ξένου
κάποτε μόνη της, γυμνή·
ἔτσι ἔζησε κοντά μου.
Τώρα πιὰ ξέρω πὼς δὲν εἶναι τίποτε πάρα πέρα
καὶ περιμένω.
Ἂν λυποῦμαι εἶναι μιὰ ὑπόθεση ἰδιωτικὴ
ὅπως τὰ συναισθήματα γιὰ τόσο ἁπλὰ πράγματα
ποὺ καθὼς λένε τά 'χουμε ξεπεράσει·

and the heart with its terrible eyes calculates
when it will run dry.
I look at the river
sudden light puffs of wind pass under the impotent sun
nothing else, the river waits;
pity those who wait.
Nothing else; that's enough for today.

. . . .
. . . .
. . . .
. . . .

THURSDAY

I saw her die many times
sometimes crying in my arms
sometimes in a stranger's arms
sometimes alone, naked;
so she lived near me.
Now at last I know there's nothing further
and I wait.
If I'm sorry, it's a private matter
like the feeling for things so simple
that, as they say, one's passed beyond them;

κι᾿ ὅμως λυποῦμαι ἀκόμη γιατὶ
δὲν ἔγινα κι᾿ ἐγὼ (ὅπως θὰ τό ἤθελα)
σὰν τὸ χορτάρι ποὺ ἄκουσα νὰ φυτρώνει
μιὰ νύχτα κοντὰ σ᾿ ἕνα πεῦκο·
γιατὶ δὲν ἀκολούθησα τὴ θάλασσα
μιὰν ἄλλη νύχτα ποὺ τραβιούνταν τὰ νερὰ
πίνοντας ἁπαλὰ τὴν πίκρα τους,
κι᾿ οὔτε κατάλαβα ὅταν ψηλάφησα τὰ ὑγρὰ φύκια
πόση τιμὴ ἀπομένει στὶς παλάμες τοῦ ἀνθρώπου.
Πέρασαν ὅλα αὐτὰ βαριὰ καὶ τελειωτικὰ
σὰν τὶς μαοῦνες μὲ τὰ ξεθωριασμένα ὀνόματα
ΕΛΕΝΗ ΤΗΣ ΣΠΑΡΤΗΣ, ΤΥΡΑΝΝΟΣ, GLORIA MUNDI
πέρασαν κάτω ἀπὸ τὰ γιοφύρια πέρα ἀπ᾿ τὶς καπνοδόχες
μὲ δυὸ σκυφτοὺς ἀνθρώπους στὴν πλώρη καὶ στὴν πρύμη
γυμνοὺς ὣς τὴ μέση·
πέρασαν, δὲν ξεχωρίζω τίποτε, μέσα στὴν πρωινὴ καταχνιὰ
μόλις ξεχώριζαν τ᾿ ἀρνιὰ κουλουριασμένα μηρυκάζοντας οὔτε
τὴ νύχτα ξεχωρίζει τὸ φεγγάρι πάνω ἀπ᾿ τὸν ποταμὸ
ποὺ περιμένει·
μόνο ἑφτὰ λόγχες βυθισμένες στὸ νερὸ
στεκάμενο καὶ χωρὶς αἷμα
καὶ κάποτε στὶς πλάκες φωτισμένες θλιβερὰ
κάτω ἀπ᾿ τὸν πύργο τὸν ἀλλοίθωρο
ζωγραφιστὸς μὲ κόκκινο καὶ κίτρινο μολύβι
δείχνοντας τὴν πληγή του ὁ Ναζωραῖος.
«Μὴ ρίχνετε τὴν καρδιά σας στὰ σκυλιά.
Μὴ ρίχνετε τὴν καρδιά σας στὰ σκυλιά».
Βουλιάζει κι᾿ ἡ φωνή της μὲ τὸ χτύπημα τοῦ ρολογιοῦ·
τὸ θέλημά σου, γύρεψα τὸ θέλημά σου.

and yet I'm sorry still because
I too didn't become (as I would have wished)
like the grass I heard sprouting
one night near a pine-tree;
because I didn't follow the sea
another night when the waters were withdrawing
gently drinking their own bitterness,
and I didn't even understand, as I groped in the damp
    seaweed,
how much honor remains in the hands of men.
All this passed by slowly and conclusively
like the barges with faded names:
HELEN OF SPARTA, TYRANNUS, GLORIA MUNDI
they passed under the bridges beyond the chimneys
with two stooping men at the prow and stern
naked to the waist;
they passed, I can't distinguish anything, in the morning fog
the sheep, curled, ruminating, barely stand out
nor does the moon stand out above
the waiting river;
only seven lances plunged in the water
stagnant, bloodless
and sometimes on the flagstones, sadly lit
under the squint-eyed castle,
drawn with red and yellow pencil:
the Nazarene, showing his wound.
"Don't throw your heart to the dogs.
Don't throw your heart to the dogs."
Her voice sinks as the clock strikes;
your will, I sought your will.

ΠΑΡΑΣΚΕΥΗ

'Από τότες πόσες φορὲς πέρασε μπροστὰ στὰ μάτια μου μιὰ γυναίκα, ποὺ τῆς ἀπόμεναν μονάχα τὰ μαλλιά, τὰ μάτια, τὸ στῆθος καὶ τίποτε ἄλλο, γοργόνα ταξιδεύοντας στὸ πέλαγο, κι' ἀνάμεσό τους κυκλοφοροῦσε τὸ φρέσκο ἀεράκι, σὰ γαλάζιο αἷμα.

ΣΑΒΒΑΤΟ

—«Δὲν ξέχασα τίποτε
ὅλα εἶναι στὴ θέση τους ταχτοποιημένα κατὰ σειρὰ περιμένοντας τὸ χέρι νὰ διαλέξει
μόνο δὲν μπόρεσα νὰ βρῶ τὰ παιδικὰ χρόνια
μήτε τὸν τόπο ποὺ γεννήθηκε ὁ ἥρωας τοῦ δράματος
μήτε τὶς πρῶτες ἐντυπώσεις
ἐκεῖνες ποὺ θυμᾶται στὴν πέμπτη πράξη
στὴν κορυφὴ τῆς δυστυχίας.
Ὅλα τ' ἄλλα, νά τα, κατὰ σειρά:
οἱ προσωπίδες γιὰ τὰ τρία κύρια συναισθήματα
καὶ τὰ ἐνδιάμεσα
τὰ φορέματα μὲ τὶς βόλτες ἕτοιμες νὰ κινηθοῦν
τὰ παραπετάσματα, τὰ φῶτα
τὰ σκοτωμένα παιδιὰ τῆς Μήδειας
τὸ φαρμάκι καὶ τὸ μαχαίρι.
Μέσα σ' αὐτὸ τὸ κουτὶ εἶναι ἡ ζωὴ ὅταν ἀρχίσει νὰ γίνεται ἀνυπόφορη,
ἂν τ' ἀφουγκραστεῖς θὰ τὴν ἀκούσεις πῶς ἀνασαίνει·

FRIDAY

Since then how many times has there passed before me a woman with only her hair, eyes, and breasts left, nothing else—mermaid traveling the seas—and with the fresh air circulating between them like blue blood.

SATURDAY

—"I haven't forgotten anything,
everything's in its place, arranged in order, waiting for the
    hand to choose;
only I couldn't find the childhood years
nor the place where the hero of the drama was born
nor the first impressions
those he recalls in the fifth act
at the height of the disaster.
All the rest, there it is, in order:
the masks for the three main emotions
and for the intermediary ones
the pleated costumes ready to move,
the curtains, the lights,
Medea's slaughtered children,
the poison and the knife.
In that box there's life when it starts getting unbearable:
if you put your ear close you'll hear it breathing;

πρόσεξε μὴν τ' ἀνοίξεις προτοῦ σφυρίξουν οἱ Εὐμενίδες.
Μέσα σ' αὐτὸ τὸ γυαλὶ βρίσκεται ὁ ἔρωτας τοῦ κορμιοῦ
καὶ στὸ ἄλλο, ποὺ εἶναι γαλάζιο, ὁ ἔρωτας τῆς ψυχῆς·
πρόσεξε μὴν τ' ἀναμίξεις,
καὶ σ' αὐτὸ τὸ συρτάρι τὸ πουκάμισο τοῦ Νέσσου
(πέμπτη πράξη, σκηνὴ τρίτη)
τὰ λόγια τὰ θυμᾶσαι ποὺ ἀρχίζουν:
'Αρκείτω βίος! 'Ιώ! 'Ιώ!
'Εδῶ εἶναι ἡ σάλπιγγα ποὺ γκρεμίζει τὸ παλάτι
καὶ φαίνεται ἡ βασίλισσα μέσα στὴν ἀνομία,
αὐτὸς εἶναι ὁ διακόπτης τῶν μικροφώνων
θὰ σ' ἀκούσουν ὣς τὰ πέρατα τοῦ κόσμου.
'Εμπρός! Προβολέα! Καλὴ τύχη!»

—«Μιὰ στιγμή, ποιὸς θὰ εἶμαι; ποιὸν θὰ σκοτώσω;
κι' οἱ ἄνθρωποι τοῦτοι ποὺ μὲ κοιτάζουν
πῶς θὰ πιστέψουν πὼς ἡ δικαιοσύνη μὲ προστατεύει;
πῶς θὰ πιστέψουν;
Ὢ νὰ μπορούσαμε ν' ἀγαπήσουμε
τουλάχιστο σὰν τὶς μέλισσες
ὄχι σὰν τὰ περιστέρια
τουλάχιστο σὰν τὰ κοχύλια
ὄχι σὰν τὶς σειρῆνες
τουλάχιστο σὰν τὰ μερμήγκια
ὄχι σὰν τὰ πλατάνια...
μὰ δὲν τοὺς βλέπεις, ὅλοι τους εἶναι τυφλοί!
Οἱ τυφλοὶ κοιμοῦνται...»

—«Θαυμάσια, μπορεῖς νὰ ἐξακολουθήσεις».

make sure you don't open it before the Furies whistle.
In that glass you'll find love of the body
and in that other glass—the blue one—love of the soul:
make sure you don't confuse them.
And in that drawer is Nessus' shirt
(Act Five, Scene Three);
you remember the speech that begins:
"Enough of life! Io! Io!"
Here's the trumpet that destroys the palace
revealing the queen in her iniquity;
that's the microphone switch—
they'll hear you at the far end of the world.
Let's go. Lights! Good luck!"

—"Just a moment, who am I going to play? Who will I kill?
And these people looking at me—
what will make them believe that justice protects me?
What will make them believe it?
O could we only love
like bees at least
not like pigeons
like shells at least
not like sirens
like ants at least
not like plane-trees . . .
But don't you see them, they're all blind!
The blind are sleeping . . ."

—"Wonderful. You can continue."

ΚΥΡΙΑΚΗ

Δυὸ βαριὰ ἄλογα καὶ ἕνα ἀργὸ ἁμάξι, αὐτὸ ἢ κάτι ἄλλο,
ἔξω ἀπὸ τὸ παράθυρό μου στὸ δρόμο
αὐτὸς ὁ θόρυβος.
Σὲ λίγο θά 'χει νυχτώσει· βλέπω νὰ μὲ κοιτάζει ἀκόμη ἕνα
ἀέτωμα γεμάτο ἀγάλματα ἀκρωτηριασμένα.
Πόσο βαριὰ εἶναι τὰ ἀγάλματα;
Προτιμῶ μιὰ στάλα αἷμα ἀπὸ ἕνα ποτήρι μελάνι.

Καλοκαίρι, 1933

SUNDAY

Two heavy horses and a slow carriage, that or something
else,
in the street outside my window:
that's the noise.
Soon it'll be dark; I see a pediment of amputated statues
still looking at me.
What do statues weigh?
I prefer a drop of blood to a glass of ink.

Summer, 1933

ΣΧΕΔΙΑ ΓΙΑ ΕΝΑ ΚΑΛΟΚΑΙΡΙ

SKETCHES FOR A SUMMER

ΕΝΑΣ ΛΟΓΟΣ ΓΙΑ ΤΟ ΚΑΛΟΚΑΙΡΙ

Γυρίσαμε πάλι στὸ φθινόπωρο, τὸ καλοκαίρι
σὰν ἕνα τετράδιο ποὺ μᾶς κούρασε γράφοντας μένει
γεμάτο διαγραφὲς ἀφηρημένα σχέδια
στὸ περιθώριο κι' ἐρωτηματικά, γυρίσαμε
στὴν ἐποχὴ τῶν ματιῶν ποὺ κοιτάζουν
στὸν καθρέφτη μέσα στὸ ἠλεχτρικὸ φῶς
σφιγμένα χείλια κι' οἱ ἄνθρωποι ξένοι
στὶς κάμαρες στοὺς δρόμους κάτω ἀπ' τὶς πιπεριὲς
καθὼς οἱ φάροι τῶν αὐτοκινήτων σκοτώνουν
χιλιάδες χλωμὲς προσωπίδες.
Γυρίσαμε· πάντα κινᾶμε γιὰ νὰ γυρίσουμε
στὴ μοναξιά, μιὰ φούχτα χῶμα, στὶς ἄδειες παλάμες.

Κι' ὅμως ἀγάπησα κάποτε τὴ λεωφόρο Συγγροῦ
τὸ διπλὸ λίκνισμα τοῦ μεγάλου δρόμου
ποὺ μᾶς ἄφηνε θαματουργὰ στὴ θάλασσα
τὴν παντοτινὴ γιὰ νὰ μᾶς πλύνει ἀπὸ τὶς ἁμαρτίες·
ἀγάπησα κάποιους ἀνθρώπους ἄγνωστους
ἀπαντημένους ξαφνικὰ στὸ ἔβγα τῆς μέρας,
μονολογώντας σὰν καπετάνιοι βουλιαγμένης ἀρμάδας,
σημάδια πὼς ὁ κόσμος εἶναι μεγάλος.
Κι' ὅμως ἀγάπησα τοὺς δρόμους τοὺς ἐδῶ, αὐτὲς τὶς κολόνες·
κι' ἂς γεννήθηκα στὴν ἄλλη ἀκρογιαλιὰ κοντὰ
σὲ βοῦρλα καὶ σὲ καλάμια νησιὰ

A WORD FOR SUMMER

We've returned to autumn again; summer,
like an exercise book we're tired of writing in, remains
full of deletions, abstract designs,
question marks in the margin; we've returned
to the season of eyes gazing
into the mirror under the electric light
closed lips and people strangers
in rooms in streets under the pepper-trees
while the headlights of cars massacre
thousands of pale masks.
We've returned; we always set out to return
to solitude, a fistful of earth, to the empty hands.

And yet I used to love Syngrou Avenue*
the double rise and fall of the great road
bringing us out miraculously to the sea
the eternal sea, to cleanse us of our sins;
I used to love certain unknown people
met suddenly at the end of day
talking to themselves like captains of a sunken armada,
evidence that the world is large.
And yet I used to love these roads here, these columns,
even though I was born on the other shore, close
to reeds and rushes, islands

πού εἶχαν νερὸ στὴν ἄμμο νὰ ξεδιψάει
ὁ κουπολάτης, κι' ἂς γεννήθηκα κοντὰ
στὴ θάλασσα πού ξετυλίγω καὶ τυλίγω στὰ δάχτυλά μου
σὰν εἶμαι κουρασμένος — δὲν ξέρω πιὰ ποῦ γεννήθηκα.

Μένει ἀκόμα τὸ κίτρινο ἀπόσταγμα τὸ καλοκαίρι
καὶ τὰ χέρια σου γγίζοντας μέδουσες πάνω στὸ νερὸ
τὰ μάτια σου ξεσκεπασμένα ξαφνικά, τὰ πρῶτα
μάτια τοῦ κόσμου, κι' οἱ θαλασσινὲς σπηλιές·
πόδια γυμνὰ στὸ κόκκινο χῶμα.
Μένει ἀκόμα ὁ ξανθὸς μαρμαρωμένος ἔφηβος τὸ καλοκαίρι
λίγο ἁλάτι πού στέγνωσε στὴ γούβα ἑνὸς βράχου
λίγες βελόνες πεύκου ὕστερα ἀπ' τὴ βροχὴ
σκόρπιες καὶ κόκκινες σὰ χαλασμένα δίχτυα.

Δὲν τὰ καταλαβαίνω αὐτὰ τὰ πρόσωπα δὲν τὰ καταλαβαίνω
μιμοῦνται κάποτε τὸ θάνατο κι' ἔπειτα ξανὰ
φέγγουν μὲ μιὰ ζωὴ πυγολαμπίδας χαμηλὴ
μὲ μιὰ προσπάθεια περιορισμένη ἀνέλπιδη
σφιγμένη ἀνάμεσα σὲ δυὸ ρυτίδες
σὲ δυὸ τραπεζάκια καφενείου κηλιδωμένα
σκοτώνουνται τὸ ἕνα μὲ τ' ἄλλο λιγοστεύουν
κολλοῦν σὰ γραμματόσημα στὰ τζάμια
τὰ πρόσωπα τῆς ἄλλης φυλῆς.

Περπατήσαμε μαζὶ μοιραστήκαμε τὸ ψωμὶ καὶ τὸν ὕπνο
δοκιμάσαμε τὴν ἴδια πίκρα τοῦ ἀποχωρισμοῦ
χτίσαμε μὲ τὶς πέτρες πού εἴχαμε τὰ σπίτια μας
πήραμε τὰ καράβια ξενιτευτήκαμε γυρίσαμε

where water gushed from the sand to quench
the thirst of a rower, even though I was born
close to the sea that I unwind and wind on my fingers
when I'm tired—I no longer know where I was born.

There still remains the yellow essence, summer,
and your hands touching medusas on the water
your eyes suddenly open, the first
eyes of the world, and the sea caves:
feet naked on the red soil.
There still remains the blond marble youth, summer,
a little salt dried in the rock's hollow
a few pine needles after the rain
scattered and red like broken nets.

I don't understand these faces I don't understand them,
sometimes they imitate death and then again
they gleam with the low life of a glow-worm
with a limited effort, hopeless,
squeezed between two wrinkles,
between two stained café tables;
they kill one another, grow smaller,
stick like postage stamps to window panes—
the faces of the other tribe.

We walked together, shared bread and sleep
tasted the same bitterness of parting
built our houses with what stones we had
set out in ships, knew exile, returned

βρήκαμε τὶς γυναῖκες μας νὰ περιμένουν
μᾶς γνώρισαν δύσκολα, κανεὶς δὲ μᾶς γνωρίζει.
Κι' οἱ σύντροφοι φόρεσαν τ' ἀγάλματα φόρεσαν τὶς γυμνὲς
ἄδειες καρέκλες τοῦ φθινοπώρου, κι' οἱ σύντροφοι
σκοτώσανε τὰ πρόσωπά τους· δὲν τὰ καταλαβαίνω.
Μένει ἀκόμα ἡ κίτρινη ἔρημο τὸ καλοκαίρι
κύματα τῆς ἄμμου φεύγοντας ὣς τὸν τελευταῖο κύκλο
ἕνας ρυθμὸς τυμπάνου ἀλύπητος ἀτέλειωτος
μάτια φλογισμένα βουλιάζοντας μέσα στὸν ἥλιο
χέρια μὲ φερσίματα πουλιῶν χαράζοντας τὸν οὐρανὸ
χαιρετώντας στίχους νεκρῶν σὲ στάση προσοχῆς
χαμένα σ' ἕνα σημεῖο ποὺ δὲν τ' ὁρίζω καὶ μὲ κυβερνᾷ·
τὰ χέρια σου γγίζοντας τὸ ἐλεύθερο κῦμα.

Φθινόπωρο, 1936

found our women waiting—
they scarcely knew us, no one knows us.
And the companions wore statues, wore the naked
empty chairs of autumn, and the companions
destroyed their own faces: I don't understand them.
There still remains the yellow desert, summer,
waves of sand receding to the final circle
a drum's beat, merciless, endless,
flaming eyes sinking into the sun
hands in the manner of birds cutting the sky
saluting ranks of the dead who stand at attention
hands lost at a point beyond my control and mastering me:
your hands touching the free wave.

Autumn, 1936

ΕΠΙΦΑΝΙΑ, 1937

Τ' ἀνθισμένο πέλαγο καὶ τὰ βουνὰ στὴ χάση τοῦ φεγγαριοῦ
ἡ μεγάλη πέτρα κοντὰ στὶς ἀραποσυκιὲς καὶ τ' ἀσφοδίλια
τὸ σταμνὶ ποὺ δὲν ἤθελε νὰ στερέψει στὸ τέλος τῆς μέρας
καὶ τὸ κλειστὸ κρεβάτι κοντὰ στὰ κυπαρίσσια καὶ τὰ μαλλιά σου
χρυσά· τ' ἄστρα τοῦ Κύκνου κι' ἐκεῖνο τ' ἄστρο ὁ 'Αλδεβαράν.

Κράτησα τὴ ζωή μου κράτησα τὴ ζωή μου ταξιδεύοντας
ἀνάμεσα στὰ κίτρινα δέντρα κατὰ τὸ πλάγιασμα τῆς βροχῆς
σὲ σιωπηλὲς πλαγιὲς φορτωμένες μὲ τὰ φύλλα τῆς ὀξιᾶς,
καμιὰ φωτιὰ στὴν κορυφή τους· βραδιάζει.
Κράτησα τὴ ζωή μου· στ' ἀριστερό σου χέρι μιὰ γραμμὴ
μιὰ χαρακιὰ στὸ γόνατό σου, τάχα νὰ ὑπάρχουν
στὴν ἄμμο τοῦ περασμένου καλοκαιριοῦ τάχα
νὰ μένουν ἐκεῖ ποὺ φύσηξε ὁ βοριὰς καθὼς ἀκούω
γύρω στὴν παγωμένη λίμνη τὴν ξένη φωνή.
Τὰ πρόσωπα ποὺ βλέπω δὲ ρωτοῦν μήτε ἡ γυναίκα
περπατώντας σκυφτὴ βυζαίνοντας τὸ παιδί της.
'Ανεβαίνω τὰ βουνά· μελανιασμένες λαγκαδιές· ὁ χιονισμένος
κάμπος, ὣς πέρα ὁ χιονισμένος κάμπος, τίποτε δὲ ρωτοῦν

EPIPHANY, 1937

The flowering sea and the mountains in the moon's waning
the great stone close to the Barbary figs and the asphodels
the jar that refused to go dry at the end of day
and the closed bed by the cypress trees and your hair
golden; the stars of the Swan and that other star, Aldebaran.

I've kept a hold on my life, kept a hold on my life, traveling
among yellow trees in driving rain
on silent slopes loaded with beech leaves
no fire on their peaks; it's getting dark.
I've kept a hold on my life; on your left hand a line
a scar at your knee, perhaps they exist
on the sand of the past summer perhaps
they remain there where the north wind blew as I hear
an alien voice around the frozen lake.
The faces I see do not ask questions nor does the woman
bent as she walks giving her child the breast.
I climb the mountains; dark ravines; the snow-covered
plain, into the distance stretches the snow-covered plain,
they ask nothing

μήτε ὁ καιρὸς κλειστὸς σὲ βουβὰ ἐρμοκλήσια μήτε
τὰ χέρια ποὺ ἁπλώνουνται γιὰ νὰ γυρέψουν, κι' οἱ δρόμοι.
Κράτησα τὴ ζωή μου ψιθυριστὰ μέσα στὴν ἀπέραντη
σιωπὴ
δὲν ξέρω πιὰ νὰ μιλήσω μήτε νὰ συλλογιστῶ· ψίθυροι
σὰν τὴν ἀνάσα τοῦ κυπαρισσιοῦ τὴ νύχτα ἐκείνη
σὰν τὴν ἀνθρώπινη φωνὴ τῆς νυχτερινῆς θάλασσας στὰ χαλίκια
σὰν τὴν ἀνάμνηση τῆς φωνῆς σου λέγοντας «εὐτυχία».
Κλείνω τὰ μάτια γυρεύοντας τὸ μυστικὸ συναπάντημα
τῶν νερῶν
κάτω ἀπ' τὸν πάγο τὸ χαμογέλιο τῆς θάλασσας τὰ κλειστὰ
πηγάδια
ψηλαφώντας μὲ τὶς δικές μου φλέβες τὶς φλέβες ἐκεῖνες
ποὺ μοῦ ξεφεύγουν
ἐκεῖ ποὺ τελειώνουν τὰ νερολούλουδα κι' αὐτὸς ὁ ἄνθρωπος
ποὺ βηματίζει τυφλὸς πάνω στὸ χιόνι τῆς σιωπῆς.
Κράτησα τὴ ζωή μου, μαζί του, γυρεύοντας τὸ νερὸ ποὺ σ'
ἀγγίζει
στάλες βαρειὲς πάνω στὰ πράσινα φύλλα, στὸ πρόσωπό σου
μέσα στὸν ἄδειο κῆπο, στάλες στὴν ἀκίνητη δεξαμενὴ
βρίσκοντας ἕναν κύκνο νεκρὸ μέσα στὰ κάτασπρα φτερά του,
δέντρα ζωντανὰ καὶ τὰ μάτια σου προσηλωμένα.

Ὁ δρόμος αὐτὸς δὲν τελειώνει δὲν ἔχει ἀλλαγή, ὅσο γυρεύεις
νὰ θυμηθεῖς τὰ παιδικά σου χρόνια, ἐκείνους ποὺ ἔφυγαν
ἐκείνους

neither time shut up in dumb chapels nor
hands outstretched to beg, nor the roads.
I've kept a hold on my life whispering in a boundless silence
I no longer know how to speak nor how to think; whispers
like the breathing of the cypress tree that night
like the human voice of the night sea on pebbles
like the memory of your voice saying "happiness."
I close my eyes looking for the secret meeting place of the
    waters
under the ice the sea's smile, the closed wells
groping with my veins for those veins that escape me
there where the water-lilies end and that man
who walks blindly across the snows of silence.
I've kept a hold on my life, with him, looking for the water
    that touches you
heavy drops on green leaves, on your face
in the empty garden, drops in the motionless reservoir
striking a swan dead in its white wings
living trees and your eyes staring.

This road has no end, has no relief, however hard you try
to recall your childhood years, those who left, those

πού χάθηκαν μέσα στὸν ὕπνο τοὺς πελαγίσιους τάφους,
ὅσο ζητᾶς τὰ σώματα πού ἀγάπησες νὰ σκύψουν
κάτω ἀπὸ τὰ σκληρὰ κλωνάρια τῶν πλατάνων ἐκεῖ
πού στάθηκε μιὰ ἀχτίδα τοῦ ἥλιου γυμνωμένη
καὶ σκίρτησε ἕνας σκύλος καὶ φτεροκόπησε ἡ καρδιά σου,
ὁ δρόμος δὲν ἔχει ἀλλαγή· κράτησα τὴ ζωή μου.

Τὸ χιόνι
καὶ τὸ νερὸ παγωμένο στὰ πατήματα τῶν ἀλόγων.

lost in sleep, in the graves of the sea,
however much you ask bodies you've loved to stoop
under the harsh branches of the plane-trees there
where a ray of the sun, naked, stood still
and a dog leapt and your heart shuddered,
the road has no relief; I've kept a hold on my life.

The snow
and the water frozen in the hoofmarks of the horses.

RAVEN

In memoriam E. A. P.

Χρόνια σὰν τὰ φτερά. Τί θυμᾶται τ' ἀκίνητο κοράκι;
τί θυμοῦνται οἱ πεθαμένοι κοντὰ στὶς ρίζες τῶν δέντρων;
Εἶχαν ἕνα χρῶμα τὰ χέρια σου σὰν τὸ μῆλο ποὺ πέφτει.
Κι' αὐτὴ ἡ φωνὴ ποὺ ξαναγυρίζει πάντα, χαμηλή.

Ἐκεῖνοι ποὺ ταξιδεύουν κοιτάζουν τὸ πανὶ καὶ τ' ἀστέρια
ἀκοῦνε τὸν ἀγέρα ἀκοῦνε πέρα ἀπ' τὸν ἀγέρα τὴν ἄλλη θά-
    λασσα
σὰν ἕνα κοχύλι κλειστὸ κοντά τους, δὲν ἀκοῦνε
τίποτε ἄλλο, δὲν ψάχνουν μέσα στοὺς ἴσκιους τῶν κυπα-
    ρισσιῶν
ἕνα χαμένο πρόσωπο, ἕνα νόμισμα, δὲ γυρεύουν
κοιτάζοντας ἕνα κοράκι σ' ἕνα ξερὸ κλωνί, τί θυμᾶται.
Μένει ἀκίνητο πάνω στὶς ὧρες μου λίγο πιὸ ψηλὰ
σὰν τὴν ψυχὴ ἑνὸς ἀγάλματος ποὺ δὲν ἔχει μάτια
εἶναι ἕνα πλῆθος μαζεμένο μέσα σ' αὐτὸ τὸ πουλὶ
χίλιοι ἄνθρωποι ξεχασμένοι σβησμένες ρυτίδες
ἐρειπωμένες ἀγκαλιὲς καὶ γέλια ποὺ δὲν τέλειωσαν
ἔργα σταματημένα σιωπηλοὶ σταθμοὶ
ἕνας ὕπνος βαρὺς ἀπὸ χρυσὰ ψιχαλίσματα.
Μένει ἀκίνητο. Κοιτάζει τὶς ὧρες μου. Τί θυμᾶται;
Εἶναι πολλὲς πληγὲς μέσα στοὺς ἀόρατους ἀνθρώπους,
    μέσα του

RAVEN

In memoriam E. A. P.

Years like wings. What does the motionless raven remember?
What do the dead close to the roots of trees remember?
Your hands had the color of an apple ready to fall,
and that voice which always returns, that low voice.

Those who travel watch the sail and the stars
they hear the wind they hear the other sea beyond the wind
near them like a closed shell, they don't hear
anything else, don't look among the cypress shadows
for a lost face, a coin, don't ask,
seeing a raven on a dry branch, what it remembers.
It remains motionless just over my hours
like the soul of an eyeless statue;
there's a whole crowd gathered in that bird
thousands of people forgotten, wrinkles obliterated
broken embraces and uncompleted laughter,
arrested works, silent stations
a deep sleep of golden spangles.
It remains motionless. It gazes at my hours. What does it
remember?
There are many wounds inside those invisible people within
it

πάθη μετέωρα περιμένοντας τὴ δεύτερη παρουσία
ἐπιθυμίες ταπεινὲς ποὺ κόλλησαν πάνω στὸ χῶμα
σκοτωμένα παιδιὰ καὶ γυναῖκες ποὺ κουράστηκαν τὴν
αὐγή.
Τάχα νὰ βαραίνει πάνω στὸ ξερὸ κλωνὶ τάχα νὰ
βαραίνει
πάνω στὶς ρίζες τοῦ κίτρινου δέντρου πάνω στοὺς
ὤμους
τῶν ἄλλων ἀνθρώπων, τὶς παράξενες φυσιογνωμίες
ποὺ δὲν τολμοῦν νὰ γγίξουν μιὰ στάλα νερὸ βυθισμένοι στὸ
χῶμα
τάχα νὰ βαραίνει πουθενά ;
Εἶχαν ἕνα βάρος τὰ χέρια σου ὅπως μέσα στὸ νερὸ
μέσα στὶς θαλασσινὲς σπηλιές, ἕνα βάρος ἀλαφρὺ χωρὶς
συλλογὴ
μὲ τὴν κίνηση κάποτε ποὺ διώχνουμε τὴν ἄσκημη σκέψη
στρώνοντας τὸ πέλαγο ὣς πέρα στὸν ὁρίζοντα στὰ νησιά.
Εἶναι βαρὺς ὁ κάμπος ὕστερ' ἀπ' τὴ βροχή· τί θυμᾶται
ἡ μαύρη στεκάμενη φλόγα πάνω στὸν γκρίζο οὐρανὸ
σφηνωμένη ἀνάμεσα στὸν ἄνθρωπο καὶ στὴν ἀνάμνηση τοῦ
ἀνθρώπου
ἀνάμεσα στὴν πληγὴ καὶ τὸ χέρι ποὺ πλήγωσε μαύρη
λόγχη,
σκοτείνιασε ὁ κάμπος πίνοντας τὴ βροχή, ἔπεσε ὁ ἀγέρας
δὲ σώνει ἡ δική μου πνοή, ποιὸς θὰ τὸ μετακινήσει ;
ἀνάμεσα στὴ μνήμη, χάσμα — ἕνα ξαφνισμένο στῆθος
ἀνάμεσα στοὺς ἴσκιους ποὺ μάχουνται νὰ ξαναγίνουν ἄντρας
καὶ γυναίκα

suspended passions waiting for the Second Coming
humble desires cleaving to the ground
children slaughtered and women exhausted at daybreak.
Does it weigh the dry branch down? Does it weigh down
the roots of the yellow tree, the shoulders
of other men, strange figures
sunk in the ground, not daring to touch even a drop of
    water?
Does it weigh down anywhere?
Your hands had a weight like hands in water
in the sea caves, a light careless weight
pushing the sea away to the horizon to the islands
with that movement we make sometimes when we dismiss
    an ugly thought.
The plain is heavy after the rain; what does the black
static flame against the gray sky remember
wedged between man and the memory of man
between the wound and the hand that inflicted the wound
    a black lance,
the plain darkened drinking the rain, the wind dropped
my own breath's not enough, who will move it?
Within memory, a gulf—a startled breast
between the shadows struggling to become man and woman
    again

ἀνάμεσα στὸν ὕπνο καὶ στὸ θάνατο στεκάμενη ζωή.

Εἶχαν μιὰ κίνηση τὰ χέρια σου πάντα πρὸς τὸν ὕπνο τοῦ
    πελάγου
χαϊδεύοντας τ' ὄνειρο ποὺ ἀνέβαινε ἥσυχα τὴ μαλαματένια
    ἀράχνη
φέρνοντας μέσα στὸν ἥλιο τὸ πλῆθος τῶν ἀστερισμῶν
τὰ κλεισμένα βλέφαρα τὰ κλεισμένα φτερά...

Κοριτσά, χειμώνας 1937

stagnant life between sleep and death.

Your hands always moved towards the sea's slumber
caressing the dream that gently ascended the golden spider
bearing into the sun the host of constellations
the closed eyelids the closed wings . . .

Koritsa, winter 1937

Ἄνθη τῆς πέτρας μπροστὰ στὴν πράσινη θάλασσα
μὲ φλέβες ποὺ μοῦ θύμιζαν ἄλλες ἀγάπες
γυαλίζοντας στ᾽ ἀργὸ ψιχάλισμα,
ἄνθη τῆς πέτρας φυσιογνωμίες
ποὺ ἦρθαν ὅταν κανένας δὲ μιλοῦσε καὶ μοῦ μίλησαν
ποὺ μ᾽ ἄφησαν νὰ τὶς ἀγγίξω ὕστερ᾽ ἀπ᾽ τὴ σιωπὴ
μέσα σὲ πεῦκα σὲ πικροδάφνες καὶ σὲ πλατάνια.

Flowers of the rock facing the green sea
with veins that reminded me of other loves
glowing in the slow fine rain,
flowers of the rock, figures
that came when no one spoke and spoke to me
that let me touch them after the silence
among pine-trees, oleanders, and plane-trees.

Τὸ ζεστὸ νερὸ μοῦ θυμίζει κάθε πρωὶ
πὼς δὲν ἔχω τίποτε ἄλλο ζωντανὸ κοντά μου.

The warm water reminds me each morning
that I have nothing else alive near me.

ΕΠΙΤΥΜΒΙΟ

Τὰ κάρβουνα μὲς στὴν ὀμίχλη
εἴτανε ρόδα ριζωμένα στὴν καρδιά σου
κι᾽ ἡ στάχτη σκέπαζε τὸ πρόσωπό σου
κάθε πρωί.

Μαδώντας ἴσκιους ἀπὸ κυπαρίσσια
ἔφυγες τ᾽ ἄλλο καλοκαίρι.

EPITAPH

Coals in the fog
were roses rooted in your heart
and the ashes covered your face
each morning.

Plucking cypress shadows
you left a summer ago.

'Ανάμεσα σὲ δυὸ πικρὲς στιγμὲς δὲν ἔχεις καιρὸ μήτε
ν' ἀνασάνεις
ἀνάμεσα στὸ πρόσωπό σου καὶ στὸ πρόσωπό σου
μιὰ τρυφερὴ μορφὴ παιδιοῦ γράφεται καὶ σβήνει.

Between two bitter moments you don't have time even to
breathe
between your face and your face
the tender form of a child takes shape and vanishes.

Μέσα στὶς θαλασσινὲς σπηλιὲς
ὑπάρχει μιὰ δίψα ὑπάρχει μιὰ ἀγάπη
ὑπάρχει μιὰ ἔκσταση,
ὅλα σκληρὰ σὰν τὰ κοχύλια
μπορεῖς νὰ τὰ κρατήσεις στὴν παλάμη σου.

Μέσα στὶς θαλασσινὲς σπηλιὲς
μέρες ὁλόκληρες σὲ κοίταζα στὰ μάτια
καὶ δὲ σὲ γνώριζα μήτε μὲ γνώριζες.

In the sea caves
there's a thirst there's a love
there's an ecstasy
all hard like shells
you can hold them in your palm.

In the sea caves
for whole days I gazed into your eyes
and I didn't know you nor did you know me.

Πάψε πιὰ νὰ γυρεύεις τὴ θάλασσα καὶ τῶν κυμάτων τὶς
προβιὲς σπρώχνοντας τὰ καΐκια
κάτω ἀπ' τὸν οὐρανὸ εἴμαστε ἐμεῖς τὰ ψάρια καὶ τὰ δέντρα
εἶναι τὰ φύκια.

Stop looking for the sea and the waves' fleece pushing the
caiques along
under the sky we are the fish and the trees are the seaweed.

ΗΜΕΡΟΛΟΓΙΟ
ΚΑΤΑΣΤΡΩΜΑΤΟΣ, Α'

Παραμένομεν εἰς τὴν αὐτὴν θέσιν ἀναμένοντες διαταγάς.

ΗΜΕΡΟΛΟΓΙΑ ΚΑΤΑΣΤΡΩΜΑΤΟΣ

Στὸ μεταξὺ πολλὲς φορὲς μοῦ φαίνεται
πὼς εἶναι πιὸ καλὰ νὰ κοιμηθεῖς παρὰ νὰ βρίσκεσαι ἔτσι χωρὶς σύντροφο
καὶ νὰ ἐπιμένεις τόσο. Καὶ τί νὰ κάνεις μέσα στὴν ἀναμονή, καὶ τί νὰ πεῖς;
Δὲν ξέρω. Κι' οἱ ποιητὲς τί χρειάζουνται σ' ἕνα μικρόψυχο καιρό;

ΦΡΕΙΔΕΡΙΚΟΣ ΧΕΛΝΤΕΡΛΙΝ, «ΤΟ ΨΩΜΙ ΚΑΙ ΤΟ ΚΡΑΣΙ»

LOGBOOK I

We remain in this position awaiting orders.

FROM LOGBOOKS

Meanwhile it sometimes seems better to me
to sleep than to be so completely without companions as we
are,
to be always waiting like this; and what's to be done or said
in the meanwhile
I don't know, and what is the use of poets in a mean-spirited
time?

FRIEDRICH HÖLDERLIN, *"BREAD AND WINE"**

Ο ΜΑΘΙΟΣ ΠΑΣΚΑΛΗΣ ΑΝΑΜΕΣΑ ΣΤΑ ΤΡΙΑΝΤΑΦΥΛΛΑ

Καπνίζω χωρὶς νὰ σταματήσω ἀπ' τὸ πρωὶ
ἂν σταματήσω τὰ τριαντάφυλλα θὰ μ' ἀγκαλιάσουν
μ' ἀγκάθια καὶ μὲ ξεφυλλισμένα πέταλα θὰ μὲ πνίξουν
φυτρώνουν στραβὰ ὅλα μὲ τὸ ἴδιο τριανταφυλλὶ
κοιτάζουν· περιμένουν νὰ ἰδοῦν κάποιον· δὲν περνᾶ κανείς·
πίσω ἀπὸ τὸν καπνὸ τῆς πίπας μου τὰ παρακολουθῶ
πάνω σ' ἕνα κοτσάνι βαριεστισμένο χωρὶς εὐωδιά,
στὴν ἄλλη ζωὴ μιὰ γυναίκα μοῦ ἔλεγε μπορεῖς νὰ γγίξεις
αὐτὸ τὸ χέρι
κι' εἶναι δικό σου αὐτὸ τὸ τριαντάφυλλο εἶναι δικό σου
μπορεῖς νὰ τὸ πάρεις
τώρα ἢ ἀργότερα, ὅταν θελήσεις.

Κατεβαίνω καπνίζοντας ὁλοένα, τὰ σκαλοπάτια
τὰ τριαντάφυλλα κατεβαίνουν μαζί μου ἐρεθισμένα
κι' ἔχουνε κάτι στὸ φέρσιμό τους ἀπ' τὴ φωνὴ
στὴ ρίζα τῆς κραυγῆς ἐκεῖ ποὺ ἀρχίζει
νὰ φωνάζει ὁ ἄνθρωπος: «μάνα» ἢ «βοήθεια»
ἢ τὶς μικρὲς ἄσπρες φωνὲς τοῦ ἔρωτα.

Εἶναι ἕνας μικρὸς κῆπος ὅλο τριανταφυλλιὲς
λίγα τετραγωνικὰ μέτρα ποὺ χαμηλώνουν μαζί μου
καθὼς κατεβαίνω τὰ σκαλοπάτια, χωρὶς οὐρανό·

MATHIOS PASKALIS AMONG THE ROSES

I've been smoking steadily all morning
if I stop the roses will embrace me
they'll choke me with thorns and fallen petals
they grow crookedly, each with the same rose color
they gaze, expecting to see someone go by; no one goes by.
Behind the smoke of my pipe I watch them
scentless on their weary stems.
In the other life a woman said to me: "You can touch this
hand,
and this rose is yours, it's yours, you can take it
now or later, whenever you like."

I go down the steps smoking still,
and the roses follow me down excited
and in their manner there's something of that voice
at the root of a cry, there where one starts shouting
"mother" or "help"
or the small white cries of love.

It's a small garden full of roses
a few square yards descending with me
as I go down the steps, without the sky;

κι᾽ ἡ θεία της ἔλεγε: «᾽Αντιγόνη ξέχασες σήμερα τὴ γυμναστική σου
στὴν ἡλικία σου δὲ φορούσα κορσέ, στὴν ἐποχή μου».
῾Η θεία της εἴταν ἕνα θλιβερὸ κορμὶ μ᾽ ἀνάγλυφες φλέβες
εἶχε πολλὲς ρυτίδες γύρω στ᾽ αὐτιὰ μιὰ ἑτοιμοθάνατη μύτη
ἀλλὰ τὰ λόγια της εἴταν γεμάτα φρόνηση πάντα.
Τὴν εἴδα μιὰ μέρα νὰ γγίζει τὸ στῆθος τῆς ᾽Αντιγόνης
σὰν τὸ μικρὸ παιδὶ ποὺ κλέβει ἕνα μῆλο.

Τάχα θὰ τὴ συναπαντήσω τὴ γριὰ γυναίκα ἔτσι ποὺ κατεβαίνω;
Μοῦ εἶπε σὰν ἔφυγα: «Ποιὸς ξέρει πότε θὰ ξαναβρεθοῦμε;»
κι᾽ ἔπειτα διάβασα τὸ θάνατό της σὲ παλιὲς ἐφημερίδες
τὸ γάμο τῆς ᾽Αντιγόνης καὶ τὸ γάμο τῆς κόρης τῆς ᾽Αντιγόνης
χωρὶς νὰ τελειώσουν τὰ σκαλοπάτια μήτε ὁ καπνός μου
ποὺ μοῦ δίνει μιὰ γέψη στοιχειωμένου καραβιοῦ
μὲ μιὰ γοργόνα σταυρωμένη τότες ποὺ εἴταν ὄμορφη, πάνω στὸ τιμόνι.

Κοριτσά, καλοκαίρι '37

and her aunt would say to her: "Antigone, you forgot your
exercises today,
at your age I never wore corsets, not in my time."
Her aunt was a pitiful creature: veins in relief,
wrinkles all around her ears, a nose ready to die;
but her words were always full of prudence.
One day I saw her touching Antigone's breast
like a small child stealing an apple.

Is it possible that I'll meet the old woman now as I go
down?
She said to me as I left: "Who knows when we'll meet
again?"
And then I read of her death in old newspapers
of Antigone's marriage and the marriage of Antigone's
daughter
without the steps coming to an end or my tobacco
which leaves on my lips the taste of a haunted ship
with a mermaid crucified to the wheel while she was still
beautiful.

Koritsa, summer '37

ΩΡΑΙΟ ΦΘΙΝΟΠΩΡΙΝΟ ΠΡΩΙ

Γιὰ τὴν κυρία Ντονογκὸ

Νά πού μ' ἀρέσουν ἐπὶ τέλους αὐτὰ τὰ βουνὰ μ' αὐτὸ τὸ φῶς
μὲ δέρμα ρυτιδωμένο σὰν τὴν κοιλιὰ τοῦ ἐλέφαντα
ὅταν τὰ μάτια του στενεύουν ἀπ' τὰ χρόνια.
Νά πού μ' ἀρέσουν αὐτὲς οἱ λεῦκες, δὲν εἶναι πολλὲς
σηκώνοντας τοὺς ὤμους μέσα στὸν ἥλιο.
Οἱ ἀψηλοὶ γκέγκηδες οἱ κοντοὶ τόσκηδες
τὸ καλοκαίρι μὲ τὰ δρεπάνια καὶ τὸ χειμώνα μὲ τὰ τσεκούρια
κι' ὅλο τὰ ἴδια ξανὰ καὶ ξανά, ἴδιες κινήσεις
στὰ ἴδια σώματα: κόπηκε ἡ μονοτονία.
Τί λέει ὁ Μουεζίνης στὴν ἄκρη τοῦ μιναρέ; γιὰ πρόσεξε!
Ἔσκυψε ν' ἀγκαλιάσει μιὰ ξανθὴ κούκλα στὸ πλαϊνὸ μπαλκόνι.
Αὐτὴ ἀνεμίζει δυὸ ρόδινα χεράκια στὸν οὐρανὸ
δὲν παραδέχεται νὰ τὴ βιάζουν.
Ὡστόσο γέρνει ὁ μιναρὲς καὶ τὸ μπαλκόνι σὰν τὸν πύργο τῆς Πίζας
ἀκοῦς μονάχα ψιθυρίσματα, δὲν εἶναι τὰ φύλλα μήτε τὸ νερὸ
«Ἀλλάχ! Ἀλλάχ!» δὲν εἶναι μήτε τ' ἀγεράκι, παράξενη προσευχή.
Ἕνας κόκορας λάλησε, πρέπει νά 'ναι ξανθὸς

FINE AUTUMN MORNING

For Mrs. Dononko

There, you see, at last I love these mountains with this light
their skin wrinkled like an elephant's belly
when his eyes shrink with age.
There, you see, I love these poplars, few as they are,
raising their shoulders into the sun.
The tall Ghegs and the short Tosks*
summer with the sickle and winter with the axe
the same things again and again, the same movements
in the same bodies: the monotony is broken.
What's the Muezzin saying from the top of his minaret?
Listen!
He's leaned over to embrace a blond doll on a nearby
balcony.
She waves two pink little hands at the sky
refusing to be ravished.
But the minaret and the balcony lean like the tower of Pisa
you hear only whispers, it isn't the leaves or the water
"Allah! Allah!" or the breeze, a strange prayer.
A cock crowed, he must be blond—

ὦ ψυχὴ ἐρωτευμένη ποὺ πέταξες στὰ ὕψη!

Νά ποὺ μ' ἀρέσουν ἐπὶ τέλους αὐτὰ τὰ βουνά, ἔτσι κουλουριασμένα
τὸ γερασμένο κοπάδι τριγύρω μου μ' αὐτὲς τὶς ρυτίδες
σκέφτηκε κανεὶς νὰ πεῖ τὴ μοίρα ἑνὸς βουνοῦ ὅπως κοιτάζει μιὰ παλάμη
σκέφτηκε κανείς;... Ὢ ἐκείνη ἡ ἐπίμονη σκέψη
κλεισμένη σ' ἕνα κουτὶ ἄδειανό, θεληματικὴ
χτυπώντας ἀδιάκοπα τὸ χαρτόνι, ὅλη τὴ νύχτα
σὰν ποντικὸς ποὺ ροκανίζει τὸ πάτωμα.
Κόπηκε ἡ μονοτονία, ὦ ἐσὺ ποὺ πέταξες στὰ ὕψη, νά ποὺ
μ' ἀρέσει
κι' αὐτὸ τὸ βουβάλι τοῦ μακεδονίτικου κάμπου τόσο ὑπομονετικὸ
τόσο ἀβίαστο, σὰ νὰ τὸ ξέρει πὼς δὲ φτάνει κανεὶς πουθενὰ
θυμίζει τ' ἀγέρωχο κεφάλι τοῦ πολεμόχαρου Βερκινγετόριξ
Tel qu'en lui-même enfin l'éternité le change.

Κοριτσά, 1937

O soul in love that has soared to the heights!

There, you see, at last I love these mountains hunched up
like this,
the ancient flock about me with these wrinkles.
Has anyone thought of telling a mountain's fortune as you
read the palm of a hand?
Has anyone thought of it? . . . O that insistent thought
shut up in an empty box, willfully
beating the cardboard without a pause all night long
like a mouse gnawing the floor.
The monotony is broken, O you who've soared to the
heights, there, you see, I love
even that buffalo on the Macedonian plain, so patient,
so unhurried, as if knowing that no one gets anywhere,
recalling the arrogant head of the warlike Vercingetorix*
*Tel qu'en lui-même enfin l'éternité le change.**

Koritsa, 1937

PIAZZA SAN NICOLO

Longtemps je me suis couché de bonne heure
τὸ σπίτι
γεμάτο γρίλιες καὶ δυσπιστία σὰν τὸ καλοκοιτάξεις στὶς
σκοτεινὲς γωνιὲς
«γιὰ χρόνια πλάγιαζα νωρὶς» ψιθυρίζει
«κοίταζα τὴν εἰκόνα τοῦ Ὕλα καὶ τὴν εἰκόνα τῆς Μαγδα-
ληνῆς
προτοῦ καλονυχτίσω κοίταζα τὸν πολυέλαιο μὲ τ' ἄσπρο
φῶς
τὰ μέταλλα ποὺ γυάλιζαν καὶ δύσκολα ἄφηνα
τὶς τελευταῖες φωνὲς τῆς μέρας».
Τὸ σπίτι σὰν τὸ καλοκοιτάξεις μέσα ἀπὸ τὶς παλιὲς κορ-
νίζες
ξυπνᾶ μὲ τὰ πατήματα τῆς μητέρας στὰ σκαλοπάτια
τὸ χέρι ποὺ φτιάνει τὰ σκεπάσματα ἢ διορθώνει τὴν κου-
νουπιέρα
τὰ χείλια ποὺ σβήνουν τὴ φλόγα τοῦ κεριοῦ.

Κι' ὅλα τοῦτα εἶναι παλιὲς ἱστορίες ποὺ δὲν ἐνδιαφέρουν
πιὰ κανέναν
δέσαμε τὴν καρδιά μας καὶ μεγαλώσαμε.
Ἡ δροσιὰ τοῦ βουνοῦ δὲν κατεβαίνει ποτὲ χαμηλότερα ἀπὸ
τὸ καμπαναρειὸ
ποὺ μετρᾶ τὶς ὧρες μονολογώντας καὶ τὸ βλέπουμε
σὰν ἔρχεται τ' ἀπόγεμα στὴν αὐλὴ

PIAZZA SAN NICOLO

*Longtemps je me suis couché de bonne heure**

the house

full of grilles and distrust when you examine it closely in its
dark corners—
"For years I used to go to bed early," it whispers
"I would gaze at the picture of Hylas and the picture of
Mary Magdalene*
before saying goodnight. I would gaze at the white light of
the candelabra
the glistening metal, and it would be difficult for me to leave
the last voices of day."
The house, when you examine its old cornices closely,
wakens with a mother's footsteps on the stairs
the hand that arranges the covers or fixes the mosquito net
the lips that put out the candle's flame.

And all this is an old story that no longer interests anyone;
we've hardened our hearts and grown up.
The mountain's coolness never descends lower than the
bell-tower
that counts out the hours in monologue, as we observe

ἡ θεία Ντάρια Ντιμιετρόβνα τὸ γένος Τροφίμοβιτς.
Ἡ δροσιὰ τοῦ βουνοῦ δὲν ἀγγίζει ποτὲ τὸ στιβαρὸ χέρι τοῦ
Ἄη Νικόλα
μήτε τὸ φαρμακοποιὸ ποὺ κοιτάζει ἀνάμεσα σὲ μιὰ κόκκινη
καὶ μιὰ πράσινη σφαίρα
σὰν ὑπερωκεάνειο μαρμαρωμένο.
Γιὰ νὰ βρεῖς τὴ δροσιὰ τοῦ βουνοῦ πρέπει ν' ἀνέβεις ψηλότερα ἀπὸ τὸ καμπαναρειὸ
κι' ἀπὸ τὸ χέρι τοῦ Ἄη Νικόλα
κάπου 70 ἢ 80 μέτρα δὲν εἶναι πολύ.
Κι' ὅμως ἐκεῖ ψιθυρίζεις ὅπως σὰν πλάγιαζες νωρὶς
καὶ μέσα στὴν εὐκολία τοῦ ὕπνου χάνονταν ἡ πίκρα τοῦ
ἀποχωρισμοῦ
ὄχι λέξεις πολλὲς δυὸ - τρεῖς μονάχα καὶ τοῦτο φτάνει
ἀφοῦ κυλᾶνε τὰ νερὰ καὶ δὲ φοβοῦνται μὴ σταματήσουν
ψιθυρίζεις ἀκουμπώντας τὸ κεφάλι στὸν ὦμο ἑνὸς φίλου
σὰ νὰ μὴν εἶχες μεγαλώσει μέσα στὸ σπίτι τὸ σιωπηλὸ
μὲ φυσιογνωμίες ποὺ βάρυναν καὶ μᾶς ἔκαμαν ἀδέξιους
ξένους.
Κι' ὅμως ἐκεῖ, λίγο ψηλότερα ἀπὸ τὸ καμπαναρειό, ἀλλάζει ἡ ζωή σου.
Δὲν εἶναι μεγάλο πράγμα ν' ἀνεβεῖς μὰ εἶναι πολὺ δύσκολο
ν' ἀλλάξεις
σὰν εἶναι τὸ σπίτι μέσα στὴν πέτρινη ἐκκλησιὰ κι' ἡ καρδιά σου μέσα στὸ σπίτι ποὺ σκοτεινιάζει
κι' ὅλες οἱ πόρτες κλειδωμένες ἀπὸ τὸ μεγάλο χέρι τ' Ἄη
Νικόλα.

Πήλιο - Κoριτσά, καλοκαίρι - φθινόπωρο '37

when aunt Daria Dimietrovna neé Trofimovitch
comes into the courtyard of an afternoon.
The mountain's coolness never touches the steady hand of
St. Nicholas
nor the druggist who looks out between a red and black
sphere
like a petrified transatlantic liner.
To find the mountain's coolness you must climb higher
than the bell-tower
and the hand of St. Nicholas
about 70 or 80 meters higher, nothing really.
Yet there you whisper as you would when going to bed early
and in the ease of sleep the bitterness of separation would
disappear
not many words, one or two only and that's enough
since the water rolls on and they're not afraid it will stop
you whisper resting your head on a friend's shoulder
as though you hadn't grown up in the silent house
with faces that became heavy and made us awkward
strangers.
Yet there, a little higher than the bell-tower, your life
changes.
It's no great matter to climb up but it's very difficult for you
to change
when the house is in the stone church and your heart in
the darkening house
and all the doors locked by the huge hand of St. Nicholas.

Pelion—Koritsa, summer-fall '37

Ο ΔΙΚΟΣ ΜΑΣ ΗΛΙΟΣ

Ὁ ἥλιος αὐτὸς εἴταν δικός μου καὶ δικός σου: τὸν μοιραστήκαμε
ποιὸς ὑποφέρει πίσω ἀπὸ τὸ χρυσαφὶ μεταξωτὸ ποιὸς πεθαίνει;
Μιὰ γυναίκα φώναζε χτυπώντας τὸ στεγνὸ στῆθος της: «Δειλοὶ
μοῦ πήραν τὰ παιδιά μου καὶ τὰ κομμάτιασαν, σεῖς τὰ σκοτώσατε
κοιτάζοντας μὲ παράξενες ἐκφράσεις τὸ βράδι τὶς πυγολαμπίδες
ἀφηρημένοι μέσα σὲ μιὰ τυφλὴ συλλογή».
Τὸ αἷμα στέγνωνε πάνω στὸ χέρι ποὺ τὸ πρασίνιζε ἕνα δέντρο
ἕνας πολεμιστὴς κοιμότανε σφίγγοντας τὴ λόγχη ποὺ τοῦ φώτιζε τὸ πλευρό.

Εἴταν δικός μας ὁ ἥλιος, δὲ βλέπαμε τίποτε πίσω ἀπὸ τὰ χρυσὰ κεντίδια
ἀργότερα ἤρθαν οἱ μαντατοφόροι λαχανιασμένοι βρώμικοι
τραυλίζοντας συλλαβὲς ἀκατανόητες
εἴκοσι μερόνυχτα πάνω στὴ στέρφα γῆς καὶ μόνο ἀγκάθια
εἴκοσι μερόνυχτα νιώθοντας ματωμένες τὶς κοιλιὲς τῶν ἀλόγων

OUR SUN

This sun was mine and yours; we shared it.
Who's suffering behind the golden silk, who's dying?
A woman beating her dry breasts cried out: "Cowards,
they've taken my children and torn them to shreds, you've
killed them
gazing at the fire-flies at dusk with a strange look,
lost in blind thought."
The blood was drying on a hand that a tree made green,
a warrior was asleep clutching the lance that flared against
his side.

It was ours, this sun, we saw nothing behind the gold
embroidery
then the messengers came, dirty and breathless,
stuttering unintelligible words
twenty days and nights on the barren earth with thorns only
twenty days and nights feeling the bellies of the horses
bleeding

κι᾽ οὔτε στιγμὴ νὰ σταματήσουν γιὰ νὰ πιοῦν τὸ νερὸ τῆς
βροχῆς.
Εἶπες νὰ ξεκουραστοῦν πρῶτα κι᾽ ἔπειτα νὰ μιλήσουν, σὲ
εἶχε θαμπώσει τὸ φῶς.
Ξεψύχησαν λέγοντας: «Δὲν ἔχουμε καιρὸ» γγίζοντας κάτι
ἀχτίδες·
ξεχνοῦσες πὼς κανεὶς δὲν ξεκουράζεται.

Οὔρλιαζε μιὰ γυναίκα: «Δειλοὶ» σὰν τὸ σκυλὶ τὴ νύχτα
θὰ εἴταν ὡραία κάποτε σὰν ἐσένα
μὲ στόμα ὑγρό, τὶς φλέβες ζωντανὲς κάτω ἀπ᾽ τὸ δέρμα
μὲ τὴν ἀγάπη.

Ὁ ἥλιος αὐτὸς εἴταν δικός μας· τὸν κράτησες ὁλόκληρο δὲ
θέλησες νὰ μ᾽ ἀκολουθήσεις
κι᾽ ἔμαθα τότε αὐτὰ τὰ πράγματα πίσω ἀπὸ τὸ χρυσάφι
καὶ τὸ μετάξι·
δὲν ἔχουμε καιρό. Σωστὰ μιλήσαν οἱ μαντατοφόροι.

and not a moment's break to drink the rain water.
You told them to rest first and then to speak, the light had
blinded you.
They died saying: "We don't have time," touching some
rays of the sun.
You'd forgotten that no one rests.

A woman howled "Cowards," like a dog in the night.
Once she would have been beautiful like you
with wet mouth, veins alive beneath the skin,
with love.

This sun was ours; you kept all of it, you didn't want to
follow me.
And it was then I found out about those things behind the
gold and the silk:
we don't have the time. The messengers were right.

Ο ΓΥΡΙΣΜΟΣ ΤΟΥ ΞΕΝΙΤΕΜΕΝΟΥ

«Παλιέ μου φίλε τί γυρεύεις;
χρόνια ξενιτεμένος ἦρθες
μὲ εἰκόνες ποὺ ἔχεις ἀναθρέψει
κάτω ἀπὸ ξένους οὐρανοὺς
μακριὰ ἀπ' τὸν τόπο τὸ δικό σου».

«Γυρεύω τὸν παλιό μου κῆπο·
τὰ δέντρα μοῦ ἔρχουνται ὣς τὴ μέση
κι' οἱ λόφοι μοιάζουν μὲ πεζούλια
κι' ὅμως σὰν εἴμουνα παιδὶ
ἔπαιζα πάνω στὸ χορτάρι
κάτω ἀπὸ τοὺς μεγάλους ἴσκιους
κι' ἔτρεχα πάνω σὲ πλαγιὲς
ὥρα πολλὴ λαχανιασμένος».

«Παλιέ μου φίλε ξεκουράσου
σιγὰ σιγὰ θὰ συνηθίσεις·
θ' ἀνηφορίσουμε μαζὶ
στὰ γνώριμά σου μονοπάτια
θὰ ξαποστάσουμε μαζὶ
κάτω ἀπ' τὸ θόλο τῶν πλατάνων
σιγὰ σιγὰ θὰ 'ρθοῦν κοντά σου
τὸ περιβόλι κι' οἱ πλαγιές σου».

THE RETURN OF THE EXILE

"My old friend, what are you looking for?
After years abroad you've come back
with images nourished
under foreign skies
far from your own country."

"I'm looking for my old garden;
the trees come to my waist
and the hills resemble terraces
yet as a child
I used to play on the grass
under great shadows
and I would run for hours
breathless over the slopes."

"My old friend, rest,
you'll get used to it little by little;
together we will climb
the paths you once knew
we will sit together
under the plane-trees' dome.
They'll come back to you little by little,
your garden and your slopes."

«Γυρεύω τὸ παλιό μου σπίτι
μὲ τ' ἀψηλὰ τὰ παραθύρια
σκοτεινιασμένα ἀπ' τὸν κισσὸ
γυρεύω τὴν ἀρχαία κολόνα
ποὺ κοίταζε ὁ θαλασσινός.
Πῶς θὲς νὰ μπῶ σ' αὐτὴ τὴ στάνη;
οἱ στέγες μοῦ ἔρχουνται ὡς τοὺς ὤμους
κι' ὅσο μακριὰ καὶ νὰ κοιτάξω
βλέπω γονατιστοὺς ἀνθρώπους
λὲς κάνουνε τὴν προσευχή τους».

«Παλιέ μου φίλε δὲ μ' ἀκοῦς;
σιγὰ σιγὰ θὰ συνηθίσεις
τὸ σπίτι σου εἶναι αὐτὸ ποὺ βλέπεις
κι' αὐτὴ τὴν πόρτα θὰ χτυπήσουν
σὲ λίγο οἱ φίλοι κι' οἱ δικοί σου
γλυκὰ νὰ σὲ καλωσορίσουν».

«Γιατί εἶναι ἀπόμακρη ἡ φωνή σου;
σήκωσε λίγο τὸ κεφάλι
νὰ καταλάβω τί μοῦ λὲς
ὅσο μιλᾶς τ' ἀνάστημά σου
ὁλοένα πάει καὶ λιγοστεύει
λὲς καὶ βυθίζεσαι στὸ χῶμα».

«Παλιέ μου φίλε συλλογίσου
σιγὰ σιγὰ θὰ συνηθίσεις

"I'm looking for my old house,
the tall windows
darkened by ivy;
I'm looking for the ancient column
known to sailors.
How can I get into this coop?
The roof comes to my shoulders
and however far I look
I see men on their knees
as though saying their prayers."

"My old friend, don't you hear me?
You'll get used to it little by little.
Your house is the one you see
and soon friends and relatives
will come knocking at the door
to welcome you back tenderly."

"Why is your voice so distant?
Raise your head a little
so that I understand you.
As you speak you grow
gradually smaller
as though you're sinking into the ground."

"My old friend, stop a moment and think:
you'll get used to it little by little.

ἡ νοσταλγία σοῦ ἔχει πλάσει
μιὰ χώρα ἀνύπαρχτη μὲ νόμους
ἔξω ἀπ' τὴ γῆς κι' ἀπ' τοὺς ἀνθρώπους».

«Πιὰ δὲν ἀκούω τσιμουδιὰ
βούλιαξε κι' ὁ στερνός μου φίλος
παράξενο πῶς χαμηλώνουν
ὅλα τριγύρω κάθε τόσο
ἐδῶ διαβαίνουν καὶ θερίζουν
χιλιάδες ἅρματα δρεπανηφόρα».

Ἀθήνα, ἄνοιξη '38

Your nostalgia has created
a non-existent country, with laws
alien to earth and man."

"Now I can't hear a sound.
My last friend has sunk.
Strange how from time to time
they level everything down.
Here a thousand scythe-bearing chariots go past
and mow everything down."

Athens, spring '38

Η ΧΩΡΑ ΤΟΥ ΑΧΩΡΗΤΟΥ

Μεγάλη Παρασκευὴ

Πέφτουν ὁλοένα σήμερα νομίσματα πάνω στὴν πολιτεία
ἀνάμεσα σὲ κάθε κόμπο σὰ μιὰ σταλαματιὰ στὸ χῶμα
ἀνοίγει μιὰ καινούργια χώρα : ἦρθε ἡ στιγμή, σηκῶστε με·

THE CONTAINER OF THE UNCONTAINABLE*

Good Friday

Bells like coins falling sound today all over the city
between each peal a new space opens
like a drop of water on the earth: the moment has come,
    raise me up.

ΔΙΑΛΕΙΜΜΑ ΧΑΡΑΣ

Εἴμασταν χαρούμενοι ὅλο ἐκεῖνο τὸ πρωὶ
θεέ μου πόσο χαρούμενοι.
Πρῶτα γυάλιζαν οἱ πέτρες τὰ φύλλα καὶ τὰ λουλούδια
ἔπειτα ὁ ἥλιος
ἕνας μεγάλος ἥλιος ὅλο ἀγκάθια μὰ τόσο ψηλὰ στὸν οὐρανό.
Μιὰ νύμφη μάζευε τὶς ἔνιες μας καὶ τὶς κρεμνοῦσε στὰ
δέντρα
ἕνα δάσος ἀπὸ δέντρα τοῦ Ἰούδα.
Ἐρωτιδεῖς καὶ σάτυροι παίζαν καὶ τραγουδούσαν
κι' ἔβλεπες ρόδινα μέλη μέσα στὶς μαῦρες δάφνες
σάρκες μικρῶν παιδιῶν.
Εἴμασταν χαρούμενοι ὅλο τὸ πρωί·
ἡ ἄβυσσο κλειστὸ πηγάδι
ὅπου χτυποῦσε τὸ τρυφερὸ πόδι ἑνὸς ἀνήλικου φαύνου
θυμᾶσαι τὸ γέλιο του : πόσο χαρούμενοι !
Ἔπειτα σύννεφα βροχὴ καὶ τὸ νοτισμένο χῶμα
ἔπαψες νὰ γελᾶς σὰν ἔγειρες μέσα στὴν καλύβα
κι' ἄνοιξες τὰ μεγάλα σου τὰ μάτια κοιτάζοντας
τὸν ἀρχάγγελο νὰ γυμνάζεται μὲ μιὰ πύρινη ρομφαία —
«Ἀνεξήγητο» εἶπες «ἀνεξήγητο
δὲν καταλαβαίνω τοὺς ἀνθρώπους
ὅσο καὶ νὰ παίζουν μὲ τὰ χρώματα
εἶναι ὅλοι τους μαῦροι».

Πεντέλη, ἄνοιξη

INTERLUDE OF JOY

That whole morning we were full of joy,
my God, how full of joy.
First, stones leaves and flowers shone
then the sun
a huge sun all thorns and so high in the sky.
A nymph collected our cares and hung them on the trees
a forest of Judas trees.
Young Loves and satyrs played there and sang
and you could see pink limbs among the black laurels
bodies of little children.
The whole morning long we were full of joy;
the abyss a closed well
tapped by the tender hoof of a young fawn.
Do you remember its laugh—how full of joy!
Then clouds rain and the wet earth.
You stopped laughing when you lay down in the hut
and opened your large eyes as you watched
the archangel practicing with a fiery sword—
"Inexplicable," you said, "inexplicable.
I don't understand people:
no matter how much they play with colors
they are all black."

Penteli, spring

ΤΟ ΦΥΛΛΟ ΤΗΣ ΛΕΥΚΑΣ

Ἔτρεμε τόσο ποὺ τὸ πῆρε ὁ ἄνεμος
ἔτρεμε τόσο πῶς νὰ μὴν τὸ πάρει ὁ ἄνεμος
πέρα μακριὰ
μιὰ θάλασσα
πέρα μακριὰ
ἕνα νησὶ στὸν ἥλιο
καὶ τὰ χέρια σφίγγοντας τὰ κουπιὰ
πεθαίνοντας τὴν ὥρα ποὺ φάνηκε τὸ λιμάνι
καὶ τὰ μάτια κλειστὰ
σὲ θαλασσινὲς ἀνεμῶνες.

Ἔτρεμε τόσο πολὺ
τὸ ζήτησα τόσο πολὺ
στὴ στέρνα μὲ τοὺς εὐκαλύπτους
τὴν ἄνοιξη καὶ τὸ φθινόπωρο
σ᾽ ὅλα τὰ δάση γυμνὰ
θεέ μου τὸ ζήτησα.

THE LEAF OF THE POPLAR

It trembled so, the wind carried it away,
it trembled so, how could the wind not carry it away
in the distance
a sea
in the distance
an island in the sun
and hands grasping the oars
dying the moment the port came into sight
and eyes closed
in sea anemones.

It trembled so much
I wanted it so much
in the cistern with the eucalyptus trees
spring and autumn
in all the woods naked
my God I wanted it.

ΑΛΛΗΛΕΓΓΥΗ

Εἶναι ἐκεῖ δὲν μπορῶ ν' ἀλλάξω
μὲ δυὸ μεγάλα μάτια πίσω ἀπ' τὸ κῦμα
ἀπὸ τὸ μέρος ποὺ φυσᾶ ὁ ἀγέρας
ἀκολουθώντας τὶς φτεροῦγες τῶν πουλιῶν
εἶναι ἐκεῖ μὲ δυὸ μεγάλα μάτια
μήπως ἄλλαξε κανεὶς ποτέ του.

Τί γυρεύετε; τὰ μηνύματά σας
ἔρχουνται ἀλλαγμένα ὣς τὸ καράβι
ἡ ἀγάπη σας γίνεται μῖσος
ἡ γαλήνη σας γίνεται ταραχὴ
καὶ δὲν μπορῶ νὰ γυρίσω πίσω
νὰ ἰδῶ τὰ πρόσωπά σας στ' ἀκρογιάλι.

Εἶναι ἐκεῖ τὰ μεγάλα μάτια
κι' ὅταν μένω καρφωμένος στὴ γραμμή μου
κι' ὅταν πέφτουν στὸν ὁρίζοντα τ' ἀστέρια
εἶναι ἐκεῖ δεμένα στὸν αἰθέρα
σὰ μιὰ τύχη πιὸ δική μου ἀπ' τὴ δική μου.

Τὰ λόγια σας συνήθεια τῆς ἀκοῆς
βουίζουν μέσα στὰ ξάρτια καὶ περνᾶνε
μήπως πιστεύω πιὰ στὴν ὕπαρξή σας
μοιραῖοι σύντροφοι, ἀνυπόστατοι ἴσκιοι.

✦

SOLIDARITY

It's there, I can't change
with two large eyes behind the wave
on the side where the wind blows
following the wings of birds
it's there with two large eyes
has anyone ever changed himself?

What are you looking for? Your messages
reach the ship altered
your love becomes hatred
your peace becomes tumult
and I can't turn back
to see your faces on the shore.

The large eyes are there
both when I keep fixed on my course
and when the stars fall on the horizon
they are there tethered to space
like a fate more mine than my own.

Your words, a habit of hearing,
hum in the rigging and are lost
do I still believe in your existence
doomed companions, unsubstantial shades?

✦

Έχασε πιὰ τὸ χρῶμα αὐτὸς ὁ κόσμος
καθὼς τὰ φύκια στ' ἀκρογιάλι τοῦ ἄλλου χρόνου
γκρίζα ξερὰ καὶ στὸ ἔλεος τοῦ ἀνέμου.

Ένα μεγάλο πέλαγο δυὸ μάτια
εὐκίνητα καὶ ἀκίνητα σὰν τὸν ἀγέρα
καὶ τὰ πανιά μου ὅσο κρατήσουν, κι' ὁ θεός μου.

This world has lost its color
like last year's seaweed on the beach
dry, gray, at the wind's mercy.

A huge sea two eyes
swift and motionless like the wind
and my sails as long as they last, and my god.

Η ΤΕΛΕΥΤΑΙΑ ΜΕΡΑ

Εἴταν ἡ μέρα συννεφιασμένη. Κανεὶς δὲν ἀποφάσιζε
φυσοῦσε ἕνας ἀγέρας ἀλαφρύς: «Δὲν εἶναι γρέγος εἶναι σιρόκος» εἶπε κάποιος.
Κάτι λιγνὰ κυπαρίσσια καρφωμένα στὴν πλαγιὰ κι' ἡ θάλασσα
γκρίζα μὲ λίμνες φωτεινές, πιὸ πέρα.
Οἱ στρατιῶτες παρουσίαζαν ὅπλα σὰν ἄρχισε νὰ ψιχαλίζει.
«Δὲν εἶναι γρέγος εἶναι σιρόκος» ἡ μόνη ἀπόφαση ποὺ ἀκούστηκε.
Κι' ὅμως τὸ ξέραμε πὼς τὴν ἄλλη αὐγὴ δὲ θὰ μᾶς ἔμενε
τίποτε πιά, μήτε ἡ γυναίκα πίνοντας πλάι μας τὸν ὕπνο
μήτε ἡ ἀνάμνηση πὼς εἴμασταν κάποτες ἄντρες,
τίποτε πιὰ τὴν ἄλλη αὐγή.

«Αὐτὸς ὁ ἀγέρας φέρνει στὸ νοῦ τὴν ἄνοιξη» ἔλεγε ἡ φίλη
περπατώντας στὸ πλευρό μου κοιτάζοντας μακριὰ «τὴν ἄνοιξη
ποὺ ἔπεσε ξαφνικὰ τὸ χειμώνα κοντὰ στὴν κλειστὴ θάλασσα.
Τόσο ἀπροσδόκητα. Πέρασαν τόσα χρόνια. Πῶς θὰ πεθάνουμε;»

Ἕνα νεκρώσιμο ἐμβατήριο τριγύριζε μὲς στὴν ψιλὴ βροχή.

THE LAST DAY

The day was cloudy. No one could come to a decision;
a light wind was blowing. "Not a north-easter, the sirocco,"
someone said.
A few slender cypresses nailed to the slope and the sea,
gray with shining pools, beyond.
The soldiers presented arms as it began to drizzle.
"Not a north-easter, the sirocco," was the only decision
heard.
And yet we knew that by the following dawn
nothing would be left to us, neither the woman drinking
sleep at our side
nor the memory that we were once men,
nothing at all by the following dawn.

"This wind reminds me of spring," said my friend
as she walked beside me gazing into the distance, "the spring
that came suddenly in winter by the closed in sea.
So unexpected. So many years have gone. How are we going
to die?"

A funeral march meandered through the thin rain.

Πῶς πεθαίνει ἕνας ἄντρας; Παράξενο κανένας δὲν τὸ συλλογίστηκε.
Κι' ὅσοι τὸ σκέφτηκαν εἴταν σὰν ἀνάμνηση ἀπὸ παλιὰ χρονικὰ
τῆς ἐποχῆς τῶν Σταυροφόρων ἢ τῆς ἐν - Σαλαμῖνι - ναυμαχίας.
Κι' ὅμως ὁ θάνατος εἶναι κάτι ποὺ γίνεται· πῶς πεθαίνει ἕνας ἄντρας;
Κι' ὅμως κερδίζει κανεὶς τὸ θάνατό του, τὸ δικό του θάνατο, ποὺ δὲν ἀνήκει σὲ κανέναν ἄλλον
καὶ τοῦτο τὸ παιχνίδι εἶναι ἡ ζωή.
Χαμήλωνε τὸ φῶς πάνω ἀπὸ τὴ συννεφιασμένη μέρα, κανεὶς δὲν ἀποφάσιζε.
Τὴν ἄλλη αὐγὴ δὲ θὰ μᾶς ἔμενε τίποτε· ὅλα παραδομένα· μήτε τὰ χέρια μας·
κι' οἱ γυναῖκες μας ξενοδουλεύοντας στὰ κεφαλόβρυσα καὶ τὰ παιδιά μας
στὰ λατομεῖα.
Ἡ φίλη μου τραγουδοῦσε περπατώντας στὸ πλευρό μου ἕνα τραγούδι σακατεμένο:
«Τὴν ἄνοιξη, τὸ καλοκαίρι, ραγιάδες...»
Θυμότανε κανεὶς γέροντες δασκάλους ποὺ μᾶς ἄφησαν ὀρφανούς.
Ἕνα ζευγάρι πέρασε κουβεντιάζοντας:
«Βαρέθηκα τὸ δειλινό, πᾶμε στὸ σπίτι μας
πᾶμε στὸ σπίτι μας ν' ἀνάψουμε τὸ φῶς».

Ἀθήνα, Φεβ. '39

How does a man die? Strange no one's thought about it.
And for those who have thought about it, it's like a
    recollection from old chronicles
from the time of the Crusades or the battle of Salamis.
Yet death is something that happens: how does a man die?
Yet each of us earns his death, his own death, which
    belongs to no one else
and this game is life.
The light was sinking over the clouded day, no one decided
    anything.
The following dawn nothing would be left to us, everything
    surrendered, even our hands,
and our woman slaves at the springheads and our children
in the quarries.*
My friend, walking beside me, was singing a disjointed song:
"In spring, in summer, slaves . . ."
One recalled old teachers who'd left us orphans.
A couple passed, talking:
"I'm sick of the dusk, let's go home,
let's go home and turn on the light."

Athens, Feb. '39

ΑΝΟΙΞΗ Μ.Χ.

Πάλι μὲ τὴν ἄνοιξη
φόρεσε χρώματα ἀνοιχτὰ
καὶ μὲ περπάτημα ἀλαφρὺ
πάλι μὲ τὴν ἄνοιξη
πάλι τὸ καλοκαίρι
χαμογελοῦσε.

Μέσα στοὺς φρέσκους ροδαμοὺς
στῆθος γυμνὸ ὣς τὶς φλέβες
πέρα ἀπ' τὴ νύχτα τὴ στεγνὴ
πέρα ἀπ' τοὺς ἄσπρους γέροντες
ποὺ συζητούσαν σιγανὰ
τί θά 'τανε καλύτερο
νὰ παραδώσουν τὰ κλειδιὰ
ἢ νὰ τραβήξουν τὸ σκοινὶ
νὰ κρεμαστοῦνε στὴ θηλειὰ
ν' ἀφήσουν ἄδεια σώματα
κεῖ ποὺ οἱ ψυχὲς δὲν ἄντεχαν
ἐκεῖ ποὺ ὁ νοῦς δὲν πρόφταινε
καὶ λύγιζαν τὰ γόνατα.

Μὲ τοὺς καινούργιους ροδαμοὺς
οἱ γέροντες ἀστόχησαν
κι' ὅλα τὰ παραδώσανε

SPRING A.D.

Again with spring
she wore light colors
and with light steps
again with spring
again with summer
she was smiling.

Among fresh blossoms
breast naked to the veins
beyond the dry night
beyond the white old men
debating quietly
whether it would be better
to give up the keys
or to pull the rope
and hang from the noose
to leave empty bodies
there where souls couldn't endure
there where the mind couldn't catch up
and knees buckled.

With the new blossoms
the old men failed
and gave up everything

ἀγγόνια καὶ δισέγγονα
καὶ τὰ χωράφια τὰ βαθιὰ
καὶ τὰ βουνὰ τὰ πράσινα
καὶ τὴν ἀγάπη καὶ τὸ βιὸς
τὴ σπλάχνιση καὶ τὴ σκεπὴ
καὶ ποταμοὺς καὶ θάλασσα·
καὶ φύγαν σὰν ἀγάλματα
κι' ἄφησαν πίσω τους σιγὴ
ποὺ δὲν τὴν ἔκοψε σπαθὶ
ποὺ δὲν τὴν πῆρε καλπασμὸς
μήτε ἡ φωνὴ τῶν ἄγουρων·
κι' ἦρθε ἡ μεγάλη μοναξιὰ
κι' ἦρθε ἡ μεγάλη στέρηση
μαζὶ μ' αὐτὴ τὴν ἄνοιξη
καὶ κάθησε κι' ἁπλώθηκε
ὡσὰν τὴν πάχνη τῆς αὐγῆς
καὶ πιάστη ἀπ' τὰ ψηλὰ κλαδιὰ
μὲς ἀπ' τὰ δέντρα γλίστρησε
καὶ τὴν ψυχή μας τύλιξε.

Μὰ ἐκείνη χαμογέλασε
φορώντας χρώματα ἀνοιχτὰ
σὰν ἀνθισμένη ἀμυγδαλιὰ
μέσα σὲ φλόγες κίτρινες
καὶ περπατοῦσε ἀνάλαφρα
ἀνοίγοντας παράθυρα
στὸν οὐρανὸ ποὺ χαίρονταν
χωρὶς ἐμᾶς τοὺς ἄμοιρους.
Κι' εἶδα τὸ στῆθος της γυμνὸ

grandchildren and great-grandchildren
the broad fields
the green mountains
love and life
compassion and shelter
rivers and sea;
and they departed like statues
leaving behind a silence
that no sword could cut
that no gallop could break
nor the voices of the young;
and the great loneliness came
the great privation
along with this spring
and settled and spread
like the frost of dawn
caught hold of the high branches
slid down the trunks of trees
and wrapped around our soul.

But she smiled
wearing light colors
like a blossoming almond tree
in yellow flames
and walked along lightly
opening windows
in the delighted sky
without us, the luckless ones.
And I saw her breast naked

τὴ μέση καὶ τὸ γόνατο
πῶς βγαίνει ἀπὸ τὴν παιδωμὴ
νὰ πάει στὰ ἐπουράνια
ὁ μάρτυρας ἀνέγγιχτος
ἀνέγγιχτος καὶ καθαρός,
ἔξω ἀπ' τὰ ψιθυρίσματα
τοῦ λαοῦ τ' ἀξεδιάλυτα
στὸν τσίρκο τὸν ἀπέραντο
ἔξω ἀπ' τὸ μαῦρο μορφασμὸ
τὸν ἱδρωμένο τράχηλο
τοῦ δήμιου π' ἀγανάχτησε
χτυπώντας ἀνωφέλευτα.

Ἔγινε λίμνη ἡ μοναξιὰ
ἔγινε λίμνη ἡ στέρηση
ἀνέγγιχτη κι' ἀχάραχτη.

16 Μαρτ. '39

the waist and the knee
who rises out of torment
like the untouched martyr
on his way to the heavens
untouched and clean
beyond the inexplicable
whispering of people
in the boundless circus
beyond the black grimace
the sweaty neck
of the exasperated executioner
striking vainly.

The loneliness now a lake
the privation now a lake
untouched and untraceable.

16 March '39

ΤΟ ΓΙΑΣΕΜΙ

Εἴτε βραδιάζει
εἴτε φέγγει
μένει λευκὸ
τὸ γιασεμί.

THE JASMIN

Whether it gets dark
or light
the jasmin stays
always white.

ΑΦΗΓΗΣΗ

Αὐτὸς ὁ ἄνθρωπος πηγαίνει κλαίγοντας
κανεὶς δὲν ξέρει νὰ πεῖ γιατί
κάποτε νομίζουν πὼς εἶναι οἱ χαμένες ἀγάπες
σὰν αὐτὲς ποὺ μᾶς βασανίζουνε τόσο
στὴν ἀκροθαλασσιὰ τὸ καλοκαίρι μὲ τὰ γραμμόφωνα.

Οἱ ἄλλοι ἄνθρωποι φροντίζουν τὶς δουλειές τους
ἀτέλειωτα χαρτιὰ παιδιὰ ποὺ μεγαλώνουν, γυναῖκες
ποὺ γερνοῦνε δύσκολα
αὐτὸς ἔχει δυὸ μάτια σὰν παπαροῦνες
σὰν ἀνοιξιάτικες κομμένες παπαροῦνες
καὶ δυὸ βρυσοῦλες στὶς κόχες τῶν ματιῶν.

Πηγαίνει μέσα στοὺς δρόμους ποτὲ δὲν πλαγιάζει
δρασκελώντας μικρὰ τετράγωνα στὴ ράχη τῆς γῆς
μηχανὴ μιᾶς ἀπέραντης ὀδύνης
ποὺ κατάντησε νὰ μὴν ἔχει σημασία.

Ἄλλοι τὸν ἄκουσαν νὰ μιλᾶ
μοναχὸ καθὼς περνοῦσε
γιὰ σπασμένους καθρέφτες πρὶν ἀπὸ χρόνια
γιὰ σπασμένες μορφὲς μέσα στοὺς καθρέφτες
ποὺ δὲν μπορεῖ νὰ συναρμολογήσει πιὰ κανείς.
Ἄλλοι τὸν ἄκουσαν νὰ λέει γιὰ τὸν ὕπνο

NARRATION

That man walks along weeping
no one knows why
sometimes they think he's weeping for lost loves
like those that torture us so much
on summer beaches with the gramophones.

Other people go about their business
endless paper, children growing up, women
ageing awkwardly.
He has two eyes like poppies
like cut spring poppies
and two trickles in the corners of his eyes.

He walks along the streets, never lies down
striding small squares on the earth's back
instrument of a boundless pain
that's finally lost all significance.

Some have heard him speak
to himself as he passed by
about mirrors broken years ago
about broken forms in the mirrors
that no one can ever put together again.
Others have heard him talk about sleep

εἰκόνες φρίκης στὸ κατώφλι τοῦ ὕπνου
πρόσωπα ἀνυπόφορα ἀπὸ τὴ στοργή.

Τὸν συνηθίσαμε εἶναι καλοβαλμένος καὶ ἥσυχος
μονάχα ποὺ πηγαίνει κλαίγοντας ὁλοένα
σὰν τὶς ἰτιὲς στὴν ἀκροποταμιὰ ποὺ βλέπεις ἀπ' τὸ τρένο
ξυπνώντας ἄσκημα κάποια συννεφιασμένη αὐγή.

Τὸν συνηθίσαμε δὲν ἀντιπροσωπεύει τίποτε
σὰν ὅλα τὰ πράγματα ποὺ ἔχετε συνηθίσει
καὶ σᾶς μιλῶ γι' αὐτὸν γιατὶ δὲ βρίσκω
τίποτε ποὺ νὰ μὴν τὸ συνηθίσατε·
προσκυνῶ.

images of horror on the threshold of sleep
faces unbearable in their tenderness.

We've grown used to him, he's presentable and quiet
only that he walks along weeping continually
like willows on a riverbank you see from the train
as you wake uncomfortably some clouded dawn.

We've grown used to him; like everything else you're used to
he doesn't stand for anything
and I talk to you about him because I can't find
anything that you're not used to;
I pay my respects.

ΠΡΩΙ

Ἄνοιξε τὰ μάτια καὶ ξεδίπλωσε
τὸ μαῦρο πανὶ πλατιὰ καὶ τέντωσέ το
ἄνοιξε τὰ μάτια καλὰ στύλωσε τὰ μάτια
προσηλώσου προσηλώσου τώρα ξέρεις
πῶς τὸ μαῦρο πανὶ ξεδιπλώνεται
ὄχι μέσα στὸν ὕπνο μήτε μέσα στὸ νερὸ
μήτε σὰν πέφτουνε τὰ βλέφαρα ρυτιδωμένα
καὶ βουλιάζουνε λοξὰ σὰν τὰ κοχύλια,
τώρα ξέρεις πῶς τὸ μαῦρο δέρμα τοῦ τυμπάνου
σκεπάζει ὁλόκληρο τὸν ὁρίζοντά σου
ὅταν ἀνοίξεις τὰ μάτια ξεκούραστος, ἔτσι.
Ἀνάμεσα στὴν ἰσημερία τῆς ἄνοιξης καὶ τὴν ἰσημερία τοῦ
φθινοπώρου
ἐδῶ εἶναι τὰ τρεχάμενα νερὰ ἐδῶ εἶναι ὁ κῆπος
ἐδῶ βουίζουν οἱ μέλισσες μὲς στὰ κλωνάρια
καὶ κουδουνίζουνε στ' αὐτιὰ ἑνὸς βρέφους
καὶ ὁ ἥλιος νά! καὶ τὰ πουλιὰ τοῦ παραδείσου
ἕνας μεγάλος ἥλιος πιὸ μεγάλος ἀπ' τὸ φῶς.

MORNING

Open your eyes and unfold
the black cloth fully and stretch it
open your eyes wide fix your eyes
concentrate concentrate now you know
that the black cloth unfolds
not in sleep nor in water
nor when the eyelids close wrinkled
and sink at an angle like shells
now you know that the black skin of the drum
fully covers your horizon
when you open your eyes rested, like this.
Between the equinox of spring and the equinox of autumn
here the running waters here the garden
here the bees sounding in the branches
and buzzing in a child's ear
and there the sun! and the birds of paradise
a huge sun greater than the light.

LES ANGES SONT BLANCS

Στὸν Henry Miller

Tout à coup Louis cessa de frotter ses jambes l' une contre l' autre et dit d' une voix lente: «Les anges sont blancs».

BALZAC

Ὅπως ὁ ναύτης στὰ ξάρτια γλίστρησε πάνω στὸν τροπικὸ
τοῦ Καρκίνου καὶ στὸν τροπικὸ τοῦ Αἰγόκερω
κι' εἴταν πολὺ φυσικὸ ποὺ δὲν μποροῦσε νὰ σταματήσει
μπροστά μας στὸ ὕψος ἀνθρώπου
ἀλλὰ μᾶς κοίταζε ὅλους ἀπὸ τὸ ὕψος τῆς πυγολαμπίδας ἢ
ἀπὸ τὸ ὕψος τοῦ πεύκου
παίρνοντας βαθιὰ τὴν ἀνάσα του στὴ δροσιὰ τῶν ἄστρων ἢ
στὴ σκόνη τῆς γῆς.
Τὸν περιστοίχιζαν γυμνὲς γυναῖκες μὲ μπρούντζινα φύλλα
ἀραποσυκιᾶς
σβησμένοι φανοστάτες ἀνεμίζοντας τοὺς κηλιδωμένους ἐπί-
δεσμους τῆς μεγάλης πολιτείας
ἀσύμμετρα κορμιὰ γεννοβολώντας κενταύρους καὶ ἀμα-
ζόνες
σὰν ἄγγιζαν τὰ μαλλιά τους τὸ Γαλαξία.

Καὶ πέρασαν μέρες ἀπὸ τὴν πρώτη στιγμὴ ποὺ μᾶς χαιρέ-
τησε βγάζοντας κι' ἀκουμπώντας τὸ κεφάλι του στὸ
σιδερένιο τραπεζάκι
καθὼς ἡ ὄψη τῆς Πολωνίας ἄλλαζε σχῆμα σὰ μελανιὰ ποὺ
τὴν πίνει τὸ στουπόχαρτο

LES ANGES SONT BLANCS

To Henry Miller

Tout à coup Louis cessa de frotter ses jambes l'une contre l'autre et dit d'une voix lente: "Les anges sont blancs."

BALZAC*

Like a sailor in the shrouds he slipped over the tropic of
 Cancer and the tropic of Capricorn
and it was natural he couldn't stand before us at a man's
 height
but looked at us all from the height of a glow-worm or from
 the height of a pine-tree
drawing his breath deeply in the dew of the stars or in the
 dust of the earth.
Naked women with bronze leaves from a Barbary fig tree
 surrounded him
extinguished lamp posts airing stained bandages of the
 great city
ungainly bodies producing Centaurs and Amazons
when their hair touched the Milky Way.

And days have passed since the first moment he greeted us
 taking his head off and placing it on the iron table
while the shape of Poland changed like ink drunk by
 blotting-paper

καὶ ταξιδεύαμε ἀνάμεσα σ' ἀκρογιαλιὲς νησιῶν γυμνὲς σὰν κόκκαλο ψαριοῦ παράξενο στὴν ἄμμο
κι' εἴταν ὁλάκερος ὁ οὐρανὸς ἕνα μεγάλο φτερὸ περιστεριοῦ μ' ἕνα ρυθμὸ σιωπῆς, ἄδειος κατάσπρος
καὶ τὰ δελφίνια κάτω ἀπὸ τὸ χρωματιστὸ νερὸ μαυρίζανε γρήγορα σὰν τὰ κινήματα τῆς ψυχῆς
ὅμοια μὲ τὰ κινήματα τῆς φαντασίας καὶ μὲ τὰ χέρια τῶν ἀνθρώπων ποὺ ψηλαφοῦν καὶ σκοτώνουνται μέσα στὸν ὕπνο
μέσα στὸ μεγάλο φλούδι τοῦ ὕπνου ποὺ μᾶς τυλίγει ἀχάρακτο, κοινὸ γιὰ ὅλους μας, ὁ κοινός μας τάφος
μὲ μικροσκοπικὰ κρύσταλλα γυαλίζοντας σπασμένα ἀπὸ τὴν κίνηση τῶν ἑρπετῶν.
Κι' ὅμως τὰ πάντα εἴταν λευκὰ γιατὶ ὁ μεγάλος ὕπνος εἶναι λευκὸς κι' ὁ μεγάλος θάνατος
ἥσυχος γαλήνιος ξεχωριστὸς μέσα σὲ μιὰ ἀπέραντη σιγή.
Καὶ τὸ κακάρισμα τῆς φραγκόκοτας τὴν αὐγὴ κι' ὁ κόκορας ποὺ λάλησε πέφτοντας σ' ἕνα βαθὺ πηγάδι
κι' ἡ φωτιὰ στὸ πλάι τοῦ βουνοῦ σηκώνοντας παλάμες ἀπὸ σούρφανο καὶ φύλλα τοῦ φθινοπώρου
καὶ τὸ καράβι μὲ τὶς διχαλωτὲς ὠμοπλάτες πιὸ τρυφερὲς ἀπὸ τὸ πλάγιασμα τῆς πρώτης μας ἀγάπης,
εἴτανε πράγματα ἀπομονωμένα πιότερο ἀκόμη καὶ ἀπὸ τὸ ποίημα
ποὺ ἄφησες σὰν ἔπεσες βαρὺς μαζὶ μὲ τὴν τελευταία του λέξη
χωρὶς νὰ ξέρεις τίποτε πιὰ μέσα στοὺς ἄσπρους βολβοὺς τῶν τυφλῶν καὶ τὰ σεντόνια

and we journeyed among shores of islands bare like strange
fish-bones on the sand
and the whole sky, empty and white, was a pigeon's huge
wing beating with a rhythm of silence
and dolphins beneath the colored water turned dark quickly
like the soul's movements
like movements of the imagination and the hands of men
who grope and kill themselves in sleep
in the huge unbroken rind of sleep that wraps around us,
common to all of us, our common grave
with brilliant minute crystals crushed by the motion of
reptiles.
And yet everything was white because the great sleep is
white and the great death
calm and serene and isolated in an endless silence.
And the cackling of the guinea-hen at dawn and the cock
that crowed falling into a deep well
and the fire on the mountain-side raising hands of smoke
and autumn leaves
and the ship with its forked shoulder-blades more tender
than the joining of our first love,
all were things isolated even beyond the poem
that you abandoned when you fell heavily along with its
last word,
knowing nothing any longer among the white eyeballs
of the blind and the sheets

πού ξεδιπλώνεις μέσα στὸν πυρετὸ γιὰ νὰ σκεπάσεις τὴν
καθημερινὴ συνοδεία
τῶν ὄντων ποὺ δὲ ματώνουν ὅσο καὶ νὰ χτυπιοῦνται μὲ τὰ
πελέκια καὶ μὲ τὰ νύχια·
εἴτανε πράγματα χωριστὰ βαλμένα ἀλλοῦ καὶ τὰ σκαλιὰ
τοῦ ἀσβέστη
κατέβαιναν ὢς τὸ κατώφλι τῶν περασμένων καὶ βρίσκανε
τὴ σιγὴ καὶ δὲν ἄνοιγε ἡ πόρτα
κι' ἔλεγες πὼς οἱ φίλοι σου χτυπούσαν δυνατὰ μὲ μιὰ μεγάλη ἀπόγνωση κι' εἴσουν κι' ἐσὺ μαζί τους
ἀλλὰ δὲν ἄκουγες τίποτε κι' ἀνέβαιναν γύρω σου βουβὰ δελφίνια μέσα στὰ φύκια.
Καὶ στύλωνες πάλι τὰ μάτια κι' ὁ ἄνθρωπος αὐτὸς μὲ τὰ
δαγκώματα τῶν τροπικῶν στὸ δέρμα
βάζοντας τὰ μαῦρα του γυαλιὰ σὰ νά 'θελε νὰ δουλέψει μὲ
τὴ φλόγα τοῦ ὀξυγόνου
ἔλεγε ταπεινὰ προσέχοντας καὶ σταματώντας στὴν κάθε του
λέξη:
«Οἱ ἄγγελοι εἶναι λευκοὶ πυρωμένοι λευκοὶ καὶ τὸ μάτι μα-
ραίνεται πού θὰ τοὺς ἀντικρίσει
καὶ δὲν ὑπάρχει ἄλλος τρόπος πρέπει νὰ γίνεις σὰν τὴν πέτρα ὅταν γυρεύεις τὴ συναναστροφή τους
κι' ὅταν γυρεύεις τὸ θαῦμα πρέπει νὰ σπείρεις τὸ αἷμα σου
στὶς ὀχτὼ γωνιὲς τῶν ἀνέμων
γιατὶ τὸ θαῦμα δὲν εἶναι πουθενὰ παρὰ κυκλοφορεῖ μέσα
στὶς φλέβες τοῦ ἀνθρώπου».

Ὕδρα-Ἀθήνα, Νοέμ. '39

that you unfolded in fever to cover the daily procession
of people who fail to bleed even when they strike themselves
with axes and nails;
they were things isolated, put somewhere else, and the steps
of whitewash
descended to the threshold of the past and found silence and
the door didn't open
and it was as if your friends, in great despair, knocked
loudly and you were with them
but you heard nothing and dolphins rose around you
dumbly in the seaweed.
And again you fixed your eyes and that man, the teethmarks
of the tropics in his skin,
putting on his dark glasses as if he were going to work with
a blowlamp,
said humbly, pausing at every word:
"The angels are white flaming white and the eye that would
confront them shrivels
and there's no other way you've got to become like stone if
you want their company
and when you look for the miracle you've got to scatter your
blood to the eight points of the wind
because the miracle is nowhere but circulating in the veins
of man."

Hydra—Athens, Nov. '39

Η ΑΠΟΦΑΣΗ ΤΗΣ ΛΗΣΜΟΝΙΑΣ

Ποιὸς θὰ μᾶς λογαριάσει τὴν ἀπόφαση τῆς λησμονιᾶς;..

Γ. Σ.

Στάσου διαβάτη μπροστὰ στὴν ἥσυχη λίμνη·
ἡ σγουρὴ θάλασσα καὶ τὰ βασανισμένα καράβια
οἱ δρόμοι ποὺ τυλίγαν βουνὰ καὶ γεννούσαν ἄστρα
ὅλα τελειώνουν ἐδῶ στὴν πλατειὰ ἐπιφάνεια.

Τώρα μπορεῖς νὰ κοιτάξεις μὲ γαλήνη τοὺς κύκνους
δές τους, εἶναι κατάσπροι σὰν τὸν ὕπνο τῆς νύχτας
χωρὶς νὰ γγίξουν πουθενὰ γλιστροῦν σ' ἕνα λιγνὸ λεπίδι
ποὺ τοὺς ὑψώνει ἐλάχιστα πάνω ἀπὸ τὰ νερά.

Σοῦ μοιάζουν ξένε, τὰ ἥσυχα φτερὰ καὶ τὰ καταλαβαίνεις
ἐνῶ σὲ κοιτάζουν μαρμαρωμένα τὰ μάτια τῶν λιονταριῶν
καὶ τὸ φύλλο τοῦ δέντρου μένει ἄγραφο στὰ ἐπουράνια
καὶ τὸ κοντύλι τρύπησε τὸν τοῖχο τῆς φυλακῆς.

Κι' ὅμως δὲν εἴταν ἄλλα τὰ πουλιὰ ποὺ σφάξαν τὶς χωριατοποῦλες
τὸ αἷμα κοκκίνιζε τὸ γάλα πάνω στὶς πλάκες τοῦ δρόμου
καὶ τ' ἄλογά τους ἀθόρυβα σὰν τὸ λειωμένο μολύβι
ρίχναν ἀδιάβαστα σχήματα μέσα στὶς γοῦρνες.

Κι' ἔσφιγγε ἡ νύχτα ὁλοένα τὸν κυρτὸ λαιμό τους
ποὺ δὲν τραγουδοῦσε γιατὶ δὲν εἴταν τρόπος νὰ πεθάνει

THE DECISION TO FORGET

*Who will calculate for us the cost of our decision to forget?**

G. S.

Stop beside the still lake, passer-by;
the curly sea and the tormented ships
the roads that wrapped mountains and gave birth to stars
all end here on this broad surface.

Now you can watch the swans calmly
look at them: all white like the night's sleep
without touching anywhere they glide on a thin blade
that lifts them barely above the water.

They're like you, stranger, the still wings, and you understand them
as the stony eyes of the lions stare at you
and the tree's leaf remains uninscribed in the heavens
and the pen pierced the prison wall.

And yet the birds that slaughtered the village girls were none other than these
the blood reddened the milk on the flagstones
and their horses cast noiselessly like molten lead
illegible shapes into the troughs.

And night suddenly tightened around their arched necks
which didn't sing because there was no way to die

ἀλλὰ χτυποῦσε θερίζοντας τὰ κόκκαλα τῶν ἀνθρώπων
τυφλά. Καὶ δρόσιζαν τὰ φτερά τους τὴ φρίκη.

Κι' αὐτὰ ποὺ γίνονταν εἶχαν τὴν ἴδια γαλήνη μὲ τοῦτα ποὺ
βλέπεις
εἶχαν τὴν ἴδια γαλήνη γιατὶ δὲν περίσσευε ψυχὴ νὰ συλλο-
γιστοῦμε
ἐκτὸς ἀπ' τὴ δύναμη νὰ χαράξουμε λίγα σημάδια στὶς
πέτρες
ποὺ ἄγγιξαν τώρα πιὰ τὸ βυθὸ κάτω ἀπ' τὴ μνήμη.

Μαζί τους κι' ἐμεῖς μακριὰ πολὺ μακριά, στάσου διαβάτη
μπροστὰ στὴν ἥσυχη λίμνη μὲ τοὺς ἄσπιλους κύκνους
ποὺ ταξιδεύουν σὰν ἄσπρα κουρέλια μέσα στὸ νοῦ σου
καὶ σὲ ξυπνᾶνε σὲ πράγματα ποὺ ἔζησες καὶ ποὺ δὲ θυμᾶσαι.

Μήτε θυμᾶσαι διαβάζοντας τὰ ψηφιά μας πάνω στὶς πέτρες·
ὡστόσο μένεις ἐκστατικὸς μαζὶ μὲ τ' ἀρνιά σου
ποὺ μεγαλώνουν τὸ σῶμα σου μὲ τὸ μαλλί τους
τώρα ποὺ νιώθεις στὶς φλέβες σου μιὰ βοὴ θυσίας.

but beat, threshing men's bones blindly.
And their wings cooled the horror.

And what then happened had the same tranquillity as what
you see before you
the same tranquillity because there wasn't a soul left for us
to consider
except the power for carving a few signs on the stones
which now have touched the depths under memory.

We too with them, far away, very far away—stop, passer-by,
beside the still lake with the spotless swans
that travel like white tatters through your mind
and waken you to things you lived yet don't remember.

Nor do you remember as you read our characters on the
stones;
even so you remain astonished together with your sheep
who enlarge your body with their wool
now that you feel in your veins a sound of sacrifice.

Ο ΒΑΣΙΛΙΑΣ ΤΗΣ ΑΣΙΝΗΣ

᾿Ασίνην τε...

ΙΛΙΑΔΑ

Κοιτάξαμε ὅλο τὸ πρωὶ γύρω γύρω τὸ κάστρο
ἀρχίζοντας ἀπὸ τὸ μέρος τοῦ ἴσκιου ἐκεῖ ποὺ ἡ θάλασσα
πράσινη καὶ χωρὶς ἀναλαμπή, τὸ στῆθος σκοτωμένου παγονιοῦ
μᾶς δέχτηκε ὅπως ὁ καιρὸς χωρὶς κανένα χάσμα.
Οἱ φλέβες τοῦ βράχου κατέβαιναν ἀπὸ ψηλὰ
στριμμένα κλήματα γυμνὰ πολύκλωνα ζωντανεύοντας
στ' ἄγγιγμα τοῦ νεροῦ, καθὼς τὸ μάτι ἀκολουθώντας τις
πάλευε νὰ ξεφύγει τὸ κουραστικὸ λίκνισμα
χάνοντας δύναμη ὁλοένα.

᾿Απὸ τὸ μέρος τοῦ ἥλιου ἕνας μακρὺς γιαλὸς ὁλάνοιχτος
καὶ τὸ φῶς τρίβοντας διαμαντικὰ στὰ μεγάλα τείχη.
Κανένα πλάσμα ζωντανὸ τ' ἀγριοπερίστερα φευγάτα
κι' ὁ βασιλιὰς τῆς ᾿Ασίνης ποὺ τὸν γυρεύουμε δυὸ χρόνια τώρα
ἄγνωστος λησμονημένος ἀπ' ὅλους κι' ἀπὸ τὸν Ὅμηρο
μόνο μιὰ λέξη στὴν ᾿Ιλιάδα κι' ἐκείνη ἀβέβαιη
ριγμένη ἐδῶ σὰν τὴν ἐντάφια χρυσὴ προσωπίδα.
Τὴν ἄγγιξες, θυμᾶσαι τὸν ἦχο της; κούφιο μέσα στὸ φῶς
σὰν τὸ στεγνὸ πιθάρι στὸ σκαμμένο χῶμα·

THE KING OF ASINE

'Ασίνην τε . . .

ILIAD*

We looked all morning round the citadel*
starting from the shaded side, there where the sea
green and without luster—breast of a slain peacock—
received us like time without an opening in it.
Veins of rock dropped down from high above,
twisted vines, naked, many-branched, coming alive
at the water's touch, while the eye following them
struggled to escape the tiresome rocking,
losing strength continually.

On the sunny side a long open beach
and the light striking diamonds on the huge walls.
No living thing, the wild doves gone
and the king of Asine, whom we've been trying to find for
two years now,
unknown, forgotten by all, even by Homer,
only one word in the *Iliad* and that uncertain,
thrown here like the gold burial mask.
You touched it, remember its sound? Hollow in the light
like a dry jar in dug earth:

κι' ὁ ἴδιος ἦχος μὲς στὴ θάλασσα μὲ τὰ κουπιά μας.
Ὁ βασιλιὰς τῆς Ἀσίνης ἕνα κενὸ κάτω ἀπ' τὴν προσωπίδα
παντοῦ μαζί μας παντοῦ μαζί μας, κάτω ἀπὸ ἕνα ὄνομα:
«Ἀσίνην τε... Ἀσίνην τε...»
καὶ τὰ παιδιά του ἀγάλματα
κι' οἱ πόθοι του φτερουγίσματα πουλιῶν κι' ὁ ἀγέρας
στὰ διαστήματα τῶν στοχασμῶν του καὶ τὰ καράβια του
ἀραγμένα σ' ἄφαντο λιμάνι·
κάτω ἀπ' τὴν προσωπίδα ἕνα κενό.

Πίσω ἀπὸ τὰ μεγάλα μάτια τὰ καμπύλα χείλια τοὺς
βοστρύχους
ἀνάγλυφα στὸ μαλαματένιο σκέπασμα τῆς ὕπαρξής μας
ἕνα σημεῖο σκοτεινὸ ποὺ ταξιδεύει σὰν τὸ ψάρι
μέσα στὴν αὐγινὴ γαλήνη τοῦ πελάγου καὶ τὸ βλέπεις:
ἕνα κενὸ παντοῦ μαζί μας.
Καὶ τὸ πουλὶ ποὺ πέταξε τὸν ἄλλο χειμώνα
μὲ σπασμένη φτερούγα
σκήνωμα ζωῆς,
κι' ἡ νέα γυναίκα ποὺ ἔφυγε νὰ παίξει
μὲ τὰ σκυλόδοντα τοῦ καλοκαιριοῦ
κι' ἡ ψυχὴ ποὺ γύρεψε τσιρίζοντας τὸν κάτω κόσμο
κι' ὁ τόπος σὰν τὸ μεγάλο πλατανόφυλλο ποὺ παρασέρνει
ὁ χείμαρρος τοῦ ἥλιου
μὲ τ' ἀρχαῖα μνημεῖα καὶ τὴ σύγχρονη θλίψη.

Κι' ὁ ποιητὴς ἀργοπορεῖ κοιτάζοντας τὶς πέτρες κι' ἀνα-
ρωτιέται

the same sound that our oars make in the sea.
The king of Asine a void under the mask
everywhere with us everywhere with us, under a name:
"'Ασίνην τε . . . 'Ασίνην τε . . ."
and his children statues
and his desires the fluttering of birds, and the wind
in the gaps between his thoughts, and his ships
anchored in a vanished port:
under the mask a void.

Behind the large eyes the curved lips the curls
carved in relief on the gold cover of our existence
a dark spot that you see traveling like a fish
in the dawn calm of the sea:
a void everywhere with us.
And the bird that flew away last winter
with a broken wing
the shelter of life,
and the young woman who left to play
with the dogteeth of summer
and the soul that sought the lower world squeaking
and the country like a large plane-leaf swept along by the
torrent of the sun
with the ancient monuments and the contemporary sorrow.

And the poet lingers, looking at the stones, and asks himself

ὑπάρχουν ἄραγε
ἀνάμεσα στὶς χαλασμένες τοῦτες γραμμὲς τὶς ἀκμὲς τὶς
αἰχμὲς τὰ κοῖλα καὶ τὶς καμπύλες
ὑπάρχουν ἄραγε
ἐδῶ ποὺ συναντιέται τὸ πέρασμα τῆς βροχῆς τοῦ ἀγέρα
καὶ τῆς φθορᾶς
ὑπάρχουν, ἡ κίνηση τοῦ προσώπου τὸ σχῆμα τῆς στοργῆς
ἐκείνων ποὺ λιγόστεψαν τόσο παράξενα μὲς στὴ
ζωή μας
αὐτῶν ποὺ ἀπόμειναν σκιὲς κυμάτων καὶ στοχασμοὶ μὲ τὴν
ἀπεραντοσύνη τοῦ πελάγου
ἢ μήπως ὄχι δὲν ἀπομένει τίποτε παρὰ μόνο τὸ βάρος
ἡ νοσταλγία τοῦ βάρους μιᾶς ὕπαρξης ζωντανῆς
ἐκεῖ ποὺ μένουμε τώρα ἀνυπόστατοι λυγίζοντας
σὰν τὰ κλωνάρια τῆς φριχτῆς ἰτιᾶς σωριασμένα μέσα στὴ
διάρκεια τῆς ἀπελπισίας
ἐνῶ τὸ ρέμα κίτρινο κατεβάζει ἀργὰ βοῦρλα ξεριζωμένα
μὲς στὸ βοῦρκο
εἰκόνα μορφῆς ποὺ μαρμάρωσε μὲ τὴν ἀπόφαση μιᾶς
πίκρας παντοτινῆς.
Ὁ ποιητὴς ἕνα κενό.

Ἀσπιδοφόρος ὁ ἥλιος ἀνέβαινε πολεμώντας
κι' ἀπὸ τὸ βάθος τῆς σπηλιᾶς μιὰ νυχτερίδα τρομαγμένη
χτύπησε πάνω στὸ φῶς σὰν τὴ σαΐτα πάνω στὸ σκουτάρι:
«Ἀσίνην τε Ἀσίνην τε...». Νά 'ταν αὐτὴ ὁ βασιλιὰς τῆς
Ἀσίνης

does there really exist
among these ruined lines, edges, points, hollows, and curves
does there really exist
here where one meets the path of rain, wind, and ruin
does there exist the movement of the face, shape of the
    tenderness
of those who've shrunk so strangely in our lives,
those who remained the shadow of waves and thoughts with
    the sea's boundlessness
or perhaps no, nothing is left but the weight
the nostalgia for the weight of a living existence
there where we now remain unsubstantial, bending
like the branches of a terrible willow-tree heaped in
    permanent despair
while the yellow current slowly carries down rushes up-
    rooted in the mud
image of a form that the sentence to everlasting bitterness
    has turned to marble:
the poet a void.

Shieldbearer, the sun climbed warring,
and from the depths of the cave a startled bat
hit the light as an arrow hits a shield:
"'Ασίνην τε . . . 'Ασίνην τε . . ." Could that be the king
    of Asine

πού τὸν γυρεύουμε τόσο προσεχτικὰ σὲ τούτη τὴν ἀκρόπολη
γγίζοντας κάποτε μὲ τὰ δάχτυλά μας τὴν ἀφή του πάνω στὶς πέτρες.

'Ασίνη, καλοκαίρι '38 - 'Αθήνα, Γεν. '40

we've been searching for so carefully on this acropolis
sometimes touching with our fingers his touch upon
the stones.

Asine, summer '38–Athens, Jan. '40

ΗΜΕΡΟΛΟΓΙΟ ΚΑΤΑΣΤΡΩΜΑΤΟΣ, Β΄

Στὴ Μαρὼ

Κάποτε συλλογίζομαι πὼς τοῦτα ἐδῶ ποὺ γράφω δὲν εἶναι ἄλλο παρὰ εἰκόνες ποὺ κεντοῦν στὸ δέρμα τους φυλακισμένοι ἢ πελαγίσιοι.

Γ. Σ.

LOGBOOK II

To Maró

Sometimes it crosses my mind that the things I write here are nothing other than images that prisoners or sailors tattoo on their skin.

G. S.

ΜΕΡΕΣ ΤΟΥ ΙΟΥΝΙΟΥ '41

Βγῆκε τὸ νέο φεγγάρι στὴν 'Αλεξάνδρεια
κρατώντας τὸ παλιὸ στὴν ἀγκαλιά του
κι' ἐμεῖς πηγαίνοντας κατὰ τὴν Πόρτα τοῦ Ἥλιου
μὲς στὸ σκοτάδι τῆς καρδιᾶς — τρεῖς φίλοι.

Ποιὸς θέλει τώρα νὰ λουστεῖ στὰ νερὰ τοῦ Πρωτέα;
Τὴ μεταμόρφωση τὴ γυρέψαμε στὰ νιάτα μας
μὲ πόθους ποὺ ἔπαιζαν σὰν τὰ μεγάλα ψάρια
σὲ πέλαγα ποὺ φύραναν ξαφνικά·
πιστεύαμε στὴν παντοδυναμία τοῦ κορμιοῦ.
Καὶ τώρα βγῆκε τὸ νέο φεγγάρι ἀγκαλιασμένο
μὲ τὸ παλιό· μὲ τ' ὄμορφο νησὶ ματώνοντας
λαβωμένο· τὸ ἤρεμο νησί, τὸ δυνατὸ νησί, τὸ ἀθῶο.
Καὶ τὰ κορμιὰ σὰν τσακισμένα κλαδιὰ
καὶ σὰν ξεριζωμένες ρίζες.

Ἡ δίψα μας
ἔνιππος φύλακας μαρμαρωμένος
στὴ σκοτεινὴ Πόρτα τοῦ Ἥλιου
δὲν ξέρει νὰ ζητήσει τίποτε: φυλάγεται
ξενιτεμένη ἐδῶ τριγύρω
κοντὰ στὸν τάφο τοῦ Μεγάλου 'Αλεξάντρου.

Κρήτη - 'Αλεξάνδρεια - Νότιος 'Αφρική, Μάης - Σεπτέμ. '41

DAYS OF JUNE '41

The new moon came out over Alexandria
with the old moon in her arms
while we were walking towards the Gate of the Sun*
in the heart's darkness—three friends.

Who wants to bathe in the waters of Proteus now?
We looked for metamorphosis in our youth
with desires that played like big fish
in seas suddenly shrinking;
we believed in the body's omnipotence.
And now the new moon has come out embracing
the old; and the beautiful island bleeding,
wounded; the calm island—the strong, the innocent island.
And the bodies like broken branches,
like roots uprooted.

Our thirst
a guard on horseback turned to marble
at the dark Gate of the Sun—
he doesn't know how to ask for anything: he stands guard
exiled somewhere around here
near the tomb of Alexander the Great.

Crete, Alexandria, South Africa, May–Sept. '41

ΥΣΤΕΡΟΓΡΑΦΟ

'Αλλὰ ἔχουν μάτια κάτασπρα χωρὶς ματόκλαδα
καὶ τὰ χέρια τους εἶναι λιγνὰ σὰν τὰ καλάμια.

Κύριε, ὄχι μ' αὐτούς. Γνώρισα
τὴ φωνὴ τῶν παιδιῶν τὴν αὐγὴ
πάνω σὲ πράσινες πλαγιὲς ροβολώντας
χαρούμενα σὰν μέλισσες καὶ σὰν
τὶς πεταλοῦδες, μὲ τόσα χρώματα.
Κύριε, ὄχι μ' αὐτούς, ἡ φωνή τους
δὲ βγαίνει κὰν ἀπὸ τὸ στόμα τους.
Στέκεται ἐκεῖ κολλημένη σὲ κίτρινα δόντια.

Δική σου ἡ θάλασσα κι' ὁ ἀγέρας
μ' ἕνα ἄστρο κρεμασμένο στὸ στερέωμα,
Κύριε, δὲν ξέρουνε πὼς εἴμαστε
ὅ,τι μποροῦμε νά εἴμαστε
γιατρεύοντας τὶς πληγές μας μὲ τὰ βότανα
ποὺ βρίσκουμε πάνω σὲ πράσινες πλαγιές,
ὄχι ἄλλες, τοῦτες τὶς πλαγιὲς κοντά μας·
πὼς ἀνασαίνουμε ὅπως μποροῦμε ν' ἀνασάνουμε
μὲ μιὰ μικρούλα δέηση κάθε πρωὶ
ποὺ βρίσκει τ' ἀκρογιάλι ταξιδεύοντας
στὰ χάσματα τῆς μνήμης—
Κύριε, ὄχι μ' αὐτούς. Ἂς γίνει ἀλλιῶς τὸ θέλημά σου.

11 Σεπτέμβρη '41

POSTSCRIPT

But their eyes are all white, without lashes
and their arms are thin as reeds.

Lord, not with these people. I've known
the voices of children at dawn
rushing down green slopes
happy as bees, happy as butterflies
with so many colors.
Lord, not with these people, their voices
don't even leave their mouths—
they stay glued to their yellow teeth.

Yours is the sea and the wind
with a star hung in the firmament.
Lord, they don't know that we are
what we are able to be
healing our wounds with herbs
found on the green slopes,
these slopes nearby, not any others;
that we breathe as we are able to breathe
with a little prayer each dawn
that reaches the shore by crossing
the chasms of memory—
Lord, not with these people. Let your will be done in some
    other way.

11 September '41

Η ΜΟΡΦΗ ΤΗΣ ΜΟΙΡΑΣ

Ἱστορισμένα παραμύθια στὴν καρδιά μας
Σὰν ἀσημένια σκούνα μπρὸς στὸ τέμπλο
Μιᾶς ἄδειας ἐκκλησιᾶς, Ἰούλιο στὸ νησί.

Γ. Σ.

Ἡ μορφὴ τῆς μοίρας πάνω ἀπ' τὴ γέννηση ἑνὸς παιδιοῦ,
γύροι τῶν ἄστρων κι' ὁ ἄνεμος μιὰ σκοτεινὴ βραδιὰ τοῦ Φλεβάρη,
γερόντισσες μὲ γιατροσόφια ἀνεβαίνοντας τὶς σκάλες ποὺ τρίζουν
καὶ τὰ ξερὰ κλωνάρια τῆς κληματαριᾶς ὁλόγυμνα στὴν αὐλή.

Ἡ μορφὴ πάνω ἀπ' τὴν κούνια ἑνὸς παιδιοῦ μιᾶς μοίρας μαυρομαντηλούσας
χαμόγελο ἀνεξήγητο καὶ βλέφαρα χαμηλωμένα καὶ στῆθος ἄσπρο σὰν τὸ γάλα
κι' ἡ πόρτα ποὺ ἄνοιξε κι' ὁ καραβοκύρης θαλασσοδαρμένος
πετώντας σὲ μιὰ μαύρη κασέλα τὸ βρεμένο σκουφί του.

Αὐτὰ τὰ πρόσωπα κι' αὐτὰ τὰ περιστατικὰ σ' ἀκολουθοῦσαν
καθὼς ξετύλιγες τὸ νῆμα στὴν ἀκρογιαλιὰ γιὰ τὰ δίχτυα
κι' ὅταν ἀκόμη ἀρμενίζοντας δευτερόπριμα κοίταζες τὸ λάκκο τῶν κυμάτων·

THE SHAPE OF FATE

Once-told fables in our heart
Like a silver schooner offered to the icons
Of an empty church, July on the island.

G. S.

The shape of fate over a child's birth,
circling of the stars and the wind on a dark night in
February,
old women with healing skills climbing the creaking stairs
and the dry branches of the vine naked in the courtyard.

Over a child's crib the shape of fate black-kerchiefed
smile inexplicable and eyelids lowered and breast white
as milk
and the door opening and the skipper, sea-whipped,
throwing his wet cap onto a black chest.

These faces and these circumstances pursued you
while you unwound the yarn for your nets on the beach
and again while you watched the hollow of waves as you
sailed on a broad reach;

σ' ὅλες τὶς θάλασσες, σ' ὅλους τοὺς κόρφους
εἴταν μαζί σου, κι' εἴταν ἡ δύσκολη ζωὴ κι' εἴταν ἡ χαρά.

Τώρα δὲν ξέρω νὰ διαβάσω παρακάτω,
γιατὶ σὲ δέσαν μὲ τὶς ἁλυσίδες, γιατὶ σὲ τρύπησαν μὲ τὴ
λόγχη,
γιατὶ σὲ χώρισαν μιὰ νύχτα μέσα στὸ δάσος ἀπὸ τὴ γυναίκα
ποὺ κοίταζε στυλώνοντας τὰ μάτια καὶ δὲν ἤξερε καθόλου
νὰ μιλήσει,
γιατὶ σοῦ στέρησαν τὸ φῶς τὸ πέλαγο τὸ ψωμί.

Πῶς πέσαμε, σύντροφε, μέσα στὸ λαγούμι τοῦ φόβου;
Δὲν εἴταν τῆς δικῆς σου μοίρας, μήτε τῆς δικῆς μου τὰ
γραμμένα,
ποτές μας δὲν πουλήσαμε μήτε ἀγοράσαμε τέτια πρα-
μάτεια·
ποιὸς εἶναι ἐκεῖνος ποὺ προστάζει καὶ σκοτώνει πίσω
ἀπὸ μᾶς;
Ἄφησε μὴ ρωτᾶς· τρία κόκκινα ἄλογα στ' ἁλώνι
γυρίζουν πάνω σ' ἀνθρώπινα κόκκαλα κι' ἔχουν τὰ μάτια
δεμένα,
ἄφησε μὴ ρωτᾶς, περίμενε· τὸ αἷμα, τὸ αἷμα
ἕνα πρωὶ θὰ σηκωθεῖ σὰν τὸν Ἅη Γιώργη τὸν καβαλάρη
γιὰ νὰ καρφώσει μὲ τὸ κοντάρι πάνω στὸ χῶμα τὸ δρά-
κοντα.

1η Ὀχτώβρη '41

on all seas, in every gulf
they were with you, and they were the hardship of life, they
were the joy.

Now I don't know how to read on:
why they bound you in chains, why they pierced you with
the spear,
why one night in the forest they parted you from the woman
who watched with startled eyes and couldn't speak at all,
why they deprived you of light, the open sea, bread.

How did we happen to fall, my friend, into the pit of fear?
It wasn't your fate, nor was it decreed for me,
we never sold or bought this kind of merchandise;
who is he who commands and murders behind our backs?
Don't ask; three red horses on the threshing floor
circle on human bones, their eyes blindfolded;
don't ask, just wait: the blood, the blood
will rise some morning like Saint George the rider
to nail the dragon to earth with his lance.

1 October '41

KERK STR. OOST, PRETORIA, TRANSVAAL

Οἱ τζακαράντες παίζοντας καστανιέτες καὶ χορεύοντας
ρίχναν γύρω στὰ πόδια τους ἕνα μενεξεδένιο χιόνι.
Ἀδιάφορα ὅλα τ' ἄλλα, κι' αὐτὸ
τὸ Βένουσμπεργκ τῆς γραφειοκρατίας μὲ τοὺς διπλοὺς
του πύργους καὶ τὰ διπλά του ἐπίχρυσα ρολόγια
ναρκωμένο βαθιὰ σὰν ἱπποπόταμος μὲς στὸ γαλάζιο.
Καὶ τρέχαν τ' αὐτοκίνητα δείχνοντας
γυαλιστερὲς πλάτες ὅπως τὰ δελφίνια.
Στὸ τέλος τοῦ δρόμου μᾶς περίμενε
δρασκελώντας ἀργόσχολα μὲς στὸ κλουβί του
ὁ ἀσημένιος φασιανὸς τῆς Κίνας
ὁ Εὐπλόκαμος Νυχθήμερος, ὅπως τὸν λένε.

Καὶ νὰ σκεφτεῖς πὼς ξεκινήσαμε ἀποχαιρετώντας
μὲ τὴν καρδιὰ γεμάτη σκάγια
τὸν Ὀνοκρόταλο τὸν Πελεκάνο — αὐτὸν
ποὺ εἶχε ἕνα ὕφος τσαλαπατημένου πρωθυπουργοῦ
στὸ ζωολογικὸ κῆπο τοῦ Καΐρου.

Ὀχτώβρης '41

KERK STR. OOST, PRETORIA, TRANSVAAL

Jacarandas playing castanets and dancing
threw around their feet a violet snow.
The rest's uninteresting, and that
Venusburg of bureaucracy with its twin
towers and its twin gilt clocks
profoundly torpid like a hippopotamus in blue sky.
And cars raced by showing
backs glistening like dolphins.
At the end of the street waiting for us—
strutting idly about its cage—
was the silver pheasant of China,
the Euplocamos Nychtemerus, as they call it.

And to think we set out, the heart full of shot,
saying goodbye
to Onokrotalus the Pelican—he
with the look of a trampled prime minister
in the zoological garden of Cairo.

October '41

Ο ΣΤΡΑΤΗΣ ΘΑΛΑΣΣΙΝΟΣ ΑΝΑΜΕΣΑ ΣΤΟΥΣ ΑΓΑΠΑΝΘΟΥΣ

Δὲν ἔχει ἀσφοδίλια, μενεξέδες, μήτε ὑάκινθους·
πῶς νὰ μιλήσεις μὲ τοὺς πεθαμένους.
Οἱ πεθαμένοι ξέρουν μονάχα τὴ γλώσσα τῶν λουλουδιῶν·
γι' αὐτὸ σωπαίνουν
ταξιδεύουν καὶ σωπαίνουν, ὑπομένουν καὶ σωπαίνουν
παρὰ δῆμον ὀνείρων, παρὰ δῆμον ὀνείρων.

Ἂν ἀρχίσω νὰ τραγουδῶ θὰ φωνάξω
κι' ἂ φωνάξω—
Οἱ ἀγάπανθοι προστάζουν σιωπὴ
σηκώνοντας ἕνα χεράκι μαβιοῦ μωροῦ τῆς Ἀραβίας
ἢ ἀκόμη τὰ πατήματα μιᾶς χήνας στὸν ἀέρα.

Εἶναι βαρὺ καὶ δύσκολο, δὲ μοῦ φτάνουν οἱ ζωντανοί·
πρῶτα γιατὶ δὲ μιλοῦν, κι' ὕστερα
γιατὶ πρέπει νὰ ρωτήσω τοὺς νεκροὺς
γιὰ νὰ μπορέσω νὰ προχωρήσω παρακάτω.
Ἀλλιῶς δὲ γίνεται, μόλις μὲ πάρει ὁ ὕπνος
οἱ σύντροφοι κόβουνε τοὺς ἀσημένιους σπάγκους
καὶ τὸ φλασκὶ τῶν ἀνέμων ἀδειάζει.
Τὸ γεμίζω κι' ἀδειάζει, τὸ γεμίζω κι' ἀδειάζει·
ξυπνῶ
σὰν τὸ χρυσόψαρο κολυμπώντας
μέσα στὰ χάσματα τῆς ἀστραπῆς,

STRATIS THALASSINOS AMONG THE AGAPANTHI*

There are no asphodels, violets, or hyacinths;
how then can you talk with the dead?
The dead know the language of flowers only;
so they keep silent
they travel and keep silent, endure and keep silent,
beyond the community of dreams, beyond the community
of dreams.*

If I start to sing I'll call out
and if I call out—
the agapanthi order silence
raising the tiny hand of a blue Arabian child
or even the footfalls of a goose in the air.

It's painful and difficult, the living are not enough for me
first because they do not speak, and then
because I have to ask the dead
in order to go on farther.
There's no other way: the moment I fall asleep
the companions cut the silver strings
and the flask of the winds empties.*
I fill it and it empties, I fill it and it empties;
I wake
like a goldfish swimming
in the lightning's crevices

κι᾿ ὁ ἀγέρας κι᾿ ὁ κατακλυσμὸς καὶ τ᾿ ἀνθρώπινα σώματα,
κι᾿ οἱ ἀγάπανθοι καρφωμένοι σὰν τὶς σαΐτες τῆς μοίρας
στὴν ἀξεδίψαστη γῆς
συγκλονισμένοι ἀπὸ σπασμωδικὰ νοήματα,
θά ᾿λεγες εἶναι φορτωμένοι σ᾿ ἕνα παμπάλαιο κάρο
κατρακυλώντας σὲ χαλασμένους δρόμους, σὲ παλιὰ καλντε-
ρίμια,
οἱ ἀγάπανθοι τ᾿ ἀσφοδίλια τῶν νέγρων :
Πῶς νὰ τὴ μάθω ἐτούτη τὴ θρησκεία ;

Τὸ πρῶτο πράγμα ποὺ ἔκανε ὁ θεὸς εἶναι ἡ ἀγάπη
ἔπειτα ἔρχεται τὸ αἷμα
κι᾿ ἡ δίψα γιὰ τὸ αἷμα
ποὺ τὴν κεντρίζει
τὸ σπέρμα τοῦ κορμιοῦ καθὼς τ᾿ ἁλάτι.
Τὸ πρῶτο πράγμα ποὺ ἔκανε ὁ θεὸς εἶναι τὸ μακρινὸ τα-
ξίδι·
ἐκεῖνο τὸ σπίτι περιμένει
μ᾿ ἕνα γαλάζιο καπνὸ
μ᾿ ἕνα σκυλὶ γερασμένο
περιμένοντας γιὰ νὰ ξεψυχήσει τὸ γυρισμό.
Μὰ πρέπει νὰ μ᾿ ἁρμηνέψουν οἱ πεθαμένοι·
εἶναι οἱ ἀγάπανθοι ποὺ τοὺς κρατοῦν ἀμίλητους,
ὅπως τὰ βάθη τῆς θάλασσας ἢ τὸ νερὸ μὲς στὸ ποτήρι.
Κι᾿ οἱ σύντροφοι μένουν στὰ παλάτια τῆς Κίρκης·
ἀκριβέ μου ᾿Ελπήνωρ ! ᾿Ηλίθιε, φτωχέ μου ᾿Ελπήνωρ !
Ἤ, δὲν τοὺς βλέπεις ;
— «Βοηθῆστε μας !» —
Στῶν Ψαρῶν τὴν ὁλόμαυρη ράχη.

Τράνσβααλ, 14 Γενάρη '42

and the wind and the flood and the human bodies
and the agapanthi nailed like the arrows of fate
to the unquenchable earth
shaken by convulsive nodding,
as if loaded on an ancient cart
jolting down gutted roads, over old cobblestones,
the agapanthi, asphodels of the negroes:
How can I grasp this religion?

The first thing God made is love
then comes blood
and the thirst for blood
roused by
the body's sperm as by salt.
The first thing God made is the long journey;
that house there is waiting
with its blue smoke
with its aged dog
waiting for the homecoming so that it can die.
But the dead must guide me;
it is the agapanthi that keep them from speaking,
like the depths of the sea or the water in a glass.
And the companions stay on in the palaces of Circe:
my dear Elpenor! My poor, foolish Elpenor!*
Or don't you see them
—"Oh help us!"—
on the blackened ridge of Psara?*

Transvaal, 14 January '42

ΕΝΑΣ ΓΕΡΟΝΤΑΣ ΣΤΗΝ ΑΚΡΟΠΟΤΑΜΙΑ

Στὸ Νάνη Παναγιωτόπουλο

Κι' ὅμως πρέπει νὰ λογαριάσουμε πῶς προχωροῦμε.
Νὰ αἰσθάνεσαι δὲ φτάνει μήτε νὰ σκέπτεσαι μήτε νὰ κινεῖσαι
μήτε νὰ κινδυνεύει τὸ σῶμα σου στὴν παλιὰ πολεμίστρα,
ὅταν τὸ λάδι ζεματιστὸ καὶ τὸ λειωμένο μολύβι αὐλακώνουνε τὰ τειχιά.

Κι' ὅμως πρέπει νὰ λογαριάσουμε κατὰ ποῦ προχωροῦμε,
ὄχι καθὼς ὁ πόνος μας τὸ θέλει καὶ τὰ πεινασμένα παιδιά μας
καὶ τὸ χάσμα τῆς πρόσκλησης τῶν συντρόφων ἀπὸ τὸν ἀντίπερα γιαλό·
μήτε καθὼς τὸ ψιθυρίζει τὸ μελανιασμένο φῶς στὸ πρόχειρο νοσοκομεῖο,
τὸ φαρμακευτικὸ λαμπύρισμα στὸ προσκέφαλο τοῦ παλικαριοῦ ποὺ χειρουργήθηκε τὸ μεσημέρι·
ἀλλὰ μὲ κάποιον ἄλλο τρόπο, μπορεῖ νὰ θέλω νὰ πῶ καθὼς
τὸ μακρὺ ποτάμι ποὺ βγαίνει ἀπὸ τὶς μεγάλες λίμνες τὶς κλειστὲς βαθιὰ στὴν 'Αφρικὴ
καὶ εἴτανε κάποτε θεὸς κι' ἔπειτα γένηκε δρόμος καὶ δωρητὴς καὶ δικαστὴς καὶ δέλτα·
ποὺ δὲν εἶναι ποτές του τὸ ἴδιο, κατὰ ποὺ δίδασκαν οἱ παλαιοὶ γραμματισμένοι,

AN OLD MAN ON THE RIVER BANK

To Nani Panayiotopoulo

And yet we should consider how we go forward.
To feel is not enough, nor to think, nor to move
nor to put your body in danger in front of an old loophole
when scalding oil and molten lead furrow the walls.

And yet we should consider towards what we go forward,
not as our pain would have it, and our hungry children
and the chasm between us and the companions calling from
the opposite shore;
nor the whispering of the bluish light in an improvised
hospital,
the pharmaceutic glimmer on the pillow of the youth
operated upon at noon;
but it should be in some other way, I would say like
the long river that emerges from the great lakes enclosed
deep in Africa,
that was once a god and then became a road and a bene-
factor, a judge and a delta;
that is never the same, as the ancient wise men taught,

κι᾿ ὡστόσο μένει πάντα τὸ ἴδιο σῶμα, τὸ ἴδιο στρῶμα, καὶ
τὸ ἴδιο Σημεῖο,
ὁ ἴδιος προσανατολισμός.

Δὲ θέλω τίποτε ἄλλο παρὰ νὰ μιλήσω ἁπλά, νὰ μοῦ δοθεῖ
ἐτούτη ἡ χάρη.
Γιατὶ καὶ τὸ τραγούδι τὸ φορτώσαμε μὲ τόσες μουσικὲς
ποὺ σιγὰ σιγὰ βουλιάζει
καὶ τὴν τέχνη μας τὴ στολίσαμε τόσο πολὺ ποὺ φαγώθηκε
ἀπὸ τὰ μαλάματα τὸ πρόσωπό της
κι᾿ εἶναι καιρὸς νὰ ποῦμε τὰ λιγοστά μας λόγια γιατὶ ἡ
ψυχή μας αὔριο κάνει πανιά.

Ἂν εἶναι ἀνθρώπινος ὁ πόνος δὲν εἴμαστε ἄνθρωποι μόνο
γιὰ νὰ πονοῦμε
γι᾿ αὐτὸ συλλογίζομαι τόσο πολύ, τοῦτες τὶς μέρες, τὸ μεγάλο ποτάμι
αὐτὸ τὸ νόημα ποὺ προχωρεῖ ἀνάμεσα σὲ βότανα καὶ σὲ
χόρτα
καὶ ζωντανὰ ποὺ βόσκουν καὶ ξεδιψοῦν κι᾿ ἀνθρώπους ποὺ
σπέρνουν καὶ ποὺ θερίζουν
καὶ σὲ μεγάλους τάφους ἀκόμη καὶ μικρὲς κατοικίες
τῶν νεκρῶν.
Αὐτὸ τὸ ρέμα ποὺ τραβάει τὸ δρόμο του καὶ ποὺ δὲν εἶναι
τόσο διαφορετικὸ ἀπὸ τὸ αἷμα τῶν ἀνθρώπων
κι᾿ ἀπὸ τὰ μάτια τῶν ἀνθρώπων ὅταν κοιτάζουν ἴσια πέρα
χωρὶς τὸ φόβο μὲς στὴν καρδιά τους,
χωρὶς τὴν καθημερινὴ τρεμούλα γιὰ τὰ μικροπράματα ἢ
ἔστω καὶ γιὰ τὰ μεγάλα·

and yet always remains the same body, the same bed, and the same Sign,
the same orientation.

I want no more than to speak simply, to be granted that grace.
Because we've loaded even our songs with so much music that they're slowly sinking
and we've decorated our art so much that its features have been eaten away by gold
and it's time to say our few words because tomorrow the soul sets sail.

If pain is human we are not human beings merely to suffer pain;
that's why I think so much these days about the great river,
that symbol which moves forward among herbs and greenery
and beasts that graze and drink, men who sow and harvest,
great tombs even and small habitations of the dead.
That current which goes its way and which is not so different from the blood of men,
from the eyes of men when they look straight ahead without fear in their hearts,
without the daily tremor for trivialities or even for important things;

ὅταν κοιτάζουν ἴσια πέρα καθὼς ὁ στρατοκόπος ποὺ συνήθισε ν' ἀναμετρᾶ τὸ δρόμο του μὲ τ' ἄστρα,
ὄχι ὅπως ἐμεῖς, τὴν ἄλλη μέρα, κοιτάζοντας τὸ κλειστὸ περιβόλι στὸ κοιμισμένο ἀράπικο σπίτι,
πίσω ἀπὸ τὰ καφασωτά, τὸ δροσερὸ περιβολάκι ν' ἀλλάζει σχῆμα, νὰ μεγαλώνει καὶ νὰ μικραίνει·
ἀλλάζοντας καθὼς κοιτάζαμε, κι' ἐμεῖς, τὸ σχῆμα τοῦ πόθου μας καὶ τῆς καρδιᾶς μας,
στὴ στάλα τοῦ μεσημεριοῦ, ἐμεῖς τὸ ὑπομονετικὸ ζυμάρι ἑνὸς κόσμου ποὺ μᾶς διώχνει καὶ ποὺ μᾶς πλάθει,
πιασμένοι στὰ πλουμισμένα δίχτυα μιᾶς ζωῆς ποὺ εἴτανε σωστὴ κι' ἔγινε σκόνη καὶ βούλιαξε μέσα στὴν ἄμμο
ἀφήνοντας πίσω της μονάχα ἐκεῖνο τὸ ἀπροσδιόριστο λίκνισμα ποὺ μᾶς ζάλισε μιᾶς ἀψηλῆς φοινικιᾶς.

Κάιρο, 20 Ἰουνίου '42

when they look straight ahead like the traveler who is used
to gauging his way by the stars,
not like us, the other day, gazing at the enclosed garden of
a sleepy Arab house,
behind the lattices the cool garden changing shape, growing
larger and smaller,
we too changing, as we gazed, the shape of our desire and
our hearts,
at the tip of midday, we the patient dough of a world that
throws us out and kneads us,
caught in the embroidered nets of a life that was whole
and then became dust and sank into the sands
leaving behind it only that vague dizzying sway of a tall
palm-tree.

Cairo, 20 June '42

Ο ΣΤΡΑΤΗΣ ΘΑΛΑΣΣΙΝΟΣ ΣΤΗ ΝΕΚΡΗ ΘΑΛΑΣΣΑ

Κάποτε βλέπεις σὲ παρεκκλήσια, χτισμένα πάνω στὶς θρυλικὲς τοποθεσίες, τὴ σχετικὴ περιγραφὴ τοῦ Εὐαγγελίου γραμμένη ἀγγλικὰ καὶ ἀπὸ κάτω: «THIS IS THE PLACE GENTLEMEN!»

ΓΡΑΜΜΑ ΤΟΥ Σ. Θ. ΑΠΟ ΤΗΝ ΙΕΡΟΥΣΑΛΗΜ

Ἱερουσαλήμ, ἀκυβέρνητη πολιτεία,
Ἱερουσαλήμ, πολιτεία τῆς προσφυγιᾶς.

Κάποτε βλέπεις τὸ μεσημέρι
στὴν ἄσφαλτο τοῦ δρόμου νὰ γλιστρᾶ
ἕνα κοπάδι μαῦρα φύλλα σκορπισμένα —
Περνοῦνε διαβατάρικα πουλιὰ κάτω ἀπ' τὸν ἥλιο
μὰ δὲ σηκώνεις τὸ κεφάλι.

Ἱερουσαλήμ, ἀκυβέρνητη πολιτεία!

Ἄγνωστες γλῶσσες τῆς Βαβέλ,
χωρὶς συγγένεια μὲ τὴ γραμματικὴ
τὸ συναξάρι μήτε τὸ ψαλτήρι
ποὺ σ' ἔμαθαν νὰ συλλαβίζεις τὸ φθινόπωρο
σὰν ἔδεναν τὶς ψαροποῦλες στὰ μουράγια·
ἄγνωστες γλῶσσες κολλημένες
σὰν ἀποτσίγαρα σβηστὰ σὲ χαλασμένα χείλια.

STRATIS THALASSINOS ON THE DEAD SEA*

Sometimes one sees in chapels built on legendary sites
the relevant Biblical description quoted in English
and beneath it: "THIS IS THE PLACE GENTLEMEN!"

LETTER OF S. T. FROM JERUSALEM

Jerusalem, ungoverned city,
Jerusalem, city of refugees.

Sometimes you see at noon
a flock of scattered black leaves
sliding across the asphalt road—
Migratory birds are passing under the sun
but you don't raise your head.

Jerusalem, ungoverned city!

Unknown tongues of Babel
without relation to the grammar,
to the Lives of the Saints or the Book of Psalms,
that they taught you to spell out in autumn
when they tied the fishing boats to the quays;
unknown tongues glued
like burned-out cigarette butts to decayed lips.

Ἱερουσαλήμ, πολιτεία τῆς προσφυγιᾶς!

Ἀλλὰ τὰ μάτια τους μιλοῦν ὅλα τὸν ἴδιο λόγο,
ὄχι τὸ λόγο ποὺ ἔγινε ἄνθρωπος, θεέ μου συμπάθα μας,
ὄχι ταξίδια γιὰ νὰ ἰδεῖς καινούργιους τόπους, ἀλλὰ
τὸ σκοτεινὸ τρένο τῆς φυγῆς ὅπου τὰ βρέφη
τρέφουνται μὲ τὴ βρώμα καὶ τὶς ἁμαρτίες τῶν γονιῶν
καὶ νιώθουν οἱ μεσόκοποι τὸ χάσμα
νὰ μεγαλώνει ἀνάμεσα στὸ σῶμα
ποὺ μένει πίσω σὰ γκαμήλα λαβωμένη
καὶ τὴν ψυχὴ μὲ τὸ ἀνεξάντλητο κουράγιο, καθὼς λένε.
Εἶναι καὶ τὰ καράβια ποὺ τοὺς ταξιδεύουν
ὀλόρθους σὰ μπαλσαμωμένους δεσποτάδες
μέσα στ' ἀμπάρια, γιὰ ν' ἀράξουν ἕνα βράδι
στὰ φύκια τοῦ βυθοῦ ἁπαλά.

Ἱερουσαλήμ, ἀκυβέρνητη πολιτεία!

Στὸν ποταμὸ Γιορδάνη
τρεῖς καλογέροι φέραν
καὶ δέσανε στὴν ὄχτη
κόκκινο τρεχαντήρι.
Τρεῖς ἀπ' τ' Ἁγιονόρος
ἁρμένισαν τρεῖς μῆνες
καὶ δέσαν σ' ἕνα κλῶνο
στὴν ὄχτη τοῦ Γιορδάνη
τοῦ πρόσφυγα τὸ τάμα.
Πεινάσανε τρεῖς μῆνες
διψάσανε τρεῖς μῆνες,

Jerusalem, city of refugees!

But their eyes all speak the same word,
not the word that became man, God forgive us,
not journeys to see new places, but
the dark train of flight where infants
are fed on the dirt and the sins of their parents
and the middle-aged feel the chasm
broaden between the body—
lagging behind like a wounded camel—
and the soul with its inexhaustible courage, as they say.
It is also the ships that carry them,
standing upright like embalmed bishops
in the holds, to moor one evening
in the seaweed of the deep, softly.

Jerusalem, ungoverned city!

To the River Jordan
three monks brought
a small red caique
and moored it to the banks.
Three from Mount Athos
sailed for three months
and moored to a branch,
on the Jordan banks,
a refugee's offering.
They hungered three months
they thirsted three months

ξαγρύπνησαν τρεῖς μῆνες
κι᾿ ἤρθαν ἀπ᾿ τ᾿ Ἁγιονόρος
ἀπ᾿ τὴ Θεσσαλονίκη
οἱ σκλάβοι καλογέροι.

Εἴμαστε ὅλοι καθὼς ἡ Νεκρὴ θάλασσα
πολλὲς ὀργιὲς κάτω ἀπ᾿ τὴν ἐπιφάνεια τοῦ Αἰγαίου.
Ἔλα μαζί μου νὰ σοῦ δείξω τὸ τοπίο:

Στὴ Νεκρὴ θάλασσα
δὲν εἶναι ψάρια
δὲν εἶναι φύκια
μήτε ἀχινοὶ
δὲν ἔχει ζωή.
Δὲν εἶναι ζωντανὰ
ποὺ ἔχουν στομάχι
γιὰ νὰ πεινοῦν
ποὺ θρέφουν νεῦρα
γιὰ νὰ πονοῦν,
THIS IS THE PLACE, GENTLEMEN!

Στὴ Νεκρὴ θάλασσα
ἡ καταφρόνια
εἶναι ἡ πραμάτεια
τοῦ κανενοῦ,
ὄξω ἀπ᾿ τὸ νοῦ.
Καρδιὰ καὶ στόχαση
πήζουν στ᾿ ἁλάτι
ποὺ εἶναι πικρὸ

stayed sleepless three months
and they came from Mount Athos
came from Salonika
the three enslaved monks.

Like the Dead Sea, we are all
many fathoms below the level of the Aegean.
Come with me and I will show you the setting:

In the Dead Sea
there are no fish
there is no seaweed
nor any sea-urchins
there is no life.
There are no creatures
that have a belly
to suffer hunger
that nourish nerves
to suffer pain,

THIS IS THE PLACE, GENTLEMEN!

In the Dead Sea
scornfulness
is no onc's tradc
no one's worry.
Heart and thought
congeal in salt
that's full of bitterness

σμίγουν τὸν κόσμο
τὸν ὀρυχτό,
THIS IS THE PLACE, GENTLEMEN!

Στὴ Νεκρὴ θάλασσα
ὀχτροὺς καὶ φίλους
παιδιά, γυναίκα
καὶ συγγενεῖς,
ἄει νὰ τοὺς βρεῖς.
Εἶναι στὰ Γόμορρα
κάτω στὸν πάτο
πολὺ εὐτυχεῖς
ποὺ δὲν προσμένουν
καμμιὰ γραφή.
GENTLEMEN,

συνεχίζουμε τὴν περιοδεία μας
πολλὲς ὀργιὲς κάτω ἀπ' τὴν ἐπιφάνεια τοῦ Αἰγαίου.

Ἰούλιος '42

and finally join
the mineral world,
THIS IS THE PLACE, GENTLEMEN!

In the Dead Sea
enemies and friends
wife and children
other relations
go and find them.
They're in Gomorrah
down on the bottom
very happy
they don't expect
any message.
GENTLEMEN,

we continue our tour
many fathoms below the level of the Aegean.

July '42

ΚΑΛΛΙΓΡΑΦΗΜΑ

Νεῖλος, «Τὰ περιστέρια»

Πανιὰ στὸ Νεῖλο,
πουλιὰ χωρὶς κελάιδισμα μὲ μιὰ φτερούγα
γυρεύοντας σιωπηλὰ τὴν ἄλλη·
ψηλαφώντας στὴν ἀπουσία τ' οὐρανοῦ
τὸ σῶμα ἑνὸς μαρμαρωμένου ἐφήβου·
γράφοντας μὲ συμπαθητικὸ μελάνι στὸ γαλάζιο
μιὰν ἀπελπιστικὴ κραυγή.

CALLIGRAPHY

Nile, "Casino des Pigeons"

Sails on the Nile,
songless birds with one wing
searching silently for the other;
groping in the sky's absence
for the body of a marble youth;
inscribing on the blue with invisible ink
a desperate cry.

ΜΕΡΕΣ Τ' ΑΠΡΙΛΗ '43

Τρουμπέτες, τράμ, βορβορυγμοί, τρίξιμο φρένων
χλωροφορμίζουν τὸ μυαλό του ὅπως μετρᾶς
ὅσο βαστᾶς κι' ἔπειτα χάνεσαι
στὴ νάρκη καὶ στὸ ἔλεος τοῦ χειρούργου.

Στοὺς δρόμους περπατᾶ μὲ προσοχή, νὰ μὴ γλιστρήσει
στὶς πεπονόφλουδες ποὺ ρίχνουν ἀδιαφόρετοι ἀραπάδες
ἢ πρόσφυγες πολιτικάντηδες καὶ τὸ σινάφι,
παραμονεύοντας: θὰ τήνε πατήσει; — δὲ θὰ τὴν πατήσει;
Ὅπως μαδᾶς μιὰ μαργαρίτα·

προχωρεῖ
κουνώντας μιὰν ὑπέρογκη ἁρμαθιὰ ἀνωφέλευτων κλειδιῶν·
τὸ στεγνὸ γαλάζιο μνημονεύει
ρεκλάμες ξεβαμμένες τῆς Ἑλληνικῆς Ἀκτοπλοΐας,
παράθυρα μανταλωμένα πάνω σὲ πρόσωπα ἀκριβά,
ἢ λίγο καθαρὸ νερὸ στὴ ρίζα ἑνὸς πλατάνου.

Προχωρεῖ πηγαίνοντας στὴ δουλειά του καθὼς
χίλια λιμάρικα σκυλιὰ τοῦ κουρελιάζουν τὰ μπατζάκια
καὶ τὸν γυμνώνουν.
Προχωρεῖ, παραπατώντας, δαχτυλοδειχτούμενος,
κι' ἕνας πηχτὸς ἀγέρας φέρνει γύρα
σκουπίδια, καβαλίνα, μπόχα καὶ καταλαλιά.

Κάιρο - Σάρια Ἐμὰντ ἐλ Ντίν, 24 Ἰουνίου '43

DAYS OF APRIL '43

Trumpets, trams, swearing, the screeching of brakes
chloroform his mind in the same way as one counts
so long as one holds out before being lost
in numbness, at the surgeon's mercy.

In the streets he walks carefully, not to slip
on melon-rinds thrown by indifferent Arabs
or refugee politicians and the clique,
they watch him: will he step on it?—Will he not?
As one plucks a daisy;

he walks on

swinging an enormous bunch of useless keys;
the dry sky recalls
faded advertisements of the Greek Coastal Steamship
Company,
windows locked on faces one loves
or a little clear water at the root of a plane-tree.

He walks on, going to his work, while
a thousand starving dogs tear his pants to shreds
and strip him naked.
He walks on, staggering, pointed at,
and a dense wind whirls around him
rubbish, dung, stench, and slander.

Cairo–Saria Emad-el-Din, 24 June '43

ΑΝΑΜΕΣΑ ΣΤΑ ΚΟΚΚΑΛΑ ΕΔΩ

Ἀνάμεσα στὰ κόκκαλα
μιὰ μουσική :
περνάει τὴν ἄμμο,
περνάει τὴ θάλασσα.
Ἀνάμεσα στὰ κόκκαλα
ἦχος φλογέρας
ἦχος τυμπάνου ἀπόμακρος
κι' ἕνα ψιλὸ κουδούνισμα,
περνάει τοὺς κάμπους τοὺς στεγνοὺς
περνάει τὴ θάλασσα μὲ τὰ δελφίνια.
Ψηλὰ βουνά, δὲ μᾶς ἀκοῦτε !
Βοήθεια ! Βοήθεια !
Ψηλὰ βουνὰ θὰ λειώσουμε, νεκροὶ μὲ τοὺς νεκρούς !

Κάιρο, Αὔγουστος '43

HERE AMONG THE BONES

Among thc bones
music:
it crosses the sand,
crosses the sea.
Among the bones
a flute's sound
the distant sound of a drum
and the faint ringing of bells
crosses the dry fields
crosses the dolphined sea.
High mountains, can't you hear us?
Help! Help!
High mountains, we will dissolve, dead among the dead!

Cairo, August '43

ΤΕΛΕΥΤΑΙΟΣ ΣΤΑΘΜΟΣ

Λίγες οἱ νύχτες μὲ φεγγάρι ποὺ μ' ἀρέσαν.
Τ' ἀλφαβητάρι τῶν ἄστρων ποὺ συλλαβίζεις
ὅπως τὸ φέρει ὁ κόπος τῆς τελειωμένης μέρας
καὶ βγάζεις ἄλλα νοήματα κι' ἄλλες ἐλπίδες,
πιὸ καθαρὰ μπορεῖς νὰ τὸ διαβάσεις.
Τώρα ποὺ κάθομαι ἄνεργος καὶ λογαριάζω
λίγα φεγγάρια ἀπόμειναν στὴ μνήμη·
νησιά, χρῶμα θλιμμένης Παναγίας, ἀργὰ στὴ χάση
ἢ φεγγαρόφωτα σὲ πολιτεῖες τοῦ βοριᾶ ρίχνοντας κάποτε
σὲ ταραγμένους δρόμους ποταμοὺς καὶ μέλη ἀνθρώπων
βαρειὰ μιὰ νάρκη.
Κι' ὅμως χτὲς βράδι ἐδῶ, σὲ τούτη τὴ στερνή μας σκάλα
ὅπου προσμένουμε τὴν ὥρα τῆς ἐπιστροφῆς μας νὰ χαράξει
σὰν ἕνα χρέος παλιό, μονέδα ποὺ ἔμεινε γιὰ χρόνια
στὴν κάσα ἑνὸς φιλάργυρου, καὶ τέλος
ἦρθε ἡ στιγμὴ τῆς πλερωμῆς κι' ἀκούγονται
νομίσματα νὰ πέφτουν πάνω στὸ τραπέζι·
σὲ τοῦτο τὸ τυρρηνικὸ χωριό, πίσω ἀπὸ τὴ θάλασσα τοῦ Σαλέρνο
πίσω ἀπὸ τὰ λιμάνια τοῦ γυρισμοῦ, στὴν ἄκρη
μιᾶς φθινοπωρινῆς μπόρας τὸ φεγγάρι
ξεπέρασε τὰ σύννεφα, καὶ γίναν
τὰ σπίτια στὴν ἀντίπερα πλαγιὰ ἀπὸ σμάλτο.

LAST STOP

Few arc the moonlit nights that I've cared for:
the alphabet of the stars—which you spell out
as much as your fatigue at the day's end allows
and from which you gather other meanings and other
    hopes—
you can then read more clearly.
Now that I sit here, idle, and think about it,*
few are the moons that remain in my memory:
islands, color of grieving Madonna, late in the waning
or moonlight in northern cities sometimes casting
over turbulent streets, rivers, and limbs of men
a heavy torpor.
Yet here last evening, in this our final port
where we wait for the hour of our return home to dawn
like an old debt: money that lay for years
in a miser's safe, and at last
the time for payment comes
and you hear the coins falling onto the table;
in this Etruscan village, behind the sea of Salerno
behind the harbors of our return, on the edge
of an autumn squall, the moon
outstripped the clouds, and houses
on the slope opposite became enamel:

Σιωπὲς ἀγαπημένες τῆς σελήνης.

Εἶναι κι' αὐτὸς ἕνας εἱρμὸς τῆς σκέψης ἕνας τρόπος
ν' ἀρχίσεις νὰ μιλᾶς γιὰ πράγματα ποὺ ὁμολογεῖς
δύσκολα, σὲ ὧρες ὅπου δὲ βαστᾶς σὲ φίλο
ποὺ ξέφυγε κρυφὰ καὶ φέρνει
μαντάτα ἀπὸ τὸ σπίτι κι' ἀπὸ τοὺς συντρόφους,
καὶ βιάζεσαι ν' ἀνοίξεις τὴν καρδιά σου
μὴ σὲ προλάβει ἡ ξενιτειὰ καὶ τὸν ἀλλάξει.
'Ερχόμαστε ἀπ' τὴν 'Αραπιά, τὴν Αἴγυπτο τὴν Παλαιστίνη
τὴ Συρία·
τὸ κρατίδιο
τῆς Κομμαγηνῆς πού 'σβησε σὰν τὸ μικρὸ λυχνάρι
πολλὲς φορὲς γυρίζει στὸ μυαλό μας,
καὶ πολιτεῖες μεγάλες ποὺ ἔζησαν χιλιάδες χρόνια
κι' ἔπειτα ἀπόμειναν τόπος βοσκῆς γιὰ τὶς γκαμοῦζες
χωράφια γιὰ ζαχαροκάλαμα καὶ καλαμπόκια.
'Ερχόμαστε ἀπ' τὴν ἄμμο τῆς ἔρημος ἀπ' τὶς θάλασσες τοῦ
Πρωτέα,
ψυχὲς μαραγκιασμένες ἀπὸ δημόσιες ἁμαρτίες,
καθένας κι' ἕνα ἀξίωμα σὰν τὸ πουλὶ μὲς στὸ κλουβί του.
Τὸ βροχερὸ φθινόπωρο σ' αὐτὴ τὴ γούβα
κακοφορμίζει τὴν πληγὴ τοῦ καθενός μας
ἢ αὐτὸ ποὺ θά 'λεγες ἀλλιῶς, νέμεση μοίρα
ἢ μοναχὰ κακὲς συνήθειες, δόλο καὶ ἀπάτη,
ἢ ἀκόμη ἰδιοτέλεια νὰ καρπωθεῖς τὸ αἷμα τῶν ἄλλων.
Εὔκολα τρίβεται ὁ ἄνθρωπος μὲς στοὺς πολέμους·
ὁ ἄνθρωπος εἶναι μαλακός, ἕνα δεμάτι χόρτο·
χείλια καὶ δάχτυλα ποὺ λαχταροῦν ἕνα ἄσπρο στῆθος

Amica silentia lunae.*

This is a train of thought, a way
to begin to speak of things you confess
uneasily, at times when you can't hold back, to a friend
who escaped secretly and who brings
word from home and from the companions,
and you hurry to open your heart
before this exile forestalls you and alters him.
We come from Arabia, Egypt, Palestine, Syria;
the little state
of Kommagene, which flickered out like a small lamp,
often comes to mind,
and great cities that lived for thousands of years
and then became pasture land for cattle,
fields for sugar-cane and corn.
We come from the sand of the desert, from the seas of
    Proteus,
souls shriveled by public sins,
each holding office like a bird in its cage.
The rainy autumn in this gorge
infects the wound of each of us
or what you might term differently: nemesis, fate,
or simply bad habits, fraud and deceit,*
or even the selfish urge to reap reward from the blood of
    others.
Man frays easily in wars;
man is soft, a sheaf of grass,
lips and fingers that hunger for a white breast

μάτια πού μισοκλείνουν στὸ λαμπύρισμα τῆς μέρας
καὶ πόδια πού θὰ τρέχανε, κι' ἂς εἶναι τόσο κουρασμένα
στὸ παραμικρὸ σφύριγμα τοῦ κέρδους.
Ὁ ἄνθρωπος εἶναι μαλακὸς καὶ διψασμένος σὰν τὸ χόρτο,
ἄπληστος σὰν τὸ χόρτο, ρίζες τὰ νεῦρα του κι' ἁπλώνουν
σὰν ἔρθει ὁ θέρος
προτιμᾶ νὰ σφυρίξουν τὰ δρεπάνια στ' ἄλλο χωράφι·
σὰν ἔρθει ὁ θέρος
ἄλλοι φωνάζουνε γιὰ νὰ ξορκίσουν τὸ δαιμονικὸ
ἄλλοι μπερδεύουνται μὲς στ' ἀγαθά τους, ἄλλοι ρητο-
    ρεύουν.
Ἀλλὰ τὰ ξόρκια τ' ἀγαθὰ τὶς ρητορεῖες,
σὰν εἶναι οἱ ζωντανοὶ μακριά, τί θὰ τὰ κάνεις;
Μήπως ὁ ἄνθρωπος εἶναι ἄλλο πράγμα;
Μὴν εἶναι αὐτὸ πού μεταδίνει τὴ ζωή;
Καιρὸς τοῦ σπείρειν, καιρὸς τοῦ θερίζειν.

Πάλι τὰ ἴδια καὶ τὰ ἴδια, θὰ μοῦ πεῖς, φίλε.
Ὅμως τὴ σκέψη τοῦ πρόσφυγα τὴ σκέψη τοῦ αἰχμάλωτου
    τὴ σκέψη
τοῦ ἀνθρώπου σὰν κατάντησε κι' αὐτὸς πραμάτεια
δοκίμασε νὰ τὴν ἀλλάξεις, δὲν μπορεῖς.
Ἴσως καὶ νά 'θελε νὰ μείνει βασιλιὰς ἀνθρωποφάγων
ξοδεύοντας δυνάμεις πού κανεὶς δὲν ἀγοράζει
νὰ σεργιανᾶ μέσα σὲ κάμπους ἀγαπάνθων
ν' ἀκούει τὰ τουμπελέκια κάτω ἀπ' τὸ δέντρο τοῦ μπαμποῦ,
καθὼς χορεύουν οἱ αὐλικοὶ μὲ τερατώδεις προσωπίδες.
Ὅμως ὁ τόπος πού τὸν πελεκοῦν καὶ πού τὸν καῖνε σὰν
    τὸ πεῦκο, καὶ τὸν βλέπεις

eyes that half-close in the radiance of day
and feet that would run, no matter how tired,
at the slightest call of profit.
Man is soft and thirsty like grass,
insatiable like grass, his nerves roots that spread;
when the harvest comes
he would rather have the scythes whistle in some other field;
when the harvest comes
some call out to exorcise the demon
some become entangled in their riches, others deliver
speeches.
But what good are exorcisms, riches, speeches
when the living are far away?
Is man ever anything else?
Isn't it this that confers life?
A time for planting, a time for harvesting.

"The same thing over and over again," you'll tell me,
friend.
But the thinking of a refugee, the thinking of a prisoner,
the thinking
of a person when he too has become a commodity—
try to change it; you can't.
Maybe he would have liked to stay king of the cannibals
wasting strength that nobody buys,
to promenade in fields of agapanthi*
to hear the drums with bamboo overhead,
as courtiers dance with prodigious masks.
But the country they're chopping up and burning like a
pine-tree—you see it

εἴτε στὸ σκοτεινὸ βαγόνι, χωρὶς νερό, σπασμένα τζάμια,
νύχτες καὶ νύχτες
εἴτε στὸ πυρωμένο πλοῖο ποὺ θὰ βουλιάξει καθὼς τὸ δείχνουν οἱ στατιστικές,
ἐτοῦτα ρίζωσαν μὲς στὸ μυαλὸ καὶ δὲν ἀλλάζουν
ἐτοῦτα φύτεψαν εἰκόνες ἴδιες μὲ τὰ δέντρα ἐκεῖνα
ποὺ ρίχνουν τὰ κλωνάρια τους μὲς στὰ παρθένα δάση
κι' αὐτὰ καρφώνουνται στὸ χῶμα καὶ ξαναφυτρώνουν·
ρίχνουν κλωνάρια καὶ ξαναφυτρώνουν δρασκελώντας
λεῦγες καὶ λεῦγες·
ἕνα παρθένο δάσος σκοτωμένων φίλων τὸ μυαλό μας.
Κι' ἂ σοῦ μιλῶ μὲ παραμύθια καὶ παραβολὲς
εἶναι γιατὶ τ' ἀκοῦς γλυκότερα, κι' ἡ φρίκη
δὲν κουβεντιάζεται γιατὶ εἶναι ζωντανὴ
γιατὶ εἶναι ἀμίλητη καὶ προχωράει·
Στάζει τὴ μέρα στάζει στὸν ὕπνο
μνησιπήμων πόνος.

Νὰ μιλήσω γιὰ ἥρωες νὰ μιλήσω γιὰ ἥρωες: ὁ Μιχάλης
ποὺ ἔφυγε μ' ἀνοιχτὲς πληγὲς ἀπ' τὸ νοσοκομεῖο
ἴσως μιλοῦσε γιὰ ἥρωες ὅταν, τὴ νύχτα ἐκείνη
ποὺ ἔσερνε τὸ ποδάρι του μὲς στὴ συσκοτισμένη πολιτεία,
οὔρλιαζε ψηλαφώντας τὸν πόνο μας· «Στὰ σκοτεινὰ
πηγαίνουμε στὰ σκοτεινὰ προχωροῦμε...»
Οἱ ἥρωες προχωροῦν στὰ σκοτεινά.

Λίγες οἱ νύχτες μὲ φεγγάρι ποὺ μ' ἀρέσουν.

Cava dei Tirreni, 5 'Οκτωβρίου '44

either in the dark train, without water, the windows broken,
night after night
or in the burning ship that according to the statistics is
bound to sink—
this has taken root in the mind and doesn't change
this has planted images like those trees
that cast their branches in virgin forests
so that they take root in the earth and sprout again;
they cast their branches that sprout again, striding mile
after mile;
our mind's a virgin forest of murdered friends.
And if I talk to you in fables and parables
it's because it's more gentle for you that way; and horror
really can't be talked about because it's alive,
because it's mute and goes on growing:
memory-wounding pain
drips by day drips in sleep.*

To speak of heroes to speak of heroes: Michael
who left the hospital with his wounds still open,
maybe he was speaking of heroes—the night
he dragged his foot through the darkened city—
when he howled, groping over our pain: "We advance in
the dark,
we move forward in the dark . . ."
The heroes move forward in the dark.

Few are the moonlit nights that I've cared for.

Cava dei Tirreni, 5 October '44

«ΚΙΧΛΗ»

Δαίμονος ἐπιπόνου καὶ τύχης χαλεπῆς ἐφήμερον σπέρμα, τί με βιάζεσθε λέγειν, ἃ ὑμῖν ἄρειον μὴ γνῶναι.

Ο ΣΕΙΛΗΝΟΣ ΣΤΟΝ ΜΙΔΑ

"THRUSH"*

Ephemeral issue of a vicious daemon and a harsh fate, why do you force me to speak of things that it would be better for you not to know.

*SILENUS TO MIDAS**

Α΄

Τὸ σπίτι κοντὰ στὴ θάλασσα

Τὰ σπίτια ποὺ εἶχα μοῦ τὰ πῆραν. Ἔτυχε
νά ᾽ναι τὰ χρόνια δίσεχτα· πολέμοι χαλασμοὶ ξενιτεμοί·
κάποτε ὁ κυνηγὸς βρίσκει τὰ διαβατάρικα πουλιὰ
κάποτε δὲν τὰ βρίσκει· τὸ κυνήγι
εἶταν καλὸ στὰ χρόνια μου, πῆραν πολλοὺς τὰ σκάγια·
οἱ ἄλλοι γυρίζουν ἢ τρελαίνουνται στὰ καταφύγια.

Μὴ μοῦ μιλᾶς γιὰ τ᾽ ἀηδόνι μήτε γιὰ τὸν κορυδαλὸ
μήτε γιὰ τὴ μικρούλα σουσουράδα
ποὺ γράφει νούμερα στὸ φῶς μὲ τὴν οὐρά της·
δὲν ξέρω πολλὰ πράγματα ἀπὸ σπίτια
ξέρω πὼς ἔχουν τὴ φυλή τους, τίποτε ἄλλο.
Καινούργια στὴν ἀρχή, σὰν τὰ μωρὰ
ποὺ παίζουν στὰ περβόλια μὲ τὰ κρόσια τοῦ ἥλιου,
κεντοῦν παραθυρόφυλλα χρωματιστὰ καὶ πόρτες
γυαλιστερὲς πάνω στὴ μέρα·
ὅταν τελειώσει ὁ ἀρχιτέκτονας ἀλλάζουν,
ζαρώνουν ἢ χαμογελοῦν ἢ ἀκόμη πεισματώνουν
μ᾽ ἐκείνους ποὺ ἔμειναν μ᾽ ἐκείνους ποὺ ἔφυγαν
μ᾽ ἄλλους ποὺ θὰ γυρίζανε ἂν μποροῦσαν
ἢ ποὺ χαθῆκαν, τώρα ποὺ ἔγινε
ὁ κόσμος ἕνα ἀπέραντο ξενοδοχεῖο.

Δὲν ξέρω πολλὰ πράγματα ἀπὸ σπίτια,
θυμᾶμαι τὴ χαρά τους καὶ τὴ λύπη τους

I

*The house near the sea**

The houses I had they took away from me. The times
happened to be unpropitious: war, destruction, exile;
sometimes the hunter hits the migratory birds,
sometimes he doesn't hit them. Hunting
was good in my time, many felt the pellet;
the rest circle aimlessly or go mad in the shelters.

Don't talk to me about the nightingale nor the lark
nor the little wagtail
inscribing figures with his tail in the light;
I don't know much about houses
I know they have their own nature, nothing else.
New at first, like babies
who play in gardens with the tassels of the sun,
they embroider colored shutters and shining doors
over the day.
When the architect's finished, they change,
they frown or smile or even grow stubborn
with those who stayed behind, with those who went away
with others who'd come back if they could
or others who disappeared, now that the world's become
a limitless hotel.

I don't know much about houses,
I remember their joy and their sorrow

καμιὰ φορά, σὰ σταματήσω·

ἀκόμη

καμιὰ φορά, κοντὰ στὴ θάλασσα, σὲ κάμαρες γυμνὲς
μ' ἕνα κρεββάτι σιδερένιο χωρὶς τίποτε δικό μου
κοιτάζοντας τὴ βραδινὴν ἀράχνη συλλογιέμαι
πὼς κάποιος ἑτοιμάζεται νὰ 'ρθεῖ, πὼς τὸν στολίζουν
μ' ἄσπρα καὶ μαῦρα ροῦχα μὲ πολύχρωμα κοσμήματα
καὶ γύρω του μιλοῦν σιγὰ σεβάσμιες δέσποινες
γκρίζα μαλλιὰ καὶ σκοτεινὲς δαντέλες,
πὼς ἑτοιμάζεται νὰ 'ρθεῖ νὰ μ' ἀποχαιρετήσει·
ἤ, μιὰ γυναίκα ἑλικοβλέφαρη βαθύζωνη
γυρίζοντας ἀπὸ λιμάνια μεσημβρινά,
Σμύρνη Ρόδο Συρακοῦσες 'Αλεξάντρεια,
ἀπὸ κλειστὲς πολιτεῖες σὰν τὰ ζεστὰ παραθυρόφυλλα,
μὲ ἀρώματα χρυσῶν καρπῶν καὶ βότανα,
πὼς ἀνεβαίνει τὰ σκαλιὰ χωρὶς νὰ βλέπει
ἐκείνους ποὺ κοιμήθηκαν κάτω ἀπ' τὴ σκάλα.

Ξέρεις τὰ σπίτια πεισματώνουν εὔκολα, σὰν τὰ γυμνώσεις.

sometimes, when I stop to think;

again

sometimes, near the sea, in naked rooms
with a single iron bed and nothing of my own
watching the evening spider, I imagine
that someone is getting ready to come, that they dress
him up*
in white and black robes, with many-colored jewels,
and around him venerable ladies,
gray hair and dark lace shawls, talk softly,
that he is getting ready to come and say goodbye to me;
or that a woman—eyelashes curled, high-girdled,
returning from southern ports,
Smyrna Rhodes Syracuse Alexandria,
from cities closed like hot shutters,
with perfume of golden fruit and herbs—
climbs the stairs without seeing
those who've fallen asleep under the stairs.

Houses, you know, grow stubborn easily when you strip
them bare.

Β΄

Ὁ ἡδονικὸς Ἐλπήνωρ

Τὸν εἶδα χτὲς νὰ σταματᾶ στὴν πόρτα
κάτω ἀπὸ τὸ παράθυρό μου· θά 'ταν
ἐφτὰ περίπου· μιὰ γυναίκα εἶταν μαζί του.
Εἶχε τὸ φέρσιμο τοῦ Ἐλπήνορα, λίγο πρὶν πέσει
νὰ τσακιστεῖ, κι' ὅμως δὲν εἶταν μεθυσμένος.
Μιλοῦσε πολὺ γρήγορα, κι' ἐκείνη
κοίταζε ἀφηρημένη πρὸς τοὺς φωνογράφους·
τὸν ἔκοβε καμιὰ φορὰ νὰ πεῖ μιὰ φράση
κι' ἔπειτα κοίταζε μ' ἀνυπομονησία
ἐκεῖ ποὺ τηγανίζουν ψάρια· σὰν τὴ γάτα.
Αὐτὸς ψιθύριζε μ' ἕνα ἀποτσίγαρο σβηστὸ στὰ χείλια:

—«Ἄκουσε ἀκόμη τοῦτο. Στὸ φεγγάρι
τ' ἀγάλματα λυγίζουν κάποτε σὰν τὸ καλάμι
ἀνάμεσα σὲ ζωντανοὺς καρποὺς—τ' ἀγάλματα·
κι' ἡ φλόγα γίνεται δροσερὴ πικροδάφνη,
ἡ φλόγα ποὺ καίει τὸν ἄνθρωπο, θέλω νὰ πῶ».

—«Εἶναι τὸ φῶς... ἴσκιοι τῆς νύχτας...».

—«Ἴσως ἡ νύχτα ποὺ ἄνοιξε, γαλάζιο ρόδι,
σκοτεινὸς κόρφος, καὶ σὲ γέμισε ἄστρα
κόβοντας τὸν καιρό.
Κι' ὅμως τ' ἀγάλματα

II

Sensual Elpenor

I saw him yesterday standing by the door
below my window; it was about
seven o'clock; there was a woman with him.
He had the look of Elpenor just before he fell
and smashed himself, yet he wasn't drunk.
He was speaking fast, and she
was gazing absently towards the gramophones;
now and then she cut him short to say a word
and then would glance impatiently
towards where they were frying fish: like a cat.
He whispered with a cigarette butt between his lips:

— "Listen to this also. In the moonlight
the statues sometimes bend like reeds
in the midst of ripe fruit—the statues;
and the flame becomes a cool oleander,
the flame that burns man, I mean."

— "It's just the light . . . shadows of the night."

— "Maybe the night that opened up, a blue pomegranate,
a dark breast, and filled you with stars,
cleaving time.

And yet the statues

λυγίζουν κάποτε, μοιράζοντας τὸν πόθο
στὰ δυό, σὰν τὸ ροδάκινο· κι᾿ ἡ φλόγα
γίνεται φίλημα στὰ μέλη κι᾿ ἀναφυλλητὸ
κι᾿ ἔπειτα φύλλο δροσερὸ ποὺ παίρνει ὁ ἄνεμος·
λυγίζουν· γίνουνται ἀλαφριὰ μ᾿ ἕνα ἀνθρώπινο βάρος.
Δὲν τὸ ξεχνᾶς».

—«Τ᾿ ἀγάλματά εἶναι στὸ μουσεῖο».

—«Ὄχι, σὲ κυνηγοῦν, πῶς δὲν τὸ βλέπεις;
θέλω νὰ πῶ μὲ τὰ σπασμένα μέλη τους,
μὲ τὴν ἀλλοτινὴ μορφή τους ποὺ δὲ γνώρισες
κι᾿ ὅμως τὴν ξέρεις.
Ὅπως ὅταν
στὰ τελευταῖα τῆς νιότης σου ἀγαπήσεις
γυναίκα ποὺ ἔμεινε ὄμορφη, κι᾿ ὅλο φοβᾶσαι,
καθὼς τὴν κράτησες γυμνὴ τὸ μεσημέρι,
τὴ μνήμη ποὺ ξυπνᾶ στὴν ἀγκαλιά σου·
φοβᾶσαι τὸ φιλὶ μὴ σὲ προδώσει
σ᾿ ἄλλα κρεββάτια περασμένα τώρα
ποὺ ὡστόσο θὰ μπορούσαν νὰ στοιχειώσουν
τόσο εὔκολα τόσο εὔκολα καὶ ν᾿ ἀναστήσουν
εἴδωλα στὸν καθρέφτη, σώματα ποὺ εἴταν μιὰ φορά·
τὴν ἡδονή τους.
Ὅπως ὅταν
γυρίζεις ἀπ᾿ τὰ ξένα καὶ τύχει ν᾿ ἀνοίξεις
παλιὰ κασέλα κλειδωμένη ἀπὸ καιρὸ
καὶ βρεῖς κουρέλια ἀπὸ τὰ ροῦχα ποὺ φοροῦσες
σὲ ὄμορφες ὧρες, σὲ γιορτὲς μὲ φῶτα

bend sometimes, dividing desire in two,
like a peach; and the flame
becomes a kiss on the limbs, a sobbing,
and then a cool leaf carried off by the wind;
they bend; they become light with a human weight.
You don't forget it."

—"The statues are in the museum."

— "No, they pursue you, why can't you see it?
I mean with their broken limbs,
with their shape from another time, a shape you don't
recognize
yet know.

It's as though
at the end of your youth you love
a woman who stayed beautiful, and you're constantly afraid,
while you hold her naked at noon,
of the memory that wakens in your embrace;
you're afraid the kiss might betray you
to other beds now of the past
which nevertheless could haunt you
so easily, so easily, and bring to life
images in the mirror, bodies once alive:
their sensuality.

It's as though
returning home from some foreign country you happen
to open
an old trunk that's been locked up a long time
and find the tatters of clothes you used to wear
on happy occasions, at festivals with many-colored lights,

πολύχρωμα, καθρεφτισμένα, πού ὅλο χαμηλώνουν
καὶ μένει μόνο τὸ ἄρωμα τῆς ἀπουσίας
μιᾶς νέας μορφῆς.
'Αλήθεια, τὰ συντρίμμια
δὲν εἶναι ἐκεῖνα· ἐσύ 'σαι τὸ ρημάδι·
σὲ κυνηγοῦν μὲ μιὰ παράξενη παρθενιὰ
στὸ σπίτι στὸ γραφεῖο στὶς δεξιώσεις
τῶν μεγιστάνων, στὸν ἀνομολόγητο φόβο τοῦ ὕπνου·
μιλοῦν γιὰ περιστατικὰ πού θά ἤθελες νὰ μὴν ὑπάρχουν
ἢ νὰ γινόντουσαν χρόνια μετὰ τὸ θάνατό σου,
κι' αὐτὸ εἶναι δύσκολο γιατὶ...»

—«Τ' ἀγάλματά εἰναι στὸ μουσεῖο.
Καληνύχτα».

—«...γιατὶ τ' ἀγάλματα δὲν εἶναι πιὰ συντρίμμια,
εἴμαστε ἐμεῖς. Τ' ἀγάλματα λυγίζουν ἀλαφριά... καληνύχτα».

'Εδῶ χωρίστηκαν. Αὐτὸς ἐπῆρε
τὴν ἀνηφόρα πού τραβάει κατὰ τὴν Ἄρκτο
κι' αὐτὴ προχώρεσε πρὸς τὸ πολύφωτο ἀκρογιάλι
ὅπου τὸ κῦμα πνίγεται στὴ βοὴ τοῦ ραδιοφώνου:

Τὸ ραδιόφωνο

—«Πανιὰ στὸ φύσημα τοῦ ἀγέρα
ὁ νοῦς δὲν κράτησε ἄλλο ἀπὸ τὴ μέρα.
Ἄρωμα πεύκου καὶ σιγὴ

mirrored, now becoming dim,
and all that remains is the perfume of the absence
of a young form.

Really, those statues are not
the fragments. You yourself are the relic;
they haunt you with a strange virginity
at home, at the office, at receptions for the celebrated,
in the unconfessed terror of sleep;
they speak of things you wish didn't exist
or would exist years after your death,
and that's difficult because . . ."

— "The statues are in the museum.
Good night."

— ". . . because the statues are no longer
fragments. We are. The statues bend lightly . . . Good
night."

At this point they separated. He took
the road leading uphill towards the North
and she moved on towards the light-flooded beach
where the waves are drowned in the noise from the radio:

The radio

—"Sails puffed out by the wind
are all that stay in the mind.
Perfume of silence and pine

εὔκολα θ' ἁπαλύνουν τὴν πληγὴ
πού ἔκαμαν φεύγοντας ὁ ναύτης
ἡ σουσουράδα ὁ κοκοβιὸς κι' ὁ μυγοχάφτης.
Γυναίκα πού ἔμεινες χωρὶς ἁφή,
ἄκουσε τῶν ἀνέμων τὴν ταφή.

Ἄδειασε τὸ χρυσὸ βαρέλι
ὁ γήλιος ἔγινε κουρέλι
σὲ μιᾶς μεσόκοπης λαιμὸ
πού βήχει καὶ δὲν ἔχει τελειωμό·
τὸ καλοκαίρι πού ταξίδεψε τὴ θλίβει
μὲ τὰ μαλάματα στοὺς ὤμους καὶ στὴν ἥβη.
Γυναίκα πού ἔχασες τὸ φῶς,
ἄκουσε, τραγουδᾶ ὁ τυφλός.

Σκοτείνιασε· κλεῖσε τὰ τζάμια·
κάνε σουραύλια μὲ τὰ χτεσινὰ καλάμια,
καὶ μὴν ἀνοίγεις ὅσο κι' ἂ χτυποῦν·
φωνάζουν μὰ δὲν ἔχουν τί νὰ ποῦν.
Πάρε κυκλάμινα, πευκοβελόνες,
κρίνα ἀπ' τὴν ἄμμο, κι' ἀπ' τὴ θάλασσα ἀνεμῶνες·
γυναίκα πού ἔχασες τὸ νοῦ,
ἄκου, περνᾶ τὸ ξόδι τοῦ νεροῦ...

—Ἀθῆναι. Ἀνελίσσονται ραγδαίως
τὰ γεγονότα πού ἤκουσε μὲ δέος
ἡ κοινὴ γνώμη. Ὁ κύριος ὑπουργὸς
ἐδήλωσεν, Δὲν μένει πλέον καιρός...
—...πάρε κυκλάμινα... πευκοβελόνες...

will soon be an anodyne
now that the sailor's set sail,
flycatcher, catfish, and wagtail.
O woman whose touch is dumb,
hear the wind's requiem.

"Drained is the golden keg
the sun's become a rag
round a middle-aged woman's neck—
who coughs and coughs without break;
for the summer that's gone she sighs,
for the gold on her shoulders, her thighs.
O woman, O sightless thing,
hear the blindman sing.

"Close the shutters: the day recedes;
make flutes from yesteryear's reeds
and don't open, knock how they may:
they shout but have nothing to say.
Take cyclamen, pine-needles, the lily,
anemones out of the sea;
O woman whose wits are lost,
listen, the water's ghost . . .

—"Athens. The public has heard
the news with alarm; it is feared
a crisis is near. The prime
minister declared: 'There is no more time . . .'
Take cyclamen . . . needles of pine . . .

κρίνα ἀπ' τὴν ἄμμο... πευκοβελόνες...
γυναίκα...
—... ὑπερτερεῖ συντριπτικῶς.
Ὁ πόλεμος...»

ΨΥΧΑΜΟΙΒΟΣ.

the lily . . . needles of pine . . .
O woman . . .
— . . . is overwhelmingly stronger
The war . . ."

SOULMONGER*

Γ'

Τὸ ναυάγιο τῆς «Κίχλης»

«Τὸ ξύλο αὐτὸ ποὺ δρόσιζε τὸ μέτωπό μου
τὶς ὧρες ποὺ τὸ μεσημέρι πύρωνε τὶς φλέβες
σὲ ξένα χέρια θέλει ἀνθίσει, Πάρ' το, σοῦ τὸ χαρίζω·
δές, εἶναι ξύλο λεμονιᾶς...»
                                        Ἄκουσα τὴ φωνὴ
καθὼς ἐκοίταζα στὴ θάλασσα νὰ ξεχωρίσω
ἕνα καράβι ποὺ τὸ βούλιαξαν ἐδῶ καὶ χρόνια·
τό 'λεγαν «Κίχλη»· ἕνα μικρὸ ναυάγιο· τὰ κατάρτια,
σπασμένα, κυματίζανε λοξὰ στὸ βάθος, σὰν πλοκάμια
ἢ μνήμη ὀνείρων, δείχνοντας τὸ σκαρί του
στόμα θαμπὸ κάποιου μεγάλου κήτους νεκροῦ
σβησμένο στὸ νερό. Μεγάλη ἁπλώνουνταν γαλήνη.

Κι' ἄλλες φωνὲς σιγὰ σιγὰ μὲ τὴ σειρά τους
ἀκολουθήσαν·. ψίθυροι φτενοὶ καὶ διψασμένοι
ποὺ βγαίναν ἀπὸ τοῦ ἥλιου τ' ἄλλο μέρος, τὸ σκοτεινό·
θά 'λεγες γύρευαν νὰ πιοῦν αἷμα μιὰ στάλα·
εἴτανε γνώριμες μὰ δὲν μπορούσα νὰ τὶς ξεχωρίσω.
Κι' ἦρθε ἡ φωνὴ τοῦ γέρου, αὐτὴ τὴν ἔνιωσα
πέφτοντας στὴν καρδιὰ τῆς μέρας
ἥσυχη, σὰν ἀκίνητη:
«Κι' ἂ μὲ δικάσετε νὰ πιῶ φαρμάκι, εὐχαριστῶ·
τὸ δίκιο σας θά 'ναι τὸ δίκιο μου· ποῦ νὰ πηγαίνω
γυρίζοντας σὲ ξένους τόπους, ἕνα στρογγυλὸ λιθάρι.

III

The wreck "Thrush"

"This wood that cooled my forehead
at times when the noon burned my veins
will flower in other hands. Take it, I'm giving it to you;
look, it's wood from a lemon-tree . . ."
I heard the voice
as I was gazing at the sea trying to make out
a ship they'd sunk there years ago;
it was called "Thrush," a small wreck; the masts,
broken, swayed at odd angles deep underwater, like
tentacles,
or the memory of dreams, marking the hull:
vague mouth of some huge dead sea-monster
extinguished in the water. Calm spread all around.

And in turn other voices*
slowly followed; whispers thin and thirsty
emerging from the other side of the sun, the dark side;
one would say they longed for a drop of blood to drink;*
familiar voices, but I couldn't distinguish one from the
other.
And then the voice of the old man reached me; I felt it
quietly falling into the heart of day,
as though motionless:
"And if you condemn me to drink poison, I thank you.
Your law will be my law; how can I go
wandering from one foreign country to another, a rolling
stone.

Τὸ θάνατο τὸν προτιμῶ·
ποιὸς πάει γιὰ τὸ καλύτερο ὁ θεὸς τὸ ξέρει».

Χῶρες τοῦ ἥλιου καὶ δὲν μπορεῖτε ν' ἀντικρίσετε τὸν ἥλιο.
Χῶρες τοῦ ἀνθρώπου καὶ δὲν μπορεῖτε ν' ἀντικρίσετε τὸν
ἄνθρωπο.

Τὸ φῶς

Καθὼς περνοῦν τὰ χρόνια
πληθαίνουν οἱ κριτὲς ποὺ σὲ καταδικάζουν·
καθὼς περνοῦν τὰ χρόνια καὶ κουβεντιάζεις μὲ λιγότερες
φωνές,
βλέπεις τὸν ἥλιο μ' ἄλλα μάτια·
ξέρεις πὼς ἐκεῖνοι ποὺ ἔμειναν, σὲ γελούσαν,
τὸ παραμίλημα τῆς σάρκας, ὁ ὅμορφος χορὸς
ποὺ τελειώνει στὴ γύμνια.
Ὅπως, τὴ νύχτα στρίβοντας στὴν ἔρμη δημοσιά,
ἄξαφνα βλέπεις νὰ γυαλίζουν τὰ μάτια ἑνὸς ζώου
ποὺ ἔφυγαν κιόλας, ἔτσι νιώθεις τὰ μάτια σου·
τὸν ἥλιο τὸν κοιτᾶς, ἔπειτα χάνεσαι μὲς στὸ σκοτάδι·
ὁ δωρικὸς χιτώνας
ποὺ ἀγγίξανε τὰ δάχτυλά σου καὶ λύγισε σὰν τὰ βουνά,
εἶναι ἕνα μάρμαρο στὸ φῶς, μὰ τὸ κεφάλι του εἶναι στὸ
σκοτάδι.
Κι' αὐτοὺς ποὺ ἀφήσαν τὴν παλαίστρα γιὰ νὰ πάρουν τὰ
δοξάρια
καὶ χτύπησαν τὸ θεληματικὸ μαραθωνοδρόμο
κι' ἐκεῖνος εἶδε τὴ σφενδόνη ν' ἀρμενίζει στὸ αἷμα
ν' ἀδειάζει ὁ κόσμος ὅπως τὸ φεγγάρι

I prefer death.
Who'll come out best only God knows."

Countries of the sun and yet you can't face the sun.
Countries of men and yet you can't face man.

The light

As the years go by
the judges who condemn you grow in number;
as the years go by and you converse with fewer voices,
you see the sun with different eyes:
you know that those who stayed behind were deceiving you
the delirium of flesh, the lovely dance
that ends in nakedness.
It's as though, turning at night into an empty highway,
you suddenly see the eyes of an animal shine,
eyes already gone; so you feel your own eyes:
you gaze at the sun, then you're lost in darkness.
The doric chiton
that swayed like the mountains when your fingers touched it
is a marble figure in the light, but its head is in darkness.
And those who abandoned the stadium to take up arms
struck the obstinate marathon runner
and he saw the track sail in blood,
the world empty like the moon,

καὶ νὰ μαραίνουνται νὰ νικηφόρα περιβόλια·
τοὺς βλέπεις μὲς στὸν ἥλιο, πίσω ἀπὸ τὸν ἥλιο.
Καὶ τὰ παιδιὰ ποὺ κάναν μακροβούτια ἀπ' τὰ μπαστούνια
πηγαίνουν σὰν ἀδράχτια γνέθοντας ἀκόμη,
σώματα γυμνὰ βουλιάζοντας μέσα στὸ μαῦρο φῶς
μ' ἕνα νόμισμα στὰ δόντια, κολυμπώντας ἀκόμη,
καθὼς ὁ γήλιος ράβει μὲ βελονιὲς μαλαματένιες
πανιὰ καὶ ξύλα ὑγρὰ καὶ χρώματα πελαγίσια·
ἀκόμη τώρα κατεβαίνουνε λοξὰ
πρὸς τὰ χαλίκια τοῦ βυθοῦ
οἱ ἄσπρες λήκυθοι.

Ἀγγελικὸ καὶ μαῦρο, φῶς,
γέλιο τῶν κυμάτων στὶς δημοσιὲς τοῦ πόντου,
δακρυσμένο γέλιο,
σὲ βλέπει ὁ γέροντας ἱκέτης
πηγαίνοντας νὰ δρασκελίσει τὶς ἀόρατες πλάκες
καθρεφτισμένο στὸ αἷμα του
ποὺ γέννησε τὸν Ἐτεοκλὴ καὶ τὸν Πολυνείκη.
Ἀγγελικὴ καὶ μαύρη, μέρα·
ἡ γλυφὴ γέψη τῆς γυναίκας ποὺ φαρμακώνει τὸ φυλακι-
σμένο
βγαίνει ἀπ' τὸ κῦμα δροσερὸ κλωνάρι στολισμένο στάλες.
Τραγούδησε μικρὴ Ἀντιγόνη, τραγούδησε, τραγούδησε...
δὲ σοῦ μιλῶ γιὰ περασμένα, μιλῶ γιὰ τὴν ἀγάπη·
στόλισε τὰ μαλλιά σου μὲ τ' ἀγκάθια τοῦ ἥλιου,
σκοτεινὴ κοπέλλα·
ἡ καρδιὰ τοῦ Σκορπιοῦ βασίλεψε,
ὁ τύραννος μέσα ἀπ' τὸν ἄνθρωπο ἔχει φύγει,

the gardens of victory wither:
you see them in the sun, behind the sun.
And the boys who dived from the bow-sprits
go like spindles twisting still,
naked bodies plunging into black light
with a coin between the teeth, swimming still,
while the sun with golden needles sews
sails and wet wood and colors of the sea;
still now they're going down obliquely,
the white lekythoi,
towards the pebbles on the sea floor.

Light, angelic and black,
laughter of waves on the sea's highways,
tear-stained laughter,
the old suppliant sees you
as he moves to cross the invisible fields—*
light mirrored in his blood,
the blood that gave birth to Eteocles and Polynices.
Day, angelic and black;
the brackish taste of woman that poisons the prisoner
emerges from the wave a cool branch adorned with drops.
Sing little Antigone, sing, O sing . . .
I'm not speaking to you about things past, I'm speaking
about love;
decorate your hair with the sun's thorns,
dark girl;
the heart of the Scorpion has set,*
the tyrant in man has fled,

κι' ὅλες οἱ κόρες τοῦ πόντου, Νηρηίδες, Γραῖες
τρέχουν στὰ λαμπυρίσματα τῆς ἀναδυομένης·
ὅποιος ποτέ του δὲν ἀγάπησε θ' ἀγαπήσει,
στὸ φῶς·

καὶ εἶσαι

σ' ἕνα μεγάλο σπίτι μὲ πολλὰ παράθυρα ἀνοιχτὰ
τρέχοντας ἀπὸ κάμαρα σὲ κάμαρα, δὲν ξέροντας ἀπὸ ποῦ
νὰ κοιτάξεις πρῶτα,
γιατὶ θὰ φύγουν τὰ πεῦκα καὶ τὰ καθρεφτισμένα βουνὰ καὶ
τὸ τιτίβισμα τῶν πουλιῶν
θ' ἀδειάσει ἡ θάλασσα, θρυμματισμένο γυαλί, ἀπὸ βοριὰ
καὶ νότο
θ' ἀδειάσουν τὰ μάτια σου ἀπ' τὸ φῶς τῆς μέρας
πὼς σταματοῦν ξαφνικὰ κι' ὅλα μαζὶ τὰ τζιτζίκια.

Πόρος, «Γαλήνη», 31 τοῦ 'Οχτώβρη 1946

and all the daughters of the sea, Nereids, Graeae,*
hurry to the radiance of the rising goddess:
whoever has never loved will love,*
in the light:

and you find yourself

in a large house with many windows open
running from room to room, not knowing from where to
look out first,*
because the pine-trees will vanish, and the mirrored mountains, and the chirping of birds
the sea will drain dry, shattered glass, from north and south
your eyes will empty of the light of day—
how suddenly and all together the cicadas stop.

Poros, "Galini," 31 October 1946

ΗΜΕΡΟΛΟΓΙΟ
ΚΑΤΑΣΤΡΩΜΑΤΟΣ, Γ΄

Στὸν κόσμο τῆς Κύπρου,
Μνήμη καὶ Ἀγάπη

...Κύπρον, οὗ μ' ἐθέσπισεν...

LOGBOOK III*

To the People of Cyprus,
in Memory and Love

"... Cyprus, where it was decreed by
*Apollo that I should live ..."**

ΑΓΙΑΝΑΠΑ, Α΄

Καὶ βλέπεις τὸ φῶς τοῦ ἥλιου καθὼς ἔλεγαν οἱ παλαιοί.
Ὡστόσο νόμιζα πὼς ἔβλεπα τόσα χρόνια
περπατώντας ἀνάμεσα στὰ βουνὰ καὶ στὴ θάλασσα
συντυχαίνοντας ἀνθρώπους μὲ τέλειες πανοπλίες·
παράξενο, δὲν πρόσεχα πὼς ἔβλεπα μόνο τὴ φωνή τους.
Εἴταν τὸ αἷμα ποὺ τοὺς ἀνάγκαζε νὰ μιλοῦν, τὸ κριάρι
ποὺ ἔσφαζα κι᾽ ἔστρωνα στὰ πόδια τους·
μὰ δὲν εἴταν τὸ φῶς ἐκεῖνο τὸ κόκκινο χαλί.
Ὅ,τι μοῦ λέγαν ἔπρεπε νὰ τὸ ψηλαφήσω
ὅπως ὅταν σὲ κρύψουν κυνηγημένο νύχτα σὲ στάβλο
ἢ φτάσεις τέλος τὸ κορμὶ βαθύκολπης γυναίκας
κι᾽ εἶναι γεμάτη ἡ κάμαρα πνιγερὲς μυρωδιές·
ὅ,τι μοῦ λέγαν δορὰ καὶ μετάξι.

Παράξενο, τὸ βλέπω ἐδῶ τὸ φῶς τοῦ ἥλιου· τὸ χρυσὸ δίχτυ
ὅπου τὰ πράγματα σπαρταροῦν σὰν τὰ ψάρια
ποὺ ἕνας μεγάλος ἄγγελος τραβᾶ
μαζὶ μὲ τὰ δίχτυα τῶν ψαράδων.

AGIANAPA I*

And you see the light of the sun as the ancients used to say.
And yet I thought I was seeing all these years
walking between the mountains and the sea
meeting by chance men in perfect armour;
strange, I didn't notice that I saw their voices only.
It was the blood that forced them to talk, the ram
that I slaughtered and spread at their feet;
but that red carpet was not the light.
Whatever they told me I had to recognize by touch
as when they hide you at night, hunted, in a stable
or when you finally reach the body of a full-breasted woman
and the room is thick with suffocating odors;
whatever they told me: fur and silk.

Strange, here I see the light of the sun; the gold net
where things quiver like fish
that a huge angel draws in
along with the nets of the fisherman.

ΟΝΕΙΡΟ

Κοιμοῦμαι κι' ἡ καρδιά μου ξαγρυπνᾶ·
κοιτάζει τ' ἄστρα στὸν οὐρανὸ καὶ τὸ δοιάκι
καὶ πῶς ἀνθοβολᾶ τὸ νερὸ στὸ τιμόνι.

DREAM

I sleep and my heart stays awake;
it gazes at the stars, the sky, and the helm,
and at how the water blossoms on the rudder.

ΛΕΠΤΟΜΕΡΕΙΕΣ ΣΤΗΝ ΚΥΠΡΟ

Στὸ ζωγράφο Διαμαντὴ

Ἡ μικρὴ κουκουβάγια εἴτανε πάντα ἐκεῖ
σκαρφαλωμένη στ' ἀνοιχτάρι τ' Ἅγιου Μάμα,
παραδομένη τυφλὰ στὸ μέλι τοῦ ἥλιου
ἐδῶ ἢ ἀλλοῦ, τώρα, στὰ περασμένα: χόρευε
μ' ἕνα τέτοιο ρυθμὸ τὸ φθινόπωρο.
Ἄγγελοι ξετυλίγανε τὸν οὐρανὸ
καὶ χάζευε ἕνας πέτρινος καμαροφρύδης
σὲ μιὰ γωνιὰ τῆς στέγης.

Τότες ἦρθε ὁ καλόγερος· σκουφί, κοντόρασο, πέτσινη ζώνη
κι' ἔπιασε νὰ πλουμίζει τὴν κολόκα.
Ἄρχισε ἀπ' τὸ λαιμό: φοινικιές, λέπια, καὶ δαχτυλίδια.
Ἔπειτα, κρατώντας στὴν πλατειὰ παλάμη τὴ στρογγυλὴ κοιλιά,
ἔβαλε τὸν παραυλακιστή, τὸν παραζυγιαστή, τὸν παραμυλωνά, καὶ τὸν κατάλαλο·
ἔβαλε τὴν ἀποστρέφουσα τὰ νήπια καὶ τὴν ἀποκαλόγρια·
καὶ στὴν ἄκρη, σχεδὸν ἀπόκρυφο, τ' ἀκοίμητο σκουλήκι.

Εἴταν ὡραῖα ὅλ' αὐτά, μιὰ περιδιάβαση.
Ὅμως τὸ ξύλινο μαγγανοπήγαδο — τ' ἀλακάτιν,
κοιμισμένο στὸν ἴσκιο τῆς καρυδιᾶς

DETAILS ON CYPRUS

To the painter Diamandí

The little owl was always there
perched on the doorkey to St. Máma,
given blindly to the honey of the sun
here or elsewhere, now, in the past:
autumn danced with just that rhythm.
Angels unwound the heavens
and a stone figure with arched eyebrows
gazed idly on a corner of the roof.

Then the monk appeared: skullcap, frock, leather belt,
and went to work decorating the gourd.*
He began at the neck: palm-trees, fish-scales, rings.
Then, cupping its round belly with a broad palm,
he added the cheating farmer, the cheating merchant, the
    cheating miller, and the slanderer;
then the infant-hater and the defrocked nun;
and at the bottom, almost hidden, the sleepless worm.

All this was fine, a casual stroll.
But the wooden well-wheel—the "alakátin"—*
asleep in the shade of the walnut tree

μισὸ στὸ χῶμα καὶ μισὸ μέσα στὸ νερό,
γιατί δοκίμασες νὰ τὸ ξυπνήσεις;
Εἶδες πῶς βόγγηξε. Κι’ ἐκείνη τὴν κραυγὴ
βγαλμένη ἀπ’ τὰ παλιὰ νεῦρα τοῦ ξύλου
γιατί τὴν εἶπες φωνὴ πατρίδας;

half in the earth and half in the water,
why did you try to wake it?
You saw how it moaned. And that cry,
brought forth from the wood's ancient nerves,
why did you call it the voice of our country?

ΕΠΙΚΑΛΕΩ ΤΟΙ ΤΗΝ ΘΕΟΝ...

Λάδι στὰ μέλη,
ἴσως ταγγὴ μυρωδιὰ
ὅπως ἐδῶ στὸ λιόμυλο
τῆς μικρῆς ἐκκλησιᾶς
στοὺς χοντροὺς πόρους
τῆς σταματημένης πέτρας.

Λάδι στὴν κόμη
στεφανωμένη μὲ σκοινί,
ἴσως καὶ ἄλλα ἀρώματα
ποὺ δὲ γνωρίσαμε
φτωχὰ καὶ πλούσια
κι᾿ ἀγαλματάκια στὰ δάχτυλα
προσφέρνοντας μικροὺς μαστούς.

Λάδι στὸν ἥλιο·
τρόμαξαν τὰ φύλλα
στοῦ ξένου τὸ σταμάτημα
καὶ βάρυνε ἡ σιγὴ
ἀνάμεσα στὰ γόνατα.
Ἔπεσαν τὰ νομίσματα·
«Ἐπικαλέω τοι τὴν θεόν...».

Λάδι στοὺς ὤμους

IN THE GODDESS' NAME
I SUMMON YOU . . . *

Oil on limbs,
maybe a rancid smell
as on the chapel's
oil-press here,
as on the rough pores
of the unturning stone.

Oil on hair
wreathed in rope
and maybe other scents
unknown to us
poor and rich
and statuettes offering
small breasts with their fingers.

Oil in the sun
the leaves shuddered
when the stranger stopped
and the silence weighed
between the knees.
The coins fell:
"In the goddess' name I summon you . . ."

Oil on the shoulders

καὶ στὴ μέση ποὺ λύγισε
γρίβα σφυρὰ στὴ χλόη,
κι' αὐτὴ ἡ πληγὴ στὸν ἥλιο
καθὼς σημαίναν τὸν ἑσπερινὸ
καθὼς μιλούσα στὸν αὐλόγυρο
μ' ἕνα σακάτη.

and the flexing waist
legs grass-dappled,
and that wound in the sun
as vespers sounded
as I spoke in the church yard
with a crippled man.

ΕΛΕΝΗ

ΤΕΥΚΡΟΣ: *... ἐς γῆν ἐναλίαν Κύπρον, οὗ μ' ἐθέσπισεν*
οἰκεῖν Ἀπόλλων, ὄνομα νησιωτικὸν
Σαλαμῖνα θέμενον τῆς ἐκεῖ χάριν πάτρας.

. . . .

ΕΛΕΝΗ: *Οὐκ ἦλθον ἐς γῆν Τρῳάδ', ἀλλ' εἴδωλον ἦν.*

. . . .

ΑΓΓΕΛΟΣ: *Τί φής;*
Νεφέλης ἄρ' ἄλλως εἴχομεν πόνους πέρι;

ΕΥΡΙΠΙΔΗΣ, *ΕΛΕΝΗ*

«Τ' ἀηδόνια δὲ σ' ἀφήνουνε νὰ κοιμηθεῖς στὶς Πλάτρες».

Ἀηδόνι ντροπαλό, μὲς στὸν ἀνασασμὸ τῶν φύλλων,
σὺ ποὺ δωρίζεις τὴ μουσικὴ δροσιὰ τοῦ δάσους
στὰ χωρισμένα σώματα καὶ στὶς ψυχὲς
αὐτῶν ποὺ ξέρουν πὼς δὲ θὰ γυρίσουν.
Τυφλὴ φωνή, ποὺ ψηλαφεῖς μέσα στὴ νυχτωμένη μνήμη
βήματα καὶ χειρονομίες· δὲ θὰ τολμοῦσα νὰ πῶ φιλήματα·
καὶ τὸ πικρὸ τρικύμισμα τῆς ξαγριεμένης σκλάβας.

«Τ' ἀηδόνια δὲ σ' ἀφήνουνε νὰ κοιμηθεῖς στὶς Πλάτρες».

Ποιὲς εἶναι οἱ Πλάτρες; Ποιὸς τὸ γνωρίζει τοῦτο τὸ νησί;
Ἔζησα τὴ ζωή μου ἀκούγοντας ὀνόματα πρωτάκουστα:

HELEN

TEUCER: . . . *in sea-girt Cyprus, where it was decreed*
by Apollo that I should live, giving the city
the name of Salamis in memory of my island home.

. . . .

HELEN: *I never went to Troy; it was a phantom.*

. . . .

SERVANT: *What? You mean it was only for a cloud that we*
struggled so much?

EURIPIDES, *HELEN**

"The nightingales won't let you sleep in Platres."*

Shy nightingale, in the breathing of the leaves,
you who bestow the forest's musical coolness
on the parted bodies, on the souls
of those who know they will not return.
Blind voice, you who grope in the darkness of memory
for footsteps and gestures—I wouldn't dare say kisses—
and the bitter raging of the slavewoman grown wild.

"The nightingales won't let you sleep in Platres."

Platres: where is Platres? And this island: who knows it?
I've lived my life hearing names I've never heard before:

καινούργιους τόπους, καινούργιες τρέλες τῶν ἀνθρώπων
ἢ τῶν θεῶν·
ἡ μοίρα μου ποὺ κυματίζει
ἀνάμεσα στὸ στερνὸ σπαθὶ ἑνὸς Αἴαντα
καὶ μιὰν ἄλλη Σαλαμίνα
μ' ἔφερε ἐδῶ σ' αὐτὸ τὸ γυρογιάλι.
Τὸ φεγγάρι
βγῆκε ἀπ' τὸ πέλαγο σὰν 'Αφροδίτη·
σκέπασε τ' ἄστρα τοῦ Τοξότη, τώρα πάει νά 'βρει
τὴν καρδιὰ τοῦ Σκορπιοῦ, κι' ὅλα τ' ἀλλάζει.
Ποῦ εἶν' ἡ ἀλήθεια;
Εἴμουν κι' ἐγὼ στὸν πόλεμο τοξότης·
τὸ ριζικό μου, ἑνὸς ἀνθρώπου ποὺ ξαστόχησε.

'Αηδόνι ποιητάρη,
σὰν καὶ μιὰ τέτοια νύχτα στ' ἀκροθαλάσσι τοῦ Πρωτέα
σ' ἄκουσαν οἱ σκλάβες Σπαρτιάτισσες κι' ἔσυραν τὸ θρῆνο,
κι' ἀνάμεσό τους — ποιὸς θὰ τό 'λεγε; — ἡ 'Ελένη!
Αὐτὴ ποὺ κυνηγούσαμε χρόνια στὸ Σκάμαντρο.
Εἴταν ἐκεῖ, στὰ χείλια τῆς ἐρήμου· τὴν ἄγγιξα, μοῦ μίλησε:
«Δὲν εἶν' ἀλήθεια, δὲν εἶν' ἀλήθεια» φώναζε.
«Δὲν μπήκα στὸ γαλαζόπλωρο καράβι.
Ποτὲ δὲν πάτησα τὴν ἀντρειωμένη Τροία».

Μὲ τὸ βαθὺ στηθόδεσμο, τὸν ἥλιο στὰ μαλλιά, κι' αὐτὸ τὸ
ἀνάστημα
ἴσκιοι καὶ χαμόγελα παντοῦ
στοὺς ὤμους στοὺς μηροὺς στὰ γόνατα·
ζωντανὸ δέρμα, καὶ τὰ μάτια

new countries, new idiocies of men
or of the gods;

 my fate, which wavers
between the last sword of some Ajax
and another Salamis,
brought me here, to this shore.

 The moon
rose from the sea like Aphrodite,
covered the Archer's stars, now moves to find
the Heart of Scorpio, and changes everything.
Truth, where's the truth?
I too was an archer in the war;
my fate: that of a man who missed his target.

Lyric nightingale,
on a night like this, by the shore of Proteus,
the Spartan slave girls heard you and began their lament,
and among them—who would have believed it?—Helen!
She whom we hunted so many years by the banks of the
 Scamander.
She was there, at the desert's lip; I touched her; she spoke
 to me:
"It isn't true, it isn't true," she cried.
"I didn't board the blue-bowed ship.
I never went to valiant Troy."

High-girdled, the sun in her hair, and that stature
shadows and smiles everywhere,
on shoulders, thighs, and knees;
the skin alive, and her eyes

μὲ τὰ μεγάλα βλέφαρα,
εἴταν ἐκεῖ, στὴν ὄχθη ἑνὸς Δέλτα.

Καὶ στὴν Τροία;

Τίποτε στὴν Τροία — ἕνα εἴδωλο.
Ἔτσι τὸ θέλαν οἱ θεοί.
Κι' ὁ Πάρης, μ' ἕναν ἴσκιο πλάγιαζε σὰ νά εἴταν πλάσμα
ἀτόφιο·
κι' ἐμεῖς σφαζόμασταν γιὰ τὴν Ἑλένη δέκα χρόνια.

Μεγάλος πόνος εἶχε πέσει στὴν Ἑλλάδα.
Τόσα κορμιὰ ριγμένα
στὰ σαγόνια τῆς θάλασσας στὰ σαγόνια τῆς γῆς·
τόσες ψυχὲς
δοσμένες στὶς μυλόπετρες, σὰν τὸ σιτάρι.
Κι' οἱ ποταμοὶ φουσκώναν μὲς στὴ λάσπη τὸ αἷμα
γιὰ ἕνα λινὸ κυμάτισμα γιὰ μιὰ νεφέλη
μιᾶς πεταλούδας τίναγμα τὸ πούπουλο ἑνὸς κύκνου
γιὰ ἕνα πουκάμισο ἀδειανό, γιὰ μιὰν Ἑλένη.
Κι' ὁ ἀδερφός μου;

Ἀηδόνι ἀηδόνι ἀηδόνι,

τ' εἶναι θεός; τί μὴ θεός; καὶ τί τ' ἀνάμεσό τους;

«Τ' ἀηδόνια δὲ σ' ἀφήνουνε νὰ κοιμηθεῖς στὶς Πλάτρες».

Δακρυσμένο πουλί,

στὴν Κύπρο τὴ θαλασσοφίλητη

ποὺ ἔταξαν γιὰ νὰ μοῦ θυμίζει τὴν πατρίδα,
ἄραξα μοναχὸς μ' αὐτὸ τὸ παραμύθι,
ἂν εἶναι ἀλήθεια πὼς αὐτό εἶναι παραμύθι,

with the large eyelids,
she was there, on the banks of a Delta.
                                        And at Troy?
At Troy, nothing: just a phantom image.
The gods wanted it so.
And Paris, Paris lay with a shadow as though it were a
    solid being;
and for ten whole years we slaughtered ourselves for Helen.

Great suffering descended on Greece.
So many bodies thrown
into the jaws of the sea, the jaws of the earth*
so many souls
fed to the millstones like grain.
And the rivers swelling, blood in their silt,
all for a linen undulation, a bit of cloud,
a butterfly's flicker, a swan's down,
an empty tunic—all for a Helen.
And my brother?
                    Nightingale nightingale nightingale,
what is a god? What is not a god? And what is there in-
    between them?

"The nightingales won't let you sleep in Platres."

Tearful bird,
                on sea-kissed Cyprus
consecrated to remind me of my country,
I moored alone with this fable,
if it's true that it is a fable,

ἂν εἶναι ἀλήθεια πὼς οἱ ἀνθρῶποι δὲ θὰ ξαναπιάσουν
τὸν παλιὸ δόλο τῶν θεῶν·
ἂν εἶναι ἀλήθεια
πὼς κάποιος ἄλλος Τεῦκρος, ὕστερα ἀπὸ χρόνια,
ἢ κάποιος Αἴαντας ἢ Πρίαμος ἢ Ἑκάβη
ἢ κάποιος ἄγνωστος, ἀνώνυμος, ποὺ ὡστόσο
εἶδε ἕνα Σκάμαντρο νὰ ξεχειλάει κουφάρια,
δὲν τό 'χει μὲς στὴ μοίρα του ν' ἀκούσει
μαντατοφόρους ποὺ ἔρχουνται νὰ ποῦνε
πὼς τόσος πόνος τόση ζωὴ
πήγαν στὴν ἄβυσσο
γιὰ ἕνα πουκάμισο ἀδειανὸ γιὰ μιὰν Ἑλένη.

if it's true that mortals will not again take up
the old deceit of the gods;
if it's true
that in future years some other Teucer,
or some Ajax or Priam or Hecuba,
or someone unknown and nameless who nevertheless saw
a Scamander overflow with corpses,
isn't fated to hear
newsbearers coming to tell him
that so much suffering, so much life,
went into the abyss
all for an empty tunic, all for a Helen.

ΜΝΗΜΗ, Α'

καὶ ἡ θάλασσα οὐκ ἔστιν ἔτι

Κι' ἐγὼ στὰ χέρια μου μόνο μ' ἕνα καλάμι·
εἴταν ἔρημη ἡ νύχτα τὸ φεγγάρι στὴ χάση
καὶ μύριζε τὸ χῶμα ἀπὸ τὴν τελευταία βροχή.
Ψιθύρισα· ἡ μνήμη ὅπου καὶ νὰ τὴν ἀγγίξεις πονεῖ,
ὁ οὐρανὸς εἶναι λίγος, θάλασσα πιὰ δὲν ὑπάρχει,
ὅ,τι σκοτώνουν τὴ μέρα τ' ἀδειάζουν μὲ κάρα πίσω ἀπ' τὴ
ράχη.

Τὰ δάχτυλά μου παίζανε ξεχασμένα μ' αὐτὴ τὴ φλογέρα
ποὺ μοῦ χάρισε ἕνας γέροντας βοσκὸς ἐπειδὴ τοῦ εἶπα καλησπέρα·
οἱ ἄλλοι ξέγραψαν κάθε χαιρετισμό·
ξυπνοῦν, ξυρίζουνται κι' ἀρχίζουν μεροκάματο τὸ σκοτωμό,
ὅπως κλαδεύεις ἢ χειρουργεῖς, μεθοδικά, χωρὶς πάθος·
ὁ πόνος νεκρὸς σὰν τὸν Πάτροκλο καὶ κανεὶς δὲν κάνει
λάθος.

Συλλογίστηκα νὰ φυσήξω ἕνα σκοπὸ κι' ἔπειτα ντράπηκα
τὸν ἄλλο κόσμο
αὐτὸν ποὺ μὲ βλέπει πέρ' ἀπ' τὴ νύχτα μὲς ἀπ' τὸ φῶς
μου
ποὺ ὑφαίνουν τὰ κορμιὰ ζωντανά, οἱ καρδιὲς γυμνὲς
κι' ἡ ἀγάπη ποὺ ἀνήκει καὶ στὶς Σεμνὲς
καθὼς καὶ στὸν ἄνθρωπο καὶ στὴν πέτρα καὶ στὸ νερὸ καὶ
στὸ χορτάρι

MEMORY I

*And there was no more sea.**

And I with only a reed in my hands.
The night was deserted, the moon waning,
earth smelled of the last rain.
I whispered: memory hurts wherever you touch it,
there's only a little sky, there's no more sea,
what they kill by day they carry away in carts and dump
behind the ridge.

I was fingering this pipe absent-mindedly;
an old shepherd gave it to me because I said good-evening
to him.
The others have abolished every kind of greeting:
they wake, shave, and start the day's work of slaughter
as one prunes or operates, methodically and without
passion;
sorrow's dead like Patroclus, and no one makes a mistake.

I thought of playing a tune and then I was ashamed of the
other world
the one that watches me from beyond the night from within
my light
woven of living bodies, naked hearts
and love that belongs to the Furies
as it belongs to man and to stone and to water and to grass

καὶ στὸ ζῶο ποὺ κοιτάει κατάματα τὸ θάνατο ποὺ ἔρχεται
νὰ τὸ πάρει.

Ἔτσι προχώρεσα στὸ σκοτεινὸ μονοπάτι
κι' ἔστριψα στὸ περβόλι μου κι' ἔσκαψα κι' ἔθαψα τὸ καλάμι
καὶ πάλι ψιθύρισα· θὰ γίνει ἡ ἀνάσταση μιὰν αὐγή,
πὼς λάμπουν τὴν ἄνοιξη τὰ δέντρα θὰ ροδαμίσει τοῦ ὄρθρου ἡ μαρμαρυγή,
θὰ ξαναγίνει τὸ πέλαγο καὶ πάλι τὸ κύμα θὰ τινάξει τὴν
'Αφροδίτη·
εἴμαστε ὁ σπόρος ποὺ πεθαίνει. Καὶ μπήκα στ' ἀδειανό μου
τὸ σπίτι.

and to the animal that looks straight into the eye of its
approaching death.

So I continued along the dark path
and turned into my garden and dug and buried the reed
and again I whispered: some morning the resurrection will
come,
dawn's dew will glisten like trees in spring,
the sea will be born again, and the wave will again fling
forth Aphrodite.
We are the seed that dies. And I entered my empty house.

Ο ΔΑΙΜΩΝ ΤΗΣ ΠΟΡΝΕΙΑΣ

... Nicosia e Famagosta
per la lor bestia si lamenti e garra...
PARADISO

... ὡς γίον ἠξεύρετε καὶ ὁ δαίμων τῆς πορνίας ὅλον τὸν κόσμον πλημμελᾶ τὸν ἐκόμπωσε τὸν ρήγαν καὶ ἔπεσεν εἰς ἁμαρτίαν...
ΧΡΟΝΙΚΟ ΤΟΥ ΜΑΧΑΙΡΑ

Ὁ Τζουὰν Βισκούντης εἶχε γράψει τὴν ἀλήθεια.
Πῶς πλέρωσε μαυλίστρες ὁ κούντη Τερουχᾶς
πῶς βρέθηκαν ἀντάμα αὐτὸς κι᾿ ἡ ρήγαινα
πῶς ἄρχισε τὸ πράμα, πῶς ξετέλειωσε,
ὅλα τῆς Λευκωσίας τὰ κοπέλια
τὸ διαλαλούσαν στὰ στενὰ καὶ στὶς πλατεῖες.
Πὼς εἴταν ἡ γραφὴ σωστὴ ποὺ ἔστειλε στὴ Φραγκιὰ στὸ
ρήγα
τὸ ξέραν οἱ συβουλατόροι.
Ὅμως τώρα
συνάχτηκαν καὶ συντυχαίναν γιὰ νὰ συβουλέψουν
τὴν Κορώνα τῆς Κύπρου καὶ τῶν Ἱεροσολύμων·
τώρα εἴταν διαταμένοι γιὰ νὰ κρίνουν
τὴ ρήγαινα Λινόρα ποὺ κρατοῦσε
ἀπ᾿ τὴ μεγάλη τὴ γενιὰ τῶν Καταλάνων·
κι᾿ εἶναι ἀνελέημονες οἱ Καταλάνοι
κι᾿ ἂν τύχαινε κι᾿ ὁ ρήγας ἐκδικιούνταν
τίποτε δὲ θὰ τό ᾿χαν ν᾿ ἀρματώσουν καὶ νὰ ᾿ρθοῦνε

THE DEMON OF FORNICATION

. . . Nicosia e Famagosta
per la lor bestia si lamenti e garra . . .

*PARADISO**

. . . even as you know that the demon of fornication assails the whole world, so he beguiled the king, and the good king fell into sin . . .

*CHRONICLE OF MAKHAIRAS**

Juan Visconti had written the truth.
How the Count of Rochas paid go-betweens,
how he and the queen were in it together,
how the thing started and how it ended
was hawked in the streets and squares
by every boy in Nicosia.
That the letter he sent to the king in France
was accurate, the counselors knew well enough.
But now
they had come together to advise
the Crown of Cyprus and Jerusalem;
now they had been ordered to judge
Queen Eleanora, descended from
a great family among the Catalans;
and the Catalans are merciless men,
so that if the king chose to avenge himself
it would be nothing for the Catalans to take up arms

καὶ νὰ τοὺς ξολοθρέψουν αὐτοὺς καὶ τὸ βιό τους.
Εἶχαν εὐθύνες τρομερὲς εὐθύνες·
ἀπὸ τὴ γνώμη τους κρέμουνταν τὸ ρηγάτο.

Πὼς ὁ Βισκούντης εἴταν τίμιος καὶ πιστὸς
βέβαια τὸ ξέραν· ὅμως βιάστηκε,
φέρθηκε ἀστόχαστα ἄμοιαστα ἄτσαλα.
Εἴταν ἀψὺς ὁ ρήγας, πῶς δὲν τὸ λογάριασε ;
καὶ μπρούμουτα στὸν πόθο τῆς Λινόρας.
Πάντα μαζί του στὰ ταξίδια τὸ πουκάμισό της
καὶ τό 'παιρνε στὴν ἀγκαλιά του σὰν κοιμούνταν·
καὶ πῆγε νὰ τοῦ γράψει ὁ ἀθεόφοβος
πὼς βρήκαν μὲ τὴν ἄρνα του τὸ κριάρι·
γράφουνται τέτια λόγια σ' ἕναν ἄρχοντα ;
Εἴταν μωρός. Τουλάχιστο ἂς θυμούνταν
πὼς ἔσφαλε κι' ὁ ρήγας· ἔκανε τὸ λιγωμένο
μά εἶχε στὸ πισωπόρτι καὶ δυὸ καῦχες.
'Αναστατώθη τὸ νησὶ σὰν ἡ Λινόρα
πρόσταξε καὶ τῆς ἔφεραν τὴ μιά, τὴ γκαστρωμένη
κι' ἄλεθαν μὲ τὸ χερομύλι πάνω στὴν κοιλιά της
πινάκι τὸ πινάκι τὸ σιτάρι.
Καὶ τὸ χειρότερο — δὲν τὸ χωράει ὁ νοῦς —
ἀφοῦ τὸ ξέρει ὁ κόσμος ὅλος πὼς ὁ ρήγας
γεννήθηκε στὸ ζώδιο τοῦ Αἰγόκερω,
πῆρε στὰ χέρια του ὁ ταλαίπωρος καλάμι
τὴ νύχτα ποὺ εἴταν στὸν Αἰγόκερω ἡ σελήνη
νὰ γράψει τί ; γιὰ κέρατα καὶ κριάρια !
Ὁ φρόνιμος τὴ μοίρα δὲν τηνε ξαγριεύει.
Ὄχι· δὲν εἴμαστε ταγμένοι γιὰ νὰ ποῦμε

and come to wipe out everyone of them, life and limb.
They had responsibilities, terrible responsibilities;
the very kingdom depended on their judgment.

That Visconti was honest and loyal
of course they knew; but he hurried things,
acted thoughtlessly, indecorously, extravagantly.
The king was irascible—how had Visconti failed
to keep that in mind?—irascible
and prostrate to Eleanora's desire:
her shift always with him when he traveled
so that he could take it in his arms at night;
and the impious Visconti went and wrote him
that they'd found the ram with his ewe—
how can you write a thing like that to a ruler?
He was a fool. At least he should have remembered
that the king too had made mistakes:
pretending to be so enraptured
while two mistresses hovered at the back door.
What an uproar on the island when Eleanora
ordered one of the two—the pregnant one—to be brought
before her
and had them lay a handmill on her belly
to grind out flour measure by measure.
And worst of all—the mind boggles—
when the whole world knows that the king
was born under the sign of Capricorn,
that miserable Visconti takes pen in hand
the very night the moon comes under Capricorn
to write what: about horns and rams!
The prudent man never tempts fate.
No; we aren't sworn to say

ποῦ εἶναι τὸ δίκιο. Τὸ δικό μας χρέος
εἶναι νὰ βροῦμε τὸ μικρότερο κακό.
Κάλλιο ἕνας νὰ πεθάνει ἀπὸ τὸ ριζικό του
παρὰ σὲ κίντυνο νὰ μποῦμε ἐμεῖς καὶ τὸ ρηγάτο.

Ἔτσι συβουλευόντουσαν ὅλη τὴ μέρα
καὶ κατὰ τὸ βασίλεμα πήγαν στὸ ρήγα
προσκύνησαν καὶ τοῦ εἶπαν πὼς ὁ Τζουὰν Βισκούντης
εἶναι ἕνας διαστρεμμένος ψεματάρης.

Κι' ὁ Τζουὰν Βισκούντης πέθανε ἀπ' τὴν πείνα σὲ μιὰ γούφα.
Μὰ στὴν ψυχὴ τοῦ ρήγα ὁ σπόρος τῆς ντροπῆς του
ἅπλωνε τὰ πλοκάμια του καὶ τὸν ἐκίνα
τό 'παθε νὰ τὸ πράξει καὶ στοὺς ἄλλους.
Κερὰ δὲν ἔμεινε ποὺ νὰ μὴ βουληθεῖ νὰ τὴν πορνέψει·
τὶς ντρόπιασε ὅλες. Φόβος κι' ἔχτρα ζευγαρώναν
καὶ γέμιζαν τὴ χώρα φόβο κι' ἔχτρα.

Ἔτσι, μὲ τὸ «μικρότερο κακό», βάδιζε ἡ μοίρα
ὣς τὴν αὐγὴ τ' Ἅγι' Ἀντωνιοῦ, μέρα Τετάρτη
πού ἦρθαν οἱ καβαλάρηδες καὶ τὸν ἐσύραν
ἀπὸ τῆς καύχας του τὴν ἀγκαλιὰ καὶ τὸν ἐσφάξαν.
«Καὶ τάπισα παρὰ οὔλους ὁ τουρκοπουλιέρης
ηὗρεν τον τυλιμένον τὸ αἷμα» λέει ὁ χρονογράφος
«κι' ἔβγαλεν τὴν μαχαίραν του καὶ κόβγει
τὰ λυμπά του μὲ τὸν αὐλὸν καὶ τοῦ εἶπε:
Γιὰ τοῦτα ἔδωκες θάνατον!».
Αὐτὸ τὸ τέλος
ὅρισε γιὰ τὸ ρήγα Πιὲρ ὁ δαίμων τῆς πορνείας.

where justice lies. Our duty
is to find the lesser of evils.
Better for one man to die because he was fated to,
than for us to put ourselves and the kingdom in danger.

So they argued through the day
and then, towards sunset, they approached the king,
bowed before him and said that Juan Visconti
was an infamous, perverted liar.

And Juan Visconti died of hunger in a dungeon.
But in the king's soul the seed of his shame
spread tentacles, and this made him long
to serve others as he had been served.
No woman escaped his ambition to fornicate;
he shamed them all. Fear and hate coupled
and filled the land with fear and hate.

In this way, with the "lesser evil," fate marched on
until the dawn of St. Anthony's day, a Wednesday,
when the knights came and dragged the king
from his mistress' embrace to slaughter him.
"And after all the others came the Turkopolier*
and found him lying in his own blood" says the Chronicler,
"And drew his sword and cut his member off
and his testicles, and said to him: For these
you dealt out death."

This was the end
appointed for King Peter by the demon of fornication.

ΤΡΕΙΣ ΜΟΥΛΕΣ

Καὶ ἐκαβαλλίκεψεν ἡ ρήγαινα ἀπάνω τῆς θαυμαστῆς μούλας τοῦ ἀνδρός της ρὲ Πιέρ, ὀνόματι Μαργαρίτα, καὶ ἔκατσεν ἀπάνω τῆς θαυμαστῆς μούλας γυναικεῖα, καὶ ἐπαράγγειλεν τοῦ σκουτιέρη της, ὀνόματι Πουτζουρέλλο, νὰ κρατῇ μετά του τὰ φτερνιστηρία της, καὶ ἄντα τοῦ νέψῃ, νὰ γυρίσῃ τὸ πόδιν της νὰ κάτσῃ ἀνθρωπινά...

ΧΡΟΝΙΚΟ ΤΟΥ ΜΑΧΑΙΡΑ

Γράμμα στὸ Μάστρο

Στὴ Δαμασκὸ μιὰ νύχτα ἀγρύπνιας
μοῦ φάνηκε τὸ πέρασμα τῆς Οὺμ Χαρὰμ
τῆς βαθυσέβαστης γενιᾶς τοῦ Προφήτη.
Ἄκουγα πέταλα σὰν ἀργυρὰ δηνάρια
κι' ἐκείνη λὲς καὶ διάβαινε λόφους ἁλάτι
κατὰ τὴ Λάρνακα, στὴ μούλα της καβάλα.
Περίμενα μέσα σὲ δροσερὰ κλωνάρια
δαγκώνοντας τὸν καρπὸ τῆς μυρτιᾶς·
τὰ μάτια μου τ' ἀγκύλωνε μιὰ ἀσπράδα
ἴσως τ' ἁλάτι ἴσως τὸ φάσμα της. Καὶ τότε
στοὺς θάμνους ἕνας ψίθυρος:
«Ἐδῶ εἴταν
ποὺ γλίστρησε τὸ ζό μου. Τούτη ἡ πέτρα
μοῦ τσάκισε τὸ διάφωτον αὐχένα
κι' ἔδωσα τὴν ψυχή μου νικηφόρα.
Ἀπ' τὴ βουλὴ τοῦ θεοῦ εἴμουν γεμάτη·

THREE MULES

And the Queen mounted on the wonderful mule called Margarita, which had belonged to her husband King Peter, and she sat upon the wonderful mule as women do; and she ordered her squire who was called Putsurello to bring her spurs with him. And she said to him: "When I make a sign to you, turn my foot over so that I sit like a man and put on my spurs."

*THE CHRONICLE OF MAKHAIRAS**

Letter to Mastro

In Damascus one sleepless night
I saw an apparition of Oum Haram,
the venerable kinswoman of the Prophet.
I heard the clatter of hooves like silver dinars,
then I saw her, seemingly crossing hills of salt
towards Larnaca, astride her mule.
I waited there among cool branches
biting the fruit of a myrtle bush;
a whiteness stung my eyes,
maybe the salt, maybe her ghost. And then
in the shrubs, a whisper:
"It was here
that my animal slipped. This stone
struck the nape of my translucent neck
and I gave up my soul triumphantly.
I was full of the will of God;

μιὰ μούλα δὲ σηκώνει τέτοιο βάρος·
μὴν τὸ ξεχνᾶς καὶ μὴν τὴν ἀδικήσεις».

Εἶπε κι' ἐχάθη. Ὡστόσο ἀκόμη τώρα
ἡ μούλα της ὁλοένα βόσκει στὸ μυαλό μου,
καθὼς καὶ ἡ ἄλλη ὁπού σταμάτησε ἡ καρδιά της
ὅταν τὴν ξεφορτώσαν ἀπ' τὰ δυὸ κιβούρια,
τοὺς δυὸ ἀδερφοὺς τοὺς ἀδικοσφαγμένους
ἀπ' τὸν τζελάτη ἐκεῖ στὸν Κουτσοβέντη.

Μὰ ἡ πιὸ τρανή, πῶς νὰ τὴν πῶ; Στὸν τόπο
ποὺ ὅσοι ἔζησαν πιὸ χαμηλὰ ἀπὸ τὰ καστέλια
λησμονηθήκαν σὰν τὸ χῶμα τοῦ ἄλλου χρόνου,
αὐτὴ ἀρμενίζει ἀκόμη στὰ φτερὰ τῆς φήμης·
τὸ ξακουσμένο ζωντανὸ τῆς ρήγαινας Λινόρας.
Στὴν κοιλιά της τὰ χρυσὰ φτερνιστήρια,
στὴ σέλα της τ' ἀξεδίψαστα λαγόνια,
στὸ γλάκι της τραντὰ τὰ στήθια ἐκεῖνα
γεμάτα σὰν τὰ ρόδια φονικό.
Κι' ὅταν Ναπολιτάνοι Γενοβέζοι καὶ Λομπάρδοι
φέραν ἀπάνω στὸ βασιλικὸ τραπέζι
σ' ἕνα ἀσημένιο δίσκο, ματωμένο
τοῦ σκοτωμένου ρήγα τὸ πουκάμισο
καὶ ξέκαμαν τὸν ἐλεεινὸν 'Ιωάννη·
λογιάζω πὼς χιχίνισε τὴ νύχτα ἐκείνη,
ἔξω ἀπὸ τὴν ἀπάθεια τῆς φυλῆς της,
καθὼς οὐρλιάζει τὸ σκυλί,
διπλοεντέληνη, χρυσοκάπουλη, στὸ στάβλο,
ἡ μούλα Μαργαρίτα.

a mule can't bear that much weight;
don't forget it, and don't wrong the mule."

She spoke and disappeared. Yet, even now
her mule still grazes in my mind,
as does that other mule, whose heart stopped dead
when they freed her of the two coffins,
the two brothers unjustly executed
by the hangman there in Koutsovendi.*

But the greatest of them all, what can I say of her? In a
country
where those who lived below the castles
were forgotten like last year's earth,
she still sails free on the wings of fame,
the celebrated beast of Queen Eleanora.
Against her belly, the golden spurs;
on her saddle, those insatiable loins;
at her trotting, those jolting breasts
ripe as pomegranates with murder.
And when Neapolitans, Genoese, and Lombards
brought to the royal table
on a silver tray, all bloody,
the shirt of the murdered king
and did in his wretched brother John,
I imagine how she must have neighed that night,
beyond the apathy of her race,
as a dog howls,
rich in trappings, golden-crouped, in the stable,
Margarita the mule.

ΠΕΝΘΕΥΣ

῾Ο ὕπνος τὸν γέμιζε ὄνειρα καρπῶν καὶ φύλλων·
ὁ ξύπνος δὲν τὸν ἄφηνε νὰ κόψει οὔτε ἕνα μοῦρο.
Κι᾿ οἱ δυὸ μαζὶ μοιράσανε τὰ μέλη του στὶς Βάκχες.

PENTHEUS

Sleep filled him with dreams of fruit and leaves;
wakefulness kept him from picking even a mulberry.
And the two together divided his limbs among the Bacchae.*

ΜΝΗΜΗ, Β΄

Ἔφεσος

Μιλοῦσε καθισμένος σ' ἕνα μάρμαρο
ποὺ ἔμοιαζε ἀπομεινάρι ἀρχαίου πυλώνα·
ἀπέραντος δεξιὰ κι' ἄδειος ὁ κάμπος
ζερβὰ κατέβαιναν ἀπ' τὸ βουνὸ τ' ἀπόσκια:
«Εἶναι παντοῦ τὸ ποίημα. Ἡ φωνή σου
καμιὰ φορὰ προβαίνει στὸ πλευρό του
σὰν τὸ δελφίνι ποὺ γιὰ λίγο συντροφεύει
μαλαματένιο τρεχαντήρι μὲς στὸν ἥλιο
καὶ πάλι χάνεται. Εἶναι παντοῦ τὸ ποίημα
σὰν τὰ φτερὰ τοῦ ἀγέρα μὲς στὸν ἀγέρα
ποὺ ἄγγιξαν τὰ φτερὰ τοῦ γλάρου μιὰ στιγμή.
Ἴδιο καὶ διάφορο ἀπὸ τὴ ζωή μας, πῶς ἀλλάζει
τὸ πρόσωπο κι' ὡστόσο μένει τὸ ἴδιο
γυναίκας ποὺ γυμνώθηκε. Τὸ ξέρει
ὅποιος ἀγάπησε· στὸ φῶς τῶν ἄλλων
ὁ κόσμος φθείρεται· μὰ ἐσὺ θυμήσου
Ἅδης καὶ Διόνυσος εἶναι τὸ ἴδιο».
Εἶπε καὶ πῆρε τὸ μεγάλο δρόμο
ποὺ πάει στ' ἀλλοτινὸ λιμάνι, χωνεμένο τώρα
πέρα στὰ βοῦρλα. Τὸ λυκόφως
θά 'λεγες γιὰ τὸ θάνατο ἑνὸς ζώου,
τόσο γυμνό.

Θυμᾶμαι ἀκόμη·

MEMORY, II

Ephesus

He spoke while sitting on what seemed to be
the marble remnant of an ancient gate;
endless the plain on the right and empty,
on the left the last shadows moved down the mountain:
"The poem is everywhere. Your voice
sometimes travels beside it
like a dolphin keeping company for a while
with a golden sloop in the sunlight,
then vanishing again. The poem is everywhere,
like the wings of the wind moved by the wind
to touch for a moment the sea gull's wings.
The same as our lives yet different too,
as a woman's face changes yet remains the same
after she strips naked. He who has loved
knows this; in the light that other people see things,
the world spoils; but you remember this:
Hades and Dionysus are the same."*
He spoke and then took the main road
that leads to the old harbor, devoured now
under the rushes there. The twilight
as if ready for the death of some animal,
so naked was it.

I remember still:

ταξίδευε σ' ἄκρες ἰωνικές, σ' ἄδεια κοχύλια θεάτρων
ὅπου μονάχα ἡ σαύρα σέρνεται στὴ στεγνὴ πέτρα,
κι' ἐγὼ τὸν ρώτησα: «Κάποτε θὰ ξαναγεμίσουν;»
Καὶ μ' ἀποκρίθηκε: «Μπορεῖ, τὴν ὥρα τοῦ θανάτου».
Κι' ἔτρεξε στὴν ὀρχήστρα οὐρλιάζοντας:
«Ἀφῆστε με ν' ἀκούσω τὸν ἀδερφό μου!»
Κι' εἴταν σκληρὴ ἡ σιγὴ τριγύρω μας
κι' ἀχάραχτη στὸ γυαλὶ τοῦ γαλάζιου.

he was traveling to Ionian shores,
to empty shells of theaters
where only the lizard slithers over the dry stones,
and I asked him: "Will they be full again some day?"
and he answered: "Maybe, at the hour of death."
And he ran across the orchestra howling
"Let me hear my brother!"
And the silence surrounding us was harsh,
leaving no trace at all on the glass of the blue.

ΣΑΛΑΜΙΝΑ ΤΗΣ ΚΥΠΡΟΣ

... Σαλαμῖνα τε
τᾶς νῦν ματρόπολις τῶνδ᾽
αἰτία στεναγμῶν.
ΑΙΣΧΥΛΟΣ, *ΠΕΡΣΕΣ*

Κάποτε ὁ ἥλιος τοῦ μεσημεριοῦ, κάποτε φοῦχτες ἡ ψιλὴ
βροχὴ
καὶ τ᾽ ἀκρογιάλι γεμάτο θρύψαλα παλιὰ πιθάρια.
᾽Ασήμαντες οἱ κολόνες· μονάχα ὁ Ἅγιος ᾽Επιφάνιος
δείχνοντας μουντά, χωνεμένη τὴ δύναμη τῆς πολύχρυσης
αὐτοκρατορίας.

Τὰ νέα κορμιὰ περάσαν ἀπ᾽ ἐδῶ, τὰ ἐρωτεμένα·
παλμοὶ στοὺς κόλπους, ρόδινα κοχύλια καὶ τὰ σφυρὰ
τρέχοντας ἄφοβα πάνω στὸ νερὸ
κι᾽ ἀγκάλες ἀνοιχτὲς γιὰ τὸ ζευγάρωμα τοῦ πόθου.
Κύριος ἐπὶ ὑδάτων πολλῶν,
πάνω σ᾽ αὐτὸ τὸ πέρασμα.

Τότες ἄκουσα βήματα στὰ χαλίκια.
Δὲν εἶδα πρόσωπα· σὰ γύρισα εἶχαν φύγει.
Ὅμως βαρειὰ ἡ φωνὴ σὰν τὸ περπάτημα καματεροῦ,
ἔμεινε ἐκεῖ στὶς φλέβες τ᾽ οὐρανοῦ στὸ κύλισμα τῆς θάλασσας
μέσα στὰ βότσαλα πάλι καὶ πάλι:

«Ἡ γῆς δὲν ἔχει κρικέλια

SALAMIS IN CYPRUS

. . . and Salamis,
whose mother-city is now
the cause of our troubles.

AESCHYLUS, *THE PERSIANS**

Sometimes the midday sun, sometimes handfuls of light rain
and the beach covered with fragments of ancient jars.
The columns insignificant; only the ruined church of St.
    Epiphanios
revealing—dark, sunken—the might of the golden Empire.

Young bodies, loved and loving, have passed by here;
throbbing breasts, shells rose-pink, feet
fearlessly skimming the water,
and arms open for the coupling of desire.
The Lord upon many waters,*
here upon this crossing.

Then I heard footsteps on the stones.
I didn't see any faces; they'd gone by the time I turned.
But the voice, heavy like the tread of oxen,
remained there in the sky's veins, in the sea's roll
over the pebbles, again and again:

"Earth has no handles

γιὰ νὰ τὴν πάρουν στὸν ὦμο καὶ νὰ φύγουν
μήτε μποροῦν, ὅσο κι' ἂν εἶναι διψασμένοι
νὰ γλυκάνουν τὸ πέλαγο μὲ νερὸ μισὸ δράμι.
Καὶ τοῦτα τὰ κορμιὰ
πλασμένα ἀπὸ ἕνα χῶμα ποὺ δὲν ξέρουν,
ἔχουν ψυχές.
Μαζεύουν σύνεργα γιὰ νὰ τὶς ἀλλάξουν,
δὲ θὰ μπορέσουν· μόνο θὰ τὶς ξεκάμουν
ἂν ξεγίνουνται οἱ ψυχές.
Δὲν ἀργεῖ νὰ καρπίσει τ' ἀστάχυ
δὲ χρειάζεται μακρὺ καιρὸ
γιὰ νὰ φουσκώσει τῆς πίκρας τὸ προζύμι,
δὲ χρειάζεται μακρὺ καιρὸ
τὸ κακὸ γιὰ νὰ σηκώσει τὸ κεφάλι,
κι' ὁ ἄρρωστος νοῦς ποὺ ἀδειάζει
δὲ χρειάζεται κακρὺ καιρὸ
γιὰ νὰ γεμίσει μὲ τὴν τρέλα,
νῆσός τις ἔστι...».

Φίλοι τοῦ ἄλλου πολέμου,
σ' αὐτὴ τὴν ἔρημη συννεφιασμένη ἀκρογιαλιὰ
σᾶς συλλογίζομαι καθὼς γυρίζει ἡ μέρα —
'Εκεῖνοι ποὺ ἔπεσαν πολεμώντας κι' ἐκεῖνοι ποὺ ἔπεσαν
χρόνια μετὰ τὴ μάχη·
ἐκεῖνοι ποὺ εἶδαν τὴν αὐγὴ μὲς ἀπ' τὴν πάχνη τοῦ θανάτου
ἤ, μὲς στὴν ἄγρια μοναξιὰ κάτω ἀπὸ τ' ἄστρα,
νιώσανε πάνω τους μαβιὰ μεγάλα
τὰ μάτια τῆς ὁλόκληρης καταστροφῆς·
κι' ἀκόμη ἐκεῖνοι ποὺ προσεύχουνταν

for them to shoulder her and carry her off,
nor can they, however thirsty,
sweeten the sea with half a dram of water.
And those bodies,
formed of a clay they know not,
have souls.
They gather tools to change them;
they won't succeed: they'll only unmake them
if souls can be unmade.
Wheat doesn't take long to ripen,
it doesn't take much time
for the yeast of bitterness to rise,
it doesn't take much time
for evil to raise its head,
and the sick mind emptying
doesn't take much time
to fill with madness:
there is an island . . . "*

Friends from the other war,
on this deserted and cloudy beach
I think of you as the day turns—
those who fell fighting and those who fell years after the
battle,
those who saw dawn through the mist of death
or, in wild solitude beneath the stars,
felt upon them the huge dark eyes
of total disaster;
and those again who prayed

ὅταν τὸ φλογισμένο ἀτσάλι πριόνιζε τὰ καράβια:
«Κύριε, βόηθα νὰ θυμόμαστε
πῶς ἔγινε τοῦτο τὸ φονικό·
τὴν ἁρπαγὴ τὸ δόλο τὴν ἰδιοτέλεια,
τὸ στέγνωμα τῆς ἀγάπης·
Κύριε, βόηθα νὰ τὰ ξεριζώσουμε...».

—Τώρα καλύτερα νὰ λησμονήσουμε πάνω σὲ τοῦτα τὰ χαλίκια·
δὲ φελᾶ νὰ μιλᾶμε·
τὴ γνώμη τῶν δυνατῶν ποιὸς θὰ μπορέσει νὰ τὴ γυρίσει;
ποιὸς θὰ μπορέσει ν' ἀκουστεῖ;
Καθένας χωριστὰ ὀνειρεύεται καὶ δὲν ἀκούει τὸ βραχνὰ τῶν ἄλλων.

—Ναί· ὅμως ὁ μαντατοφόρος τρέχει
κι' ὅσο μακρὺς κι' ἂν εἶναι ὁ δρόμος του, θὰ φέρει
σ' αὐτοὺς ποὺ γύρευαν ν' ἁλυσοδέσουν τὸν Ἑλλήσποντο
τὸ φοβερὸ μήνυμα τῆς Σαλαμίνας.

Φωνὴ Κυρίου ἐπὶ τῶν ὑδάτων.
Νῆσός τις ἔστι.

Σαλαμίνα, Κύπρος, Νοέμβρης '53

when flaming steel sawed the ships:
"Lord, help us to keep in mind
the causes of this slaughter:
greed, dishonesty, selfishness,
the desiccation of love;
Lord, help us to root these out . . . "*

— Now, on this pebbled beach, it's better to forget;
talking doesn't do any good;
who can change the attitude of those with power?
Who can make himself heard?
Each dreams separately without hearing anyone else's
    nightmare.

— True. But the messenger moves swiftly
and however long his journey, he'll bring
to those who tried to shackle the Hellespont
the terrible news from Salamis.

Voice of the Lord upon the waters.
There is an island.

Salamis, Cyprus, November '53

ΕΥΡΙΠΙΔΗΣ, ΑΘΗΝΑΙΟΣ

Γέρασε ἀνάμεσα στὴ φωτιὰ τῆς Τροίας
καὶ στὰ λατομεῖα τῆς Σικελίας.

Τοῦ ἄρεσαν οἱ σπηλιὲς στὴν ἀμμουδιὰ κι' οἱ ζωγραφιὲς τῆς
    θάλασσας.
Εἶδε τὶς φλέβες τῶν ἀνθρώπων
σὰν ἕνα δίχτυ τῶν θεῶν, ὅπου μᾶς πιάνουν σὰν τ' ἀγρίμια·
προσπάθησε νὰ τὸ τρυπήσει.
Εἴταν στρυφνός, οἱ φίλοι του εἴταν λίγοι·
ἦρθε ὁ καιρὸς καὶ τὸν σπαράξαν τὰ σκυλιά.

EURIPIDES THE ATHENIAN

He grew old between the fires of Troy
and the quarries of Sicily.

He liked seashore caves and pictures of the sea.
He saw man's veins
as a net the gods made to catch us in like wild beasts:
he tried to pierce it.
He was a sour man, his friends were few;
when the time came he was torn to pieces by dogs.*

͂ΕΓΚΩΜΗ

Εἴταν πλατὺς ὁ κάμπος καὶ στρωτός· ἀπὸ μακριὰ φαι-
νόνταν
τὸ γύρισμα χεριῶν ποὺ σκάβαν.
Στὸν οὐρανὸ τὰ σύννεφα πολλὲς καμπύλες, κάπου κάπου
μιὰ σάλπιγγα χρυσὴ καὶ ρόδινη· τὸ δείλι.
Στὸ λιγοστὸ χορτάρι καὶ στ' ἀγκάθια τριγυρίζαν
ψιλὲς ἀποβροχάρισσες ἀνάσες· θά 'χε βρέξει
πέρα στὶς ἄκρες τὰ βουνὰ ποὺ ἔπαιρναν χρῶμα.

Κι' ἐγὼ προχώρεσα πρὸς τοὺς ἀνθρώπους ποὺ δουλεύαν,
γυναῖκες κι' ἄντρες μὲ τ' ἀξίνια σὲ χαντάκια.
Εἴταν μιὰ πολιτεία παλιά· τειχιὰ δρόμοι καὶ σπίτια
ξεχώριζαν σὰν πετρωμένοι μυῶνες κυκλώπων,
ἡ ἀνατομία μιᾶς ξοδεμένης δύναμης κάτω ἀπ' τὸ μάτι
τοῦ ἀρχαιολόγου τοῦ ναρκοδότη ἢ τοῦ χειρούργου.
Φαντάσματα καὶ ὑφάσματα, χλιδὴ καὶ χείλια, χωνεμένα
καὶ τὰ παραπετάσματα τοῦ πόνου διάπλατα ἀνοιχτὰ
ἀφήνοντας νὰ φαίνεται γυμνὸς κι' ἀδιάφορος ὁ τάφος.

Κι' ἀνάβλεψα πρὸς τοὺς ἀνθρώπους ποὺ δουλεύαν
τοὺς τεντωμένους ὤμους καὶ τὰ μπράτσα ποὺ χτυπούσαν
μ' ἕνα ρυθμὸ βαρὺ καὶ γρήγορο τούτη τὴ νέκρα
σὰ νὰ περνοῦσε στὰ χαλάσματα ὁ τροχὸς τῆς μοίρας.

͂Αξαφνα περπατούσα καὶ δὲν περπατούσα

ENGOMI*

Broad the plain and level; from a distance you could see
arms circling as they dug.
In the sky, the clouds all curves, here and there
a trumpet golden and rose: the sunset.
In the meager grass and the thorns
stirred light after-shower air: it had rained
there on the peaks of the mountains that now took on color.

And I moved on towards those at work,
women and men digging with picks in trenches.
It was an ancient city; walls, streets, and houses
stood out like the petrified muscles of cyclopes,
the anatomy of spent strength under the eye
of the archaeologist, anaesthetist, or surgeon.
Phantoms and fabrics, luxury and lips, buried
and the curtains of pain spread wide open
to reveal, naked and indifferent, the tomb.

And I looked up towards those at work,
the stretched shoulders and the arms that struck
this dead silence with a rhythm heavy and swift
as though the wheel of fate were passing through the ruins.

Suddenly I was walking and did not walk

κοίταζα τὰ πετούμενα πουλιά, κι' εἴταν μαρμαρωμένα
κοίταζα τὸν αἰθέρα τ' οὐρανοῦ, κι' εἴτανε θαμπωμένος
κοίταζα τὰ κορμιὰ ποὺ πολεμούσαν, κι' εἶχαν μείνει
κι' ἀνάμεσό τους ἕνα πρόσωπο τὸ φῶς ν' ἀνηφορίζει.
Τὰ μαλλιὰ μαῦρα χύνουνταν στὴν τραχηλιά, τὰ φρύδια
εἴχανε τὸ φτερούγισμα τῆς χελιδόνας, τὰ ρουθούνια
καμαρωτὰ πάνω ἀπ' τὰ χείλια, καὶ τὸ σῶμα
ἔβγαινε ἀπὸ τὸ χεροπάλεμα ξεγυμνωμένο
μὲ τ' ἄγουρα βυζιὰ τῆς ὁδηγήτρας,
χορὸς ἀκίνητος.

Κι' ἐγὼ χαμήλωσα τὰ μάτια μου τριγύρω:
κορίτσια ζύμωναν, καὶ ζύμη δὲν ἀγγίζαν
γυναῖκες γνέθανε, τ' ἀδράχτια δὲ γυρίζαν
ἀρνιὰ ποτίζουνταν, κι' ἡ γλώσσα τους στεκόταν
πάνω ἀπὸ πράσινα νερὰ ποὺ ἔμοιαζαν κοιμισμένα
κι' ὁ ζευγὰς ἔμενε μ' ἀνάερη τὴ βουκέντρα.
Καὶ ξανακοίταξα τὸ σῶμα ἐκεῖνο ν' ἀνεβαίνει·
εἴχανε μαζευτεῖ πολλοί, μερμήγκια,
καὶ τὴ χτυπούσαν μὲ κοντάρια καὶ δὲν τὴ λαβώναν.
Τώρα ἡ κοιλιά της ἔλαμπε σὰν τὸ φεγγάρι
καὶ πίστευα πὼς ὁ οὐρανὸς εἴταν ἡ μήτρα
ποὺ τὴν ἐγέννησε καὶ τὴν ξανάπαιρνε, μάνα καὶ βρέφος.
Τὰ πόδια της μεῖναν ἀκόμη μαρμαρένια
καὶ χάθηκαν· μιὰ ἀνάληψη.
                                        Ὁ κόσμος
ξαναγινόταν ὅπως εἴταν, ὁ δικός μας
μὲ τὸν καιρὸ καὶ μὲ τὸ χῶμα.
                                        Ἀρώματα ἀπὸ σκίνο

I looked at the flying birds, and they had stopped stone dead
I looked at the sky's air, and it was full of wonder
I looked at the bodies laboring, and they were still
and among them the light bringing forth a face.
The black hair spilled over the collar, the eyebrows
had the motion of a swallow's wings, the nostrils
arched above the lips, and the body
emerged from the struggling arms stripped
with the unripe breasts of the Virgin,
a motionless dance.

And I lowered my eyes to look all around:
girls kneaded, but they didn't touch the dough
women spun, but the spindles didn't turn
lambs were being watered, but their tongues hung still
above green waters that seemed asleep
and the ploughman stood fixed with his staff poised.*
And I looked again at that body ascending;
people had gathered like ants,
and they struck her with lances but didn't wound her.
Her belly now shone like the moon
and I thought the sky was the womb
that bore her and now took her back, mother and child.
Her feet stayed marble still
and vanished: an Assumption.

                                        The world
became again as it had been, ours:
the world of time and earth.

                                        Aromas of terebinth

πήραν νὰ ξεκινήσουν στὶς παλιὲς πλαγιὲς τῆς μνήμης
κόρφοι μέσα στὰ φύλλα, χείλια ὑγρά·
κι' ὅλα στεγνώσαν μονομιᾶς στὴν πλατωσιὰ τοῦ κάμπου
στῆς πέτρας τὴν ἀπόγνωση στὴ δύναμη τὴ φαγωμένη
στὸν ἄδειο τόπο μὲ τὸ λιγοστὸ χορτάρι καὶ τ' ἀγκάθια
ὅπου γλιστροῦσε ξέγνοιαστο ἕνα φίδι,
ὅπου ξοδεύουνε πολὺ καιρὸ γιὰ νὰ πεθάνουν.

began to stir on the old slopes of memory
breasts among leaves, lips moist;
and all went dry at once on the length of the plain,
in the stone's despair, in eroded power,
in that empty place with the meager grass and the thorns
where a snake slithered heedless,
where they take a long time to die.

RHYMED POEMS
(1924-1953)*

ΣΤΡΟΦΗ

Σὴν χάριν

TURNING POINT

Σὴν χάριν

ΚΟΧΥΛΙΑ, ΣΥΝΝΕΦΑ

Μὰ ὅλα γιὰ μένα σφάλασι καὶ πάσιν ἄνω κάτω,
γιὰ μὲ ξαναγεννήθηκεν ἡ φύση τῶν πραμάτω.

Ο ΕΡΩΤΟΚΡΙΤΟΣ

SHELLS, CLOUDS

But everything went wrong for me and upside down,
the nature of things was reborn for me.

*THE EROTOKRITOS**

ΣΤΡΟΦΗ

Στιγμή, σταλμένη ἀπὸ ἕνα χέρι
ποὺ εἶχα τόσο ἀγαπήσει
μὲ πρόφταξες ἴσια στὴ δύση
σὰ μαῦρο περιστέρι.

Ὁ δρόμος ἄσπριζε μπροστά μου,
ἁπαλὸς ἀχνὸς ὕπνου
στὸ γέρμα ἑνὸς μυστικοῦ δείπνου...
Στιγμὴ σπυρὶ τῆς ἄμμου,

ποὺ κράτησες μονάχη σου ὅλη
τὴν τραγικὴ κλεψύδρα
βουβή, σὰ νά εἶχε δεῖ τὴν Ὕδρα
στὸ οὐράνιο περιβόλι.

TURNING POINT

Moment, sent by a hand
I had loved so much,
you reached me just at sunset
like a black pigeon.

The road whitened before me,
soft breath of sleep
at the close of a last supper . . .
Moment, grain of sand,

alone you kept the whole
tragic clepsydra dumb,
as though it had seen the Hydra*
in the heavenly garden.

ΑΡΓΑ ΜΙΛΟΥΣΕΣ

’Αργὰ μιλοῦσες μπρὸς στὸν ἥλιο
καὶ τώρα εἶναι σκοτάδι
κι’ εἴσουν τῆς μοίρας μου τὸ ὑφάδι
σύ, ποὺ θὰ λέγαν Μπίλιω.

Πέντε στιγμές· καὶ τί ἔχει γίνει
γύρω στὴν οἰκουμένη;
Μιὰ ἄγραφτη ἀγάπη ξεγραμμένη
κι’ ἕνα στεγνὸ λαγήνι

κι’ εἶναι σκοτάδι... Ποῦ εἶναι ὁ τόπος
κι’ ἡ γύμνια σου ὣς τὴ μέση,
θεέ μου, κι’ ἡ πιὸ ἀκριβή μου θέση
καὶ τῆς ψυχῆς σου ὁ τρόπος!

SLOWLY YOU SPOKE

Slowly you spoke before the sun
and now it's dark
and you were my fate's woof
you, whom they'd call Billio.

Five seconds; and what's happened
in the wide world?
An unwritten love rubbed out
and a dry pitcher

and it's dark . . . Where is the place
and your nakedness to the waist,
my God, and my favorite spot
and the style of your soul!

Η ΛΥΠΗΜΕΝΗ

Στὴν πέτρα τῆς ὑπομονῆς
κάθησες πρὸς τὸ βράδι
μὲ τοῦ ματιοῦ σου τὸ μαυράδι
δείχνοντας πὼς πονεῖς·

κι' εἶχες στὰ χείλια τὴ γραμμὴ
ποὺ εἶναι γυμνὴ καὶ τρέμει
σὰν ἡ ψυχὴ γίνεται ἀνέμη
καὶ δέουνται οἱ λυγμοί·

κι' εἶχες στὸ νοῦ σου τὸ σκοπὸ
ποὺ ξεκινᾶ τὸ δάκρυ
κι' είσουν κορμὶ ποὺ ἀπὸ τὴν ἄκρη
γυρίζει στὸν καρπό·

μὰ τῆς καρδιᾶς σου ὁ σπαραγμὸς
δὲ βόγγηξε κι' ἐγίνη
τὸ νόημα ποὺ στὸν κόσμο δίνει
ἔναστρος οὐρανός.

THE SORROWING GIRL

On the stone of patience
you sat at nightfall,
the black of your eye
revealing your pain;

on your lips the line
that's naked and trembles
when the soul spins
and sobs plead;

in your mind the motive
that starts tears
and you were a body that from the verge
returns to fruitfulness;

but your heart's anguish
was unmoaning, became
what gives the world
a starfilled sky.

ΑΥΤΟΚΙΝΗΤΟ

Στὴ δημοσιὰ σὰν ἀγκαλιὰ
δίκλωνη ἑνὸς διαβήτη,
τοῦ ἀγέρα δάχτυλα στὴ χήτη
καὶ μίλια στὴν κοιλιά,

οἱ δυό μας φεύγαμε ἀδειανοὶ
βιτσιὰ γιὰ τὸ ἤπιο βλέμμα·
φτιασίδι ὁ νοῦς, φτιασίδι τὸ αἷμα
γυμνοί! γυμνοί! γυμνοί!

... Σ' ἕνα κρεβάτι μ' ἀψηλὸ
κι' ἀλαφρὺ προσκεφάλι
πῶς ξεγλιστροῦσε ἀλάργα ἡ ζάλη
σὰν ψάρι στὸ γιαλό...

Στὴ δίκλωνη τὴ δημοσιὰ
φεύγαμε κορμιὰ μόνο
μὲ τὶς καρδιὲς στὸν κάθε κλῶνο
χώρια, ζερβὰ-δεξιά.

AUTOMOBILE

On the highway like the forked embrace
of a pair of compasses,
fingers of wind in the hair
and miles in the belly,

the two of us were leaving, empty,
whiplash for the mild gaze;
the mind make-up, the blood make-up
naked, naked, naked!

. . . On a bed, the pillow
high and light,
how the dizziness slipped away
like a fish in the sea . . .

On the two-branched highway
we were leaving, bodies only,
with our hearts on each branch
separate, one right, one left.

ΑΡΝΗΣΗ

Στὸ περιγιάλι τὸ κρυφὸ
κι᾿ ἄσπρο σὰν περιστέρι
διψάσαμε τὸ μεσημέρι·
μὰ τὸ νερὸ γλυφό.

Πάνω στὴν ἄμμο τὴν ξανθὴ
γράψαμε τ᾿ ὄνομά της·
ὡραῖα ποὺ φύσηξεν ὁ μπάτης
καὶ σβήστηκε ἡ γραφή.

Μὲ τί καρδιά, μὲ τί πνοή,
τί πόθους καὶ τί πάθος
πήραμε τὴ ζωή μας· λάθος!
κι᾿ ἀλλάξαμε ζωή.

DENIAL

On the secret seashore
white like a pigeon
we thirsted at noon:
but the water was brackish.

On the golden sand
we wrote her name;
but the sea-breeze blew
and the writing vanished.

With what spirit, what heart,
what desire and passion
we lived our life: a mistake!
So we changed our life.

ΟΙ ΣΥΝΤΡΟΦΟΙ ΣΤΟΝ ΑΔΗ

νήπιοι, οἳ κατὰ βοῦς Ὑπερίονος Ἠελίοιο
ἤσθιον· αὐτὰρ ὁ τοῖσιν ἀφείλετο νόστιμον ἦμαρ.

ΟΔΥΣΣΕΙΑ

Ἀφοῦ μᾶς μέναν παξιμάδια
τί κακοκεφαλιὰ
νὰ φᾶμε στὴν ἀκρογιαλιὰ
τοῦ Ἥλιου τ' ἀργὰ γελάδια

ποὺ τὸ καθένα κι' ἕνα κάστρο
γιὰ νὰ τὸ πολεμᾶς
σαράντα χρόνους καὶ νὰ πᾶς
νὰ γίνεις ἥρωας κι' ἄστρο!

Πεινούσαμε στῆς γῆς τὴν πλάτη,
σὰ φάγαμε καλὰ
πέσαμε ἐδῶ στὰ χαμηλὰ
ἀνίδεοι καὶ χορτάτοι.

THE COMPANIONS IN HADES

fools, who ate the cattle of Helios Hyperion;
but he deprived them of the day of their return.

*ODYSSEY**

Since we still had some hardtack
what stupidity
to eat while on shore
the Sun's slow cattle,

for each was a castle
you'd have to battle
forty years and become
a hero and a star!

On the earth's back we hungered,
but when we'd eaten well
we fell to these lower regions
mindless and satisfied.

FOG

Say it with a ukulele

«Πές της το μ' ἕνα γιουκαλίλι...»
γρινιάζει κάποιος φωνογράφος·
πές μου τί νὰ τῆς πῶ, Χριστέ μου,
τώρα συνήθισα μονάχος.

Μὲ φυσαρμόνικες πού σφίγγουν
φτωχοὶ μὴ βρέξει καὶ μὴ στάξει
ὅλο καὶ κράζουν τοὺς ἀγγέλους
κι' εἶναι οἱ ἀγγέλοι τους μαράζι.

Κι' οἱ ἀγγέλοι ἀνοίξαν τὰ φτερά τους
μὰ χάμω χνώτισαν ὁμίχλες
δόξα σοι ὁ θεός, ἀλλιῶς θὰ πιάναν
τὶς φτωχιές μας ψυχὲς σὰν τσίχλες.

Κι' εἶναι ἡ ζωὴ ψυχρὴ ψαρίσια
—Ἔτσι ζεῖς; — Ναί! Τί θὲς νὰ κάνω·
τόσοι καὶ τόσοι εἶναι οἱ πνιμένοι
κάτω στῆς θάλασσας τὸν πάτο.

Τὰ δέντρα μοιάζουν μὲ κοράλλια
πού κάπου ξέχασαν τὸ χρῶμα
τὰ κάρα μοιάζουν μὲ καράβια
πού βούλιαξαν καὶ μεῖναν μόνα...

FOG

*Say it with a ukulele**

"Say it with a ukulele. . ."
grumbles some gramophone;
Christ, tell me what to say to her
now that I'm used to my loneliness?

With accordions squeezed
by well-dressed beggars
they call on the angels
and their angels are hell.

And the angels opened their wings
but below the mists condensed
thank God, for otherwise they'd catch
our poor souls like thrushes.

And life's cold as a fish
—Is that how you live?—Yes, how else?
So many are the drowned
down on the sea's bed.

Trees are like corals
their color gone,
carts are like ships
sunken and lonely. . .

«Πές της το μ' ένα γιουκαλίλι...»
Λόγια γιὰ λόγια, κι' ἄλλα λόγια ;
'Αγάπη, ποῦ 'ναι ἡ ἐκκλησιά σου
βαρέθηκα πιὰ στὰ μετόχια.

"Α ! νά 'ταν ἡ ζωή μας ἴσια
πῶς θὰ τὴν παίρναμε κατόπι
μ' ἀλλιῶς ἡ μοίρα τὸ βουλήθη
πρέπει νὰ στρίψεις σὲ μιὰ κόχη.

Καὶ ποιά εἶν' ἡ κόχη ; Ποιὸς τὴν ξέρει ;
Τὰ φῶτα φέγγουνε τὰ φῶτα
ἄχνα ! δὲ μᾶς μιλοῦν οἱ πάχνες
κι' ἔχουμε τὴν ψυχὴ στὰ δόντια.

Τάχα παρηγοριὰ θὰ βροῦμε ;
'Η μέρα φόρεσε τὴ νύχτα
ὅλα εἶναι νύχτα, ὅλα εἶναι νύχτα
κάτι θὰ βροῦμε ζήτα - ζήτα...

«Πές της το μ' ένα γιουκαλίλι...»
Βλέπω τὰ κόκκινά της νύχια
μπρὸς στὴ φωτιὰ πῶς θὰ γυαλίζουν
καὶ τὴ θυμᾶμαι μὲ τὸ βῆχα.

Λονδίνο, Χριστούγεννα 1924

"Say it with a ukulele. . ."
Words for words, and more words?
Love, where's your church,
I'm tired of this hermitage.

Ah, were life but straight
how we'd live it then!
But it's fated otherwise,
you have to turn in a small corner.

And what corner is it? Who knows?
Lights shine on lights
pallidly, the hoarfrosts are dumb,
and our soul's in our teeth.

Will we find consolation?
Day put on night—
everything is night, everything is night—
we'll find something, if we search. . .

"Say it with a ukulele. . ."
I see her red nails—
how they must glow in firelight—
and I recall her when I cough.

London, Christmas 1924

ΤΟ ΥΦΟΣ ΜΙΑΣ ΜΕΡΑΣ

We plainly saw that not a soul lived in that fated vessel!

EDGAR ALLAN POE

Τὸ ὕφος μιᾶς μέρας ποὺ ζήσαμε πρὶν δέκα χρόνια σὲ ξένο
τόπο
ὁ αἰθέρας μιᾶς παμπάλαιης στιγμῆς ποὺ φτερούγισε κι᾽ ἐχάθη σὰν ἄγγελος Κυρίου
ἡ φωνὴ μιᾶς γυναίκας λησμονημένης μὲ τόση φρόνηση καὶ
μὲ τόσο κόπο·
ἕνα τέλος ἀπαρηγόρητο, μαρμαρωμένο βασίλεμα κάποιου
Σεπτεμβρίου.

Καινούργια σπίτια σκονισμένες κλινικὲς ἐξανθηματικὰ παράθυρα φερετροποιεῖα...
Συλλογίστηκε κανένας τί ὑποφέρει ἕνας εὐαίσθητος φαρμακοποιὸς ποὺ διανυχτερεύει;
᾽Ακαταστασία στὴν κάμαρα: συρτάρια παράθυρα πόρτες
ἀνοίγουν τὸ στόμα τους σὰν ἄγρια θηρία·
ἕνας ἀπαυδισμένος ἄνθρωπος ρίχνει τὰ χαρτιὰ ψάχνει
ἀστρονομίζεται γυρεύει.

Στενοχωριέται: ἃ χτυπήσουν τὴν πόρτα ποιὸς θ᾽ ἀνοίξει;
῎Αν ἀνοίξει βιβλίο ποιὸν θὰ κοιτάξει; ῎Αν ἀνοίξει τὴν
ψυχή του ποιὸς θὰ κοιτάξει; ῾Αλυσίδα.
Ποῦ ᾽ναι ἡ ἀγάπη ποὺ κόβει τὸν καιρὸ μονοκόμματα στὰ
δυὸ καὶ τὸν ἀποσβολώνει;

THE MOOD OF A DAY

We plainly saw that not a soul lived in that fated vessel!
EDGAR ALLAN POE*

The mood of a day that we lived ten years ago in a foreign country
the airy spirit of an ancient moment that took on wings and vanished like an angel of the Lord
the voice of a woman forgotten with such care and such pain
an end inconsolable, the marble setting of some September.

New houses dusty clinics exanthematic windows coffin-shops . . .
Has anyone considered the suffering of a sensitive pharmacist on night duty?
The room in a mess: drawers windows doors open their mouths like wild animals;
a tired man lays out the cards, searches, astrologizes, scrutinizes.

He worries: if they knock at the door who will open it? If he opens a book whom will he look at? If he opens his soul who will look? Chain.
Where is love that with one stroke cuts time in two and stuns it?

Λόγια μονάχα καὶ χειρονομίες. Μονότροπος μονόλογος
μπροστὰ σ' ἕναν καθρέφτη κάτω ἀπὸ μιὰ ρυτίδα.
Σὰ μιὰ στάλα μελάνι σὲ μαντήλι ἡ πλήξη ἁπλώνει.

Πέθαναν ὅλοι μέσα στὸ καραβι, μὰ τὸ καράβι ἀκολουθάει
τὸ στοχασμό του ποὺ ἄρχισε σὰν ἄνοιξε ἀπὸ τὸ λιμάνι
πῶς μεγαλώσαν τὰ νύχια τοῦ καπετάνιου... κι' ὁ ναύκληρος
ἀξούριστος πού 'χε τρεῖς ἐρωμένες σὲ κάθε σκάλα...
Ἡ θάλασσα φουσκώνει ἀργά, τ' ἄρμενα καμαρώνουν κι'
ἡ μέρα πάει νὰ γλυκάνει.
Τρία δελφίνια μαυρολογοῦν γυαλίζοντας, χαμογελᾶ ἡ γοργόνα, κι' ἕνας ναύτης γνέφει ξεχασμένος στὴ γάμπια καβάλα.

Words only and gestures. A monotonous monologue in front of a mirror under a wrinkle.
Like a drop of ink on a handkerchief, the boredom spreads.

Everyone in the ship is dead, but the ship follows the purpose with which it began when it put out from the harbor
how the captain's nails grew . . . and the boatswain, who had three mistresses in every port, unshaven . . .
The sea swells slowly, the rigging fills with pride, and the day is turning mild.
Three dolphins flash black, glistening; the mermaid smiles, and a forgotten sailor waves astride the yardarm.

ΡΟΥΚΕΤΑ

Δὲν εἶναι οὔτε ἡ θάλασσα
δὲν εἶναι οὔτε ὁ κόσμος
τὸ γαλάζιο αὐτὸ φῶς
στὰ δάχτυλά μας

κάτω ἀπὸ τὰ βλέφαρα
χίλιες ἀντένες
ψάχνουν ζαλισμένες
τὸν οὐρανὸ

κόκκινο γαρούφαλο
μοναχὸ στὴ γλάστρα
στάθηκες σὰν ἔγραφα
μπρός μου σὰν ἀγάπη

εἴταν μιὰ ἐλαφίνα
κίτρινη σὰ θειάφι
κι' εἴταν ἕνας πύργος
ἀπὸ χρυσάφι

μέτρησαν τὰ χρόνια τους
πέντε κοράκια
μάλωσαν καὶ σκόρπισαν
σὰν πεντάλφα

ROCKET

It isn't the sea
it isn't the world
this blue light
on our fingers

under the eyelids
a thousand antennae
grope giddily
to find the sky

red carnation
alone in your vase
you stood as I wrote
like love before me

there was a deer
yellow as sulphur
there was a tower
built of gold

five crows
counted their years
quarrelled and scattered
like a pentacle

τὰ μαλλιὰ τῆς ὄμορφης
τ' ἄσπρισαν τὰ κρίνα
στὸ κορμὶ τῆς ὄμορφης
ἔγραψα βιβλία.

Δὲν μπορῶ νὰ ζῶ
ὅλο μὲ παγόνια
μήτε νὰ ταξιδεύω μερόνυχτα
μέσα στὰ μάτια τῆς γοργόνας.

lilies whitened
the beloved's hair
on the beloved's body
I wrote whole books.

I can't live
only with peacocks,
nor travel always
in the mermaid's eyes.

ΡΙΜΑ

Χείλια, φρουροὶ τῆς ἀγάπης μου ποὺ εἶταν νὰ σβήσει
χέρια, δεσμὰ τῆς νιότης μου ποὺ εἶταν νὰ φύγει
χρῶμα προσώπου χαμένου κάπου στὴ φύση
δέντρα.. πουλιὰ.. κυνήγι..

Κορμί, μαῦρο μὲς στὸ λιοπύρι σὰν τὸ σταφύλι
κορμὶ πλούσιο καράβι μου, ποῦ ταξιδεύεις;
Εἶναι ἡ ὥρα ποὺ πνίγεται τὸ δείλι
καὶ κουράζομαι ψάχνοντας τὰ ἐρέβη...

(Ἡ ζωή μας κάθε μέρα λιγοστεύει).

RHYME

Lips, guardians of my love that was to fade
hands, bonds of my youth that was to go
color of a face lost in nature somewhere
trees . . . birds . . . hunting . . .

Body, black in the sun's heat like a grape
body, my rich ship, where are you traveling?
It's the hour when twilight drowns
and I tire searching the darkness . . .

(Our life shrinks every day).

ΕΡΩΤΙΚΟΣ ΛΟΓΟΣ

Ἔστι δὲ φῦλον ἐν ἀνθρώποισι ματαιότατον,
ὅστις αἰσχύνων ἐπιχώρια παπταίνει τὰ πόρσω,
μεταμώνια θηρεύων ἀκράντοις ἐλπίσιν.

ΠΙΝΔΑΡΟΣ

EROTIKOS LOGOS

There is a most vain class among men which, despising ordinary things, fixes its eyes on distant things, pursuing empty air with idle hopes . . .

PINDAR*

Α′

Ρόδο τῆς μοίρας, γύρευες νὰ βρεῖς νὰ μᾶς πληγώσεις
μὰ ἔσκυβες σὰν τὸ μυστικὸ ποὺ πάει νὰ λυτρωθεῖ
κι᾽ εἴταν ὡραῖο τὸ πρόσταγμα ποὺ δέχτηκες νὰ δώσεις
κι᾽ εἴταν τὸ χαμογέλιο σου σὰν ἕτοιμο σπαθί.

Τοῦ κύκλου σου τὸ ἀνέβασμα ζωντάνευε τὴ χτίση
ἀπὸ τ᾽ ἀγκάθι σου ἔφευγε τοῦ δρόμου ὁ στοχασμὸς
ἡ ὁρμή μας γλυκοχάραζε γυμνὴ νὰ σ᾽ ἀποχτήσει
ὁ κόσμος εἴταν εὔκολος· ἕνας ἁπλὸς παλμός.

Β′

Τὰ μυστικὰ τῆς θάλασσας ξεχνιοῦνται στ᾽ ἀκρογιάλια
ἡ σκοτεινάγρα τοῦ βυθοῦ ξεχνιέται στὸν ἀφρό·
λάμπουνε ξάφνου πορφυρὰ τῆς μνήμης τὰ κοράλλια..
Ὢ μὴν ταράξεις.. πρόσεξε ν᾽ ἀκούσεις τ᾽ ἀλαφρὸ

ξεκίνημά της... τ᾽ ἄγγιξες τὸ δέντρο μὲ τὰ μῆλα
τὸ χέρι ἁπλώθη κι᾽ ἡ κλωστὴ δείχνει καὶ σὲ ὁδηγεῖ..
Ὤ σκοτεινὸ ἀνατρίχιασμα στὴ ρίζα καὶ στὰ φύλλα
νά ᾽σουν ἐσὺ ποὺ θά ᾽φερνες τὴν ξεχασμένη αὐγή!

I

Rose of fate, you looked for ways to wound us
and yet you bent like the secret about to be released
and the command you chose to give us was beautiful
and your smile was like a ready sword.

The ascent of your cycle livened creation
from your thorn emerged the way's thought
our impulse dawned naked to possess you
the world was easy: a simple pulsation.

II

The secrets of the sea are forgotten on the shores
the darkness of the depths is forgotten on the surf;
the corals of memory suddenly shine purple . . .
O do not stir . . . listen to hear its light

motion . . . you touched the tree with the apples
the hand reached out, the thread points the way and guides
    you . . .
O dark shivering in the roots and the leaves
if it were but you who would bring the forgotten dawn!

Στὸν κάμπο τοῦ ἀποχωρισμοῦ νὰ ξανανθίζουν κρίνα
μέρες ν' ἀνοίγουνται ὥριμες, οἱ ἀγκάλες τ' οὐρανοῦ
νὰ φέγγουν στὸ ἀντηλάρισμα τὰ μάτια μόνο ἐκεῖνα
ἁγνὴ ἡ ψυχὴ νὰ γράφεται σὰν τὸ τραγούδι αὐλοῦ..

Ἡ νύχτα νά 'ταν ποὺ ἔκλεισε τὰ μάτια; Μένει ἀθάλη,
σὰν ἀπὸ δοξαριοῦ νευρὰ μένει πνιχτὸ βουητό,
μιὰ στάχτη κι' ἕνας ἴλιγγος στὸ μαῦρο γυρογιάλι
κι' ἕνα πυκνὸ φτερούγισμα στὴν εἰκασία κλειστό.

Ρόδο τοῦ ἀνέμου, γνώριζες μὰ ἀνέγνωρους μᾶς πῆρες
τὴν ὥρα ποὺ θεμέλιωνε γιοφύρια ὁ λογισμὸς
νὰ πλέξουνε τὰ δάχτυλα καὶ νὰ διαβοῦν δυὸ μοῖρες
καὶ νὰ χυθοῦν στὸ χαμηλὸ κι' ἀναπαμένο φῶς.

Γ'

Ὦ σκοτεινὸ ἀνατρίχιασμα στὴ ρίζα καὶ στὰ φύλλα!
Πρόβαλε ἀνάστημα ἄγρυπνο στὸ πλῆθος τῆς σιωπῆς
σήκωσε τὸ κεφάλι ἀπὸ τὰ χέρια τὰ καμπύλα
τὸ θέλημά σου νὰ γενεῖ καὶ νὰ μοῦ ξαναπεῖς

τὰ λόγια ποὺ ἄγγιζαν καὶ σμίγαν τὸ αἷμα σὰν ἀγκάλη·
κι' ἂς γείρει ὁ πόθος σου βαθὺς σὰν ἴσκιος καρυδιᾶς
καὶ νὰ μᾶς πλημμυράει μὲ τῶν μαλλιῶν σου τὴ σπατάλη
ἀπὸ τὸ χνούδι τοῦ φιλιοῦ στὰ φύλλα τῆς καρδιᾶς.

May lilies blossom again on the meadow of separation
may days open mature, the embrace of the heavens,*
may those eyes alone shine in the glare
the pure soul be outlined like the song of a flute.

Was it night that shut its eyes? Ashes remain,
as from the string of a bow a choked hum remains,
ash and dizziness on the black shore
and dense fluttering imprisoned in surmise.

Rose of the wind, you knew but took us unknowing
at a time when thought was building bridges
so that fingers would knit and two fates pass by
and spill into the low and rested light.

III

O dark shivering in the roots and the leaves!
Come forth sleepless form in the gathering silence
raise your head from your curved arms
so that your will be done and you tell me again

the words that touched and merged with the blood like an
embrace;
and let your desire, deep like the shade of a walnut tree,
bend
and flood us with your lavish hair
from the down of the kiss to the leaves of the heart.

Χαμήλωναν τὰ μάτια σου κι᾽ εἶχες τὸ χαμογέλιο
ποὺ ἀνιστορούσαν ταπεινὰ ζωγράφοι ἀλλοτινοί.
Λησμονημένο ἀνάγνωσμα σ᾽ ἕνα παλιὸ εὐαγγέλιο
τὸ μίλημά σου ἀνάσαινε κι᾽ ἡ ἀνάλαφρη φωνή:

«Εἶναι τὸ πέρασμα τοῦ χρόνου σιγαλὸ κι᾽ ἀπόκοσμο
κι᾽ ὁ πόνος ἁπαλὰ μὲς στὴν ψυχή μου λάμνει
χαράζει ἡ αὐγὴ τὸν οὐρανό, τ᾽ ὄνειρο μένει ἀπόντιστο
κι᾽ εἶναι σὰ νὰ διαβαίνουν μυρωμένοι θάμνοι.

Μὲ τοῦ ματιοῦ τ᾽ ἀλάφιασμα, μὲ τοῦ κορμιοῦ τὸ ρόδισμα
ξυπνοῦν καὶ κατεβαίνουν σμάρι περιστέρια
μὲ περιπλέκει χαμηλὸ τὸ κυκλωτὸ φτερούγισμα
ἀνθρώπινο ἄγγιγμα στὸν κόρφο μου τ᾽ ἀστέρια.

Τὴν ἀκοή μου ὡς νά ᾽σμιξε κοχύλι βουίζει ὁ ἀντίδικος
μακρινὸς κι᾽ ἀξεδιάλυτος τοῦ κόσμου ὁ θρῆνος
μά εἶναι στιγμὲς καὶ σβήνουνται καὶ βασιλεύει δίκλωνος
ὁ λογισμὸς τοῦ πόθου μου, μόνος ἐκεῖνος.

Λὲς κι᾽ εἶχα ἀναστηθεῖ γυμνὴ σὲ μιὰ παρμένη θύμηση
σὰν ἦρθες γνώριμος καὶ ξένος, ἀκριβέ μου
νὰ μοῦ χαρίσεις γέρνοντας τὴν ἀπέραντη λύτρωση
ποὺ γύρευα ἀπὸ τὰ γοργὰ σεῖστρα τοῦ ἀνέμου...»

Τὸ ραγισμένο ἡλιόγερμα λιγόστεψε κι᾽ ἐχάθη
κι᾽ ἔμοιαζε πλάνη νὰ ζητᾶς τὰ δῶρα τ᾽ οὐρανοῦ.
Χαμήλωναν τὰ μάτια σου. Τοῦ φεγγαριοῦ τ᾽ ἀγκάθι
βλάστησε καὶ φοβήθηκες τοὺς ἴσκιους τοῦ βουνοῦ.

You lowered your eyes and you had the smile
that masters of another time humbly painted.
A forgotten reading from an ancient gospel
breathed your words and your light voice:

"The passing of time is soft and unworldly
and pain floats lightly in my soul
dawn breaks in the heavens, the dream remains afloat
and it's as if scented shrubs were passing.

"With my eyes' startling, with my body's blush
a flock of doves awakens and descends
their low, circling flight entangles me
the stars are a human touch on my breast.

"I hear, as in a sea shell, the distant
adverse and confused lament of the world
but these are moments only, they disappear,
and the two-branched thought of my desire reigns alone.

"It seemed I'd risen naked in a vanished recollection
when you came, strange and familiar, my beloved
to grant me, bending, the boundless deliverance
I was seeking from the wind's quick rattle . . ."

The broken sunset declined and was gone
and it seemed a delusion to ask for the gifts of the sky.
You lowered your eyes. The moon's thorn blossomed
and you became afraid of the mountain's shadows.

..Μὲς στὸν καθρέφτη ἡ ἀγάπη μας, πῶς πάει καὶ λιγοστεύει
μέσα στὸν ὕπνο τὰ ὄνειρα, σκολειὸ τῆς λησμονιᾶς
μέσα στὰ βάθη τοῦ καιροῦ, πῶς ἡ καρδιὰ στενεύει
καὶ χάνεται στὸ λίκνισμα μιᾶς ξένης ἀγκαλιᾶς..

Δ′

Δυὸ φίδια ὡραῖα κι᾿ ἀλαργινά, τοῦ χωρισμοῦ πλοκάμια
σέρνουνται καὶ γυρεύουνται στὴ νύχτα τῶν δεντρῶν,
γιὰ μιὰν ἀγάπη μυστικὴ σ᾿ ἀνεύρετα θολάμια
ἀκοίμητα γυρεύουνται δὲν πίνουν καὶ δὲν τρῶν.

Μὲ γύρους μὲ λυγίσματα κι᾿ ἡ ἀχόρταγή τους γνώμη
κλώθει, πληθαίνει, στρίβει, ἁπλώνει κρίκους στὸ κορμὶ
ποὺ κυβερνοῦν ἀμίλητοι τοῦ ἔναστρου θόλου οἱ νόμοι
καὶ τοῦ ἀναδεύουν τὴν πυρὴ κι᾿ ἀσίγαστη ἀφορμή.

Τὸ δάσος στέκει ριγηλὸ τῆς νύχτας ἀντιστύλι
κι᾿ εἶναι ἡ σιγὴ τάσι ἀργυρὸ ὅπου πέφτουν οἱ στιγμὲς
ἀντίχτυποι ξεχωρισμένοι, ὁλόκληροι, μιὰ σμίλη
προσεχτικὴ ποὺ δέχουνται πελεκητὲς γραμμές..

Αὐγάζει ξάφνου τὸ ἄγαλμα. Μὰ τὰ κορμιὰ ἔχουν σβήσει
στὴ θάλασσα στὸν ἄνεμο στὸν ἥλιο στὴ βροχή.
Ἔτσι γεννιοῦνται οἱ ὀμορφιὲς ποὺ μᾶς χαρίζει ἡ φύση
μὰ ποιὸς νὰ ξέρει ἂν πέθανε στὸν κόσμο μιὰ ψυχή.

. . In the mirror how our love diminishes
in sleep the dreams, school of forgetfulness
in the depths of time, how the heart contracts
and vanishes in the rocking of a foreign embrace . .

IV

Two serpents, beautiful, apart, tentacles of separation
crawl and search, in the night of the trees,
for a secret love in hidden retreats;
sleepless they search, they neither drink nor eat.

Circling, twisting, their insatiable intent
spins, multiplies, turns, spreads rings on the body
which the laws of the starry dome silently govern,
stirring its hot, irrepressible frenzy.

The forest stands as a shivering pillar for night
and the silence is a silver cup where moments fall
echoes distinct, whole, a careful chisel
sustained by carved lines . . .

The statue suddenly dawns. But the bodies have vanished
in the sea in the wind in the sun in the rain.
So the beauties nature grants us are born
but who knows if a soul hasn't died in the world.

Στὴ φαντασία θὰ γύριζαν τὰ χωρισμένα φίδια
(Τὸ δάσος λάμπει μὲ πουλιὰ βλαστοὺς καὶ ροδαμούς)
μένουν ἀκόμη τὰ σγουρὰ γυρέματά τους, ἴδια
τοῦ κύκλου τὰ γυρίσματα ποὺ φέρνουν τοὺς καημούς.

Ε΄

Ποῦ πῆγε ἡ μέρα ἡ δίκοπη ποὺ εἶχε τὰ πάντα ἀλλάξει;
Δὲ θὰ βρεθεῖ ἕνας ποταμὸς νά 'ναι γιὰ μᾶς πλωτός;
Δὲ θὰ βρεθεῖ ἕνας οὐρανὸς τὴ δρόσο νὰ σταλάξει
γιὰ τὴν ψυχὴ ποὺ νάρκωσε κι' ἀνάθρεψε ὁ λωτός;

Στὴν πέτρα τῆς ὑπομονῆς προσμένουμε τὸ θᾶμα
ποὺ ἀνοίγει τὰ ἐπουράνϊα κι' εἶν' ὅλα βολετὰ
προσμένουμε τὸν ἄγγελο σὰν τὸ πανάρχαιο δρᾶμα
τὴν ὥρα ποὺ τοῦ δειλινοῦ χάνουνται τ' ἀνοιχτὰ

τριαντάφυλλα... Ρόδο ἄλικο τοῦ ἀνέμου καὶ τῆς μοίρας,
μόνο στὴ μνήμη ἀπόμεινες, ἕνας βαρὺς ρυθμὸς
ρόδο τῆς νύχτας πέρασες, τρικύμισμα πορφύρας
τρικύμισμα τῆς θάλασσας... Ὁ κόσμος εἶναι ἁπλός.

Ἀθήνα, Ὀχτώβρης '29 - Δεκέμβρης '30

The parted serpents must have circled in fantasy
(the forest glitters with birds, shoots, blossoms)
their wavy searching still remains,
like the turnings of the cycle that bring sorrow.

V

Where is the double-edged day that had changed everything?
Won't there be a navigable river for us?
Won't there be a sky to drop dew
for the soul benumbed and nourished by the lotus?

On the stone of patience we wait for the miracle
that opens the heavens and makes all things possible
we wait for the herald as in the ancient drama
at the moment when the open roses of twilight

disappear . . . Red rose of the wind and of fate,
you remained in memory only, a heavy rhythm
rose of the night, you passed, undulating purple
undulation of the sea . . . The world is simple.

Athens, October '29–December '30

Η ΣΤΕΡΝΑ

Στὸ Γιῶργο Ἀποστολίδη

Βρέθηκα στὴν ἀνάγκη νὰ βάλω τὸ νοσοκομεῖο τοῦ Δὸν Χουὰν Ταβέρα μὲ τὴ μορφὴ μοντέλου, γιατὶ ὄχι μόνο ἐρχότανε νὰ σκεπάσει τὴν πύλη τοῦ Βισάγκρα, ἀλλὰ καὶ ὁ θόλος του ἀνέβαινε μὲ τρόπο ποὺ ξεπερνοῦσε τὴν πόλη, κι᾽ ἔτσι μιὰ ποὺ τό ᾽βαλα σὰ μοντέλο καὶ τὸ μετακίνησα ἀπὸ τὸν τόπο του, μοῦ φαίνεται προτιμότερο νὰ δείξω τὴν πρόσοψή του παρὰ τὶς ἄλλες του μεριές. Ὅσο γιὰ τὴ θέση του μέσα στὴν πόλη φαίνεται στὸ χάρτη.

ΔΟΜΗΝΙΚΟΣ ΘΕΟΤΟΚΟΠΟΥΛΟΣ

THE CISTERN

To George Apostolidis

I found I had to put the hospital of Don Juan Tavera in the form of a model, because not only did it nearly cover the gate of Visagra, but also its dome rose so that it dominated the town; and once I'd put it in to look like a model and had shifted it from its place, it seemed to me preferable to show its façade rather than its other sides. As for its position in the town, that appears on the map.

DOMENIKOS THEOTOKOPOULOS*

’Εδῶ, στὸ χῶμα ρίζωσε μιὰ στέρνα
μονιὰ κρυφοῦ νεροῦ ποὺ θησαυρίζει.
Σκεπή της βήματα ἠχερά. Τ’ ἀστέρια
δὲ σμίγουν τὴν καρδιά της. Κάθε μέρα
πληθαίνει, ἀνοιγοκλεῖ, δὲν τὴν ἀγγίζει.

’Ανοίγει ὁ πάνω κόσμος σὰ ριπίδι
καὶ παίζει μὲ τὸ φύσημα τοῦ ἀνέμου
μ’ ἕνα ρυθμὸ ποὺ ξεψυχάει στὸ δείλι
φτεροκοπάει ἀνέλπιδα καὶ σφύζει
στὸ σφύριγμα τοῦ πόνου τοῦ γραμμένου.

Στὸ πύργωμα τοῦ θόλου ἀνέλεης νύχτας
πατοῦνε οἱ ἔνιες κι’ οἱ χαρὲς διαβαίνουν
μὲ τὸ γοργὸ κροτάλισμα τῆς μοίρας
πρόσωπα ἀνάβουν λάμπουν μιὰ στιγμὴ
καὶ σβήνουνται σ’ ἕνα σκοτάδι ἐβένου.

Μορφὲς ποὺ φεύγουν! ‘Ορμαθοὶ τὰ μάτια
κυλοῦν βαλμένα σ’ ἕνα αὐλάκι πίκρα
καὶ τῆς μεγάλης μέρας τὰ σημάδια
τὶς παίρνουν καὶ τὶς φέρνουν πιὸ σιμὰ
στὴ μαύρη γῆς ποὺ δὲ γυρεύει λύτρα.

Here in the earth a cistern has taken root
den of secret water that gathers there.
Its roof, resounding steps. The stars
don't blend with its heart. Each day
grows, opens and shuts, doesn't touch it.

The world above opens like a fan
and plays with the wind's breath
in a rhythm that expires at sunset
flaps its wings hopelessly and throbs
at the whistling of a destined suffering.

On the curve of the dome of a pitiless night
cares tread, joys move by
with fate's quick rattle
faces light up, shine a moment
and die out in an ebony darkness.

Faces that go! In rows, the eyes
roll in a gutter of bitterness
and the signs of the great day
take them up and bring them closer
to the black earth that asks no ransom.

Στὸ χῶμα γέρνει τὸ κορμὶ τοῦ ἀνθρώπου
γιὰ ν' ἀπομείνει ἡ διψασμένη ἀγάπη·
μαρμαρωμένο στ' ἄγγιγμα τοῦ χρόνου
τὸ ἄγαλμα πέφτει γυμνὸ στὸν ἁδρὸ
κόρφο ποὺ τὸ γλυκαίνει ἀγάλι-ἀγάλι.

Δάκρυα γυρεύει ἡ δίψα τῆς ἀγάπης
τὰ τριαντάφυλλα σκύβουν — ἡ ψυχή μας
στὰ φύλλα ἀκούγεται ὁ παλμὸς τῆς πλάσης
τὸ ἀπόβραδο σιμώνει σὰ διαβάτης
ὕστερα ἡ νύχτα κι' ὕστερα τὸ μνῆμα.

Μὰ ἐδῶ στὸ χῶμα ρίζωσε μιὰ στέρνα
κρυφὴ μονιά, ζεστή, ποὺ θησαυρίζει
κάθε κορμιοῦ τὸ βόγγο στὸν ἀγέρα
τὴ μάχη μὲ τὴ νύχτα μὲ τὴ μέρα
πληθαίνει ὁ κόσμος, πάει, δὲν τὴν ἀγγίζει.

Περνοῦνε οἱ ὧρες, ἥλιοι καὶ φεγγάρια,
μὰ τὸ νερὸ ἔχει δέσει σὰν καθρέφτης·
ἡ ἀπαντοχὴ μὲ τὰ ὀρθάνοιχτα μάτια
ὅταν βυθίσουν ὅλα τὰ πανιὰ
στὴν ἄκρη τοῦ πελάγου ποὺ τὴ θρέφει.

Μόνη, καὶ στὴν καρδιά της τόσο πλῆθος
μόνη, καὶ στὴν καρδιά της τόσος μόχθος
καὶ τόσος πόνος, στάλα-στάλα μόνος
τὰ δίχτυα ρίχνοντας μακριὰ στὸν κόσμο
ποὺ ζεῖ μ' ἕνα κυμάτισμα πικρό.

Man's body bends to earth
so that thirsty love remain;
turned into marble at time's touch,
the statue falls naked on the ripe breast
that sweetens it softly.

The thirst of love looks for tears
the roses bend—our soul;
the pulse of nature sounds on the leaves
dusk approaches like a passer-by
then night, then the grave.

But here in the earth a cistern has taken root
warm, secret den that hoards
the groan of each body in the air
the battle with night, with day
the world grows, passes, does not touch it.

Time goes by, suns and moons,
but the water has hardened like a mirror:
expectation open-eyed
when all the sails sink
at the edge of the sea that nourishes it.

Alone, and in its heart such a crowd
alone, and in its heart such labor
and such pain, drop by drop alone
casting its nets far into a world
that lives with bitter undulation.

Σὰν ἄνοιξε τὸ κῦμα ἀπ' τὴν ἀγκάλη
νά 'τανε στὴν ἀγκάλη νὰ τελειώσει
νά 'τανε τὴν ἀγάπη στ' ἀκρογιάλι
πρὶν σπάσει τὴ γραμμή του νὰ μᾶς δώσει
τὸ κῦμα ὡς ἔμεινε στὴν ἄμμο ἀφρός.

Μιὰ ζεστασιὰ ἁπλωμένη σὰν προβιὰ
ἥμερη σὰν τὸ κοιμισμένο ἀγρίμι
ποὺ ξέφυγε ἥσυχα τὸ καρδιοχτύπι
καὶ χτύπησε στὸν ὕπνο νὰ ζητήσει
τὸ περιβόλι ὅπου σταλάζει ἀσήμι.

Κι' ἕνα κορμὶ κρυφό, βαθειὰ κραυγὴ
βγαλμένη ἀπὸ τὸ σπήλαιο τοῦ θανάτου
σὰν τὸ νερὸ ζωηρὸ μέσα στ' αὐλάκι
σὰν τὸ νερὸ ποὺ λάμπει στὸ χορτάρι
μονάχο καὶ μιλεῖ στὶς μαῦρες ρίζες...

Ὦ! πιὸ κοντὰ στὴ ρίζα τῆς ζωῆς μας
ἀπὸ τὴ σκέψη μας κι' ἀπὸ τὴν ἔνια!
Ὢ πιὸ κοντὰ ἀπὸ τὸ σκληρὸ ἀδερφό μας
ποὺ μᾶς κοιτάει μὲ βλέφαρα κλεισμένα
κι' ἀπὸ τὴ λόγχη ἀκόμα στὸ πλευρό μας!

Ὦ! ν' ἁπαλύνει ξάφνω στὴν ἁφή μας
τὸ δέρμα τῆς σιωπῆς ποὺ μᾶς στενεύει,
νὰ λησμονήσουμε, θεοί, τὸ κρῖμα
ποὺ ὅλο πληθαίνει κι' ὅλο μᾶς βαραίνει,
νὰ βγοῦμε ἀπὸ τὴ γνώση κι' ἀπ' τὴν πείνα!

When the wave moved out of the embrace
would that it ended in the embrace
would that it gave us love on the shore
before breaking its line
the wave, as it remained foam on the sand.

A warmth stretched out like hide
tame like a sleeping beast
that calmly avoided fear
and knocked on sleep to ask
for the garden where silver drops.

And a body hidden, deep cry
let out from the cave of death
like water lively in the ditch
like water shining on the grass
alone, talking to the black roots . . .

O nearer the root of our life
than our thoughts and our anxiety!
O nearer than our stern brother
who looks at us with eyelids closed,
and nearer than the spear still in our side!

O if the skin of silence now constricting us
would only soften suddenly at our touch
so that we might forget, O gods, the sin
that daily grows and weighs upon us,
so that we might escape the knowledge and the hunger!

Μαζεύοντας τὸν πόνο τῆς πληγῆς μας
νὰ βγοῦμε ἀπὸ τὸν πόνο τῆς πληγῆς μας
μαζεύοντας τὴν πίκρα τοῦ κορμιοῦ μας
νὰ βγοῦμε ἀπὸ τὴν πίκρα τοῦ κορμιοῦ μας
ρόδα ν' ἀνθίσουν στὸ αἷμα τῆς πληγῆς μας.

Ὅλα νὰ γίνουνε ξανὰ σὰν πρῶτα
στὰ δάχτυλα στὰ μάτια καὶ στὰ χείλια
ν' ἀφήσουμε τὴ γερασμένη ἀρρώστια
πουκάμισο ποὺ ἀφήσανε τὰ φίδια
κίτρινο μὲς στὰ πράσινα τριφύλλια.

Μεγάλη ἀγάπη κι' ἄχραντη, γαλήνη!
Μέσα στὴ ζωντανὴ θέρμη ἕνα βράδι
λύγισες ταπεινά, γυμνὴ καμπύλη,
λευκὴ φτερούγα πάνω ἀπ' τὸ κοπάδι
σὰν ἁπαλὴ στὸν κρόταφο παλάμη.

Τὸ πέλαγο ποὺ σ' ἔφερε σὲ πῆρε
πέρα στὶς λεμονιὲς τὶς ἀνθισμένες
τώρα ποὺ γλυκοξύπνησαν οἱ μοῖρες
χίλιες μορφὲς μὲ τρεῖς ἁπλὲς ρυτίδες
στὸν ἐπιτάφιο συνοδεία βαλμένες.

Σέρνουνε μοιρολόγια οἱ μυροφόρες
ν' ἀκολουθήσει ἡ ἐλπίδα τῶν ἀνθρώπων
στὰ μάτια σφηνωμένη μὲ τὶς φλόγες
φωτίζοντας τὸ χῶμα τὸ τυφλὸ
ποὺ ἱδρώνει ἀπὸ τῆς ἄνοιξης τὸν κόπο.

Gathering up the pain of our wound
so that we may escape the pain of our wound
gathering up the body's bitterness
so that we may escape the body's bitterness
so that roses may bloom in the blood of our wound.

May everything become as it was at first
to fingers eyes and lips
may we throw off the aged sickness,
skin shed by snakes
yellow in the green clover.

Great and immaculate love, serenity!
In the lively fever one night
you bent humbly, naked curve,
white wing over the flock,
like a light palm on the temple.

The sea that brought you carried you away
to the blossoming lemon-trees
now that the fates have woken gently,
a thousand faces with three plain wrinkles,
placed in escort to the epitaph.*

The myrrh-bearers drag their dirges
so that man's hope may follow
wedged in the eyes by flames
lighting the blind earth
that sweats from the effort of spring.

Φλόγες τοῦ πέρα κόσμου, πυροφάνια
πάνω στὴν ἄνοιξη ποὺ σήμερα ἀναβλύζει,
ἴσκιοι θλιμμένοι στὰ νεκρὰ στεφάνια
βήματα... βήματα... ἡ ἀργὴ καμπάνα
μιὰ σκοτεινὴ ἁλυσίδα ξετυλίγει —

«Πεθαίνουμε! Πεθαίνουν οἱ θεοί μας!..»
Τὰ μάρμαρα τὸ ξέρουν ποὺ κοιτάζουν
σὰν ἄσπρη χαραυγὴ πάνω στὸ θῦμα
ξένα, γεμάτα βλέφαρα, συντρίμμια
καθὼς περνοῦν τὰ πλήθη τοῦ θανάτου.

. . . .
. . . .
. . . .
. . . .
. . . .

Περάσανε μακριά, μὲ τὸν καημό τους
ζεστὸ κοντὰ στὰ χαμηλὰ ἁγιοκέρια
ποὺ γράφανε στὸ σκυφτὸ μέτωπό τους
τὴ ζωὴ πασίχαρη στὰ μεσημέρια
ὅταν σβηστοῦν τὰ μάγια καὶ τ' ἀστέρια.

Μὰ ἡ νύχτα δὲν πιστεύει στὴν αὐγὴ
κι' ἡ ἀγάπη ζεῖ τὸ θάνατο νὰ ὑφαίνει
ἔτσι, σὰν τὴν ἐλεύθερη ψυχή,
μιὰ στέρνα ποὺ διδάσκει τὴ σιγὴ
μέσα στὴν πολιτεία τὴ φλογισμένη.

Flames of the world beyond, candles
over Spring surging forth today,
mournful shadows on dead wreaths
footsteps . . . footsteps . . . the slow bell
unwinds a dark chain.

We are dying! Our gods are dying! . . .
The marble statues know it, looking down
like white dawn upon the victim
alien, full of eyelids, fragments,
as the crowds of death pass by.

. . . .
. . . .
. . . .
. . . .
. . . .

They passed into the distance, their sorrow
hot near the lowered church candles
that inscribed on their bent foreheads
the life full of joy at noon
when magic spells and the stars expire.

But night does not believe in dawn
and love lives to weave death
thus, like a free soul,
a cistern that teaches silence
in the flaming city.

ΠΑΝΤΟΥΜ

Τ' ἀστέρια κρατοῦν ἕναν κόσμο δικό τους
στὸ πέλαγο σέρνουν φωτιὲς τὰ καράβια
ψυχή μου λυτρώσου ἀπ' τὸν κρίκο τοῦ σκότους
πικρὴ φλογισμένη ποὺ δέεσαι μ' εὐλάβεια.

Στὸ πέλαγο σέρνουν φωτιὲς τὰ καράβια
ἡ νύχτα στενεύει καὶ στέκει σὰν ξένη
πικρὴ φλογισμένη ποὺ δέεσαι μ' εὐλάβεια
ψυχή μου γνωρίζεις ποιὸς νόμος σὲ δένει.

Ἡ νύχτα στενεύει καὶ στέκει σὰν ξένη
στὸ μαῦρο μετάξι τὰ φῶτα ἔχουν σβήσει
ψυχή μου γνωρίζεις ποιὸς νόμος σὲ δένει
καὶ τί θὰ σοῦ μείνει καὶ τί θὰ σ' ἀφήσει.

Στὸ μαῦρο μετάξι τὰ φῶτα ἔχουν σβήσει
ἀκούγουνται μόνο τοῦ χρόνου τὰ σεῖστρα·
καὶ τί θὰ σοῦ μείνει καὶ τί θὰ σ' ἀφήσει
ἂν τύχει κι' ἀστράψει ἡ βουβὴ πολεμίστρα.

Ἀκούγουνται μόνο τοῦ χρόνου τὰ σεῖστρα
μετάλλινη στήλη στοῦ πόνου τὴν ἄκρη
ἂν τύχει κι' ἀστράψει ἡ βουβὴ πολεμίστρα
οὔτε ὄνειρο θά 'βρεις νὰ δώσει ἕνα δάκρυ.

PANTOUM

The stars contain a world of their own
ships drag fires over the sea
my soul, inflamed and bitter as you pray devoutly,
free yourself from the link of darkness.

Ships drag fires over the sea
night shrinks and stays still as though a stranger
my soul, inflamed and bitter as you pray devoutly,
you recognize the law that binds you.

Night shrinks and stays still as though a stranger
the lights have gone out over the black silk
my soul, recognize the law that binds you,
and what will stay with you, what abandon you.

The lights have gone out over the black silk
there's no sound but the rattle of time;
what will stay with you, what abandon you
should the dumb loophole explode with a flash.

There's no sound but the rattle of time
metallic column at the limit of pain
should the dumb loophole explode with a flash
you won't find even a dream to shed a tear.

Μετάλλινη στήλη στοῦ πόνου τὴν ἄκρη
ψηλώνει ἡ στιγμὴ σὰ μετέωρο λεπίδι
οὔτε ὄνειρο θά 'βρεις νὰ δώσει ἕνα δάκρυ
στὸ πλῆθος σου τὸ ἄυλο ποὺ σφίγγει σὰ φίδι.

Ψηλώνει ἡ στιγμὴ σὰ μετέωρο λεπίδι
σὰν τί νὰ προσμένει νὰ πέσει ἡ γαλήνη;
στὸ πλῆθος σου τὸ ἄυλο ποὺ σφίγγει σὰ φίδι
δὲν εἶναι οὐρανὸς μηδὲ ἀγγέλου εὐφροσύνη.

Σὰν τί νὰ προσμένει νὰ πέσει ἡ γαλήνη;
Σ' ἀνθρώπους κλειστοὺς ποὺ μετροῦν τὸν καημό τους
δὲν εἶναι οὐρανὸς μηδὲ ἀγγέλου εὐφροσύνη
τ' ἀστέρια κρατοῦν ἕναν κόσμο δικό τους.

Metallic column at the limit of pain
the moment rises like a suspended blade
you won't find even a dream to shed a tear
among your immaterial throng that constricts like a snake.

The moment rises like a suspended blade
why does peace delay its coming?
Among your immaterial throng that constricts like a snake
there's no heaven nor angelic happiness.

Why does peace delay its coming?
Among the taciturn counting their sorrow
there's no heaven nor angelic happiness:
the stars contain a world of their own.

ΤΡΙΖΟΝΙΑ

Τὸ σπίτι γέμισε τριζόνια
χτυποῦν σὰν ἄρρυθμα ρολόγια
λαχανιασμένα. Καὶ τὰ χρόνια

ποὺ ζοῦμε σὰν αὐτὰ χτυποῦν
καθὼς οἱ δίκαιοι σιωποῦν
σὰ νὰ μὴν εἶχαν τί νὰ ποῦν.

Κάποτε τ' ἄκουσα στὸ Πήλιο
νὰ σκάβουνε γοργὰ ἕνα σπήλαιο
μέσα στὴ νύχτα. Ἀλλὰ τὸ φύλλο

τῆς μοίρας τώρα τὸ γυρίσαμε
καὶ μᾶς γνωρίσατε καὶ σᾶς γνωρίσαμε
ἀπὸ τοὺς ὑπερβόρειους ἴσαμε

τοὺς νέγρους τοῦ ἰσημερινοῦ
ποὺ ἔχουνε σῶμα χωρὶς νοῦ
καὶ ποὺ φωνάζουν σὰν πονοῦν.

Κι' ἐγὼ πονῶ κι' ἐσεῖς πονεῖτε
μὰ δὲ φωνάζουμε καὶ μήτε
κὰν ψιθυρίζουμε, γιατὶ

CRICKETS

The house is full of crickets
beating like rhythmless clocks
out of breath. And the times

we live beat that way too
while the just remain silent
as though they had nothing to say.

Once in Pelion I heard them
swiftly digging a cave
into the night. But now

we've flipped the leaf of fate
and you've known us as we've known you
from those who live in the north

to the negroes at the equator
all body without mind
who bellow when in pain.

I suffer and you suffer
but we don't yell or cry
or whisper even, because

ἡ μηχανὴ εἶναι βιαστικὴ
στὴ φρίκη καὶ στὴν καταφρόνια
στὸ θάνατο καὶ στὴ ζωή,

Τὸ σπίτι γέμισε τριζόνια.

Πρετόρια, 16 Γενάρη '42

the machine is very quick
at horror and contempt
at death and life,

The house is full of crickets.

Pretoria, 16 January '42

ΘΕΑΤΡΙΝΟΙ, Μ.Α.

Στήνουμε θέατρα καὶ τὰ χαλνοῦμε
ὅπου σταθοῦμε κι' ὅπου βρεθοῦμε
στήνουμε θέατρα καὶ σκηνικά,
ὅμως ἡ μοίρα μας πάντα νικᾶ

καὶ τὰ σαρώνει καὶ μᾶς σαρώνει
καὶ τοὺς θεατρίνους καὶ τὸ θεατρώνη
ὑποβολέα καὶ μουσικοὺς
στοὺς πέντε ἀνέμους τοὺς βιαστικούς.

Σάρκες, λινάτσες, ξύλα, φτιασίδια,
ρίμες, αἰσθήματα, πέπλα, στολίδια,
μάσκες, λιογέρματα, γόοι καὶ κραυγὲς
κι' ἐπιφωνήματα καὶ χαραυγὲς

ριγμένα ἀνάκατα μαζὶ μ' ἐμᾶς
(πές μου ποῦ πᾶμε; πές μου ποῦ πᾶς;)
πάνω ἀπ' τὸ δέρμα μας γυμνὰ τὰ νεῦρα
σὰν τὶς λουρίδες ὀνάγρου ἢ ζέβρα

γυμνὰ κι' ἀνάερα, στεγνὰ στὴν κάψα
(πότε μᾶς γέννησαν; πότε μᾶς θάψαν;)
καὶ τεντωμένα σὰν τὶς χορδὲς
μιᾶς λύρας ποὺ ὁλοένα βουίζει. Δὲς

ACTORS, MIDDLE EAST

We put up theaters and tear them down
wherever we happen to find ourselves
we put up theaters and set the stage
but our fate always triumphs in the end

and sweeps them away as it sweeps us too
actors and the actors' manager
prompter and musicians all disappear
scattered to the five hungry winds.

Bodies, mats, wood, make-up
rhymes, feelings, veils, jewelry
masks, sunsets, wails and howls
exclamations and suns rising

cast off helter-skelter along with us
(where are we going? where are you going?)
nerves naked upon our skin
like the stripes of an onager or zebra

exposed and naked, dry and burning
(when were we born? when buried?)
and taut like the strings of a lyre
incessantly humming. Look also

καὶ τὴν καρδιά μας· ἕνα σφουγγάρι,
στὸ δρόμο σέρνεται καὶ στὸ παζάρι
πίνοντας τὸ αἷμα καὶ τὴ χολὴ
καὶ τοῦ τετράρχη καὶ τοῦ ληστῆ.

Μέση Ἀνατολή, Αὔγουστος '43

at our heart: a sponge
dragged through the street and market place
soaking up the blood and bile
of both the tetrarch and the thief.

Middle East, August '43

ΑΓΙΑΝΑΠΑ, Β′

Ἄνοιξη 1156

Στίχοι γιὰ μουσικὴ

Κάτω ἀπ' τὴ γέρικη συκομουριὰ
τρελὸς ὁ ἀγέρας ἔπαιζε
μὲ τὰ πουλιὰ μὲ τὰ κλωνιὰ
καὶ δὲ μᾶς ἔκραινε.

Ὥρα καλή σου ἀνάσα τῆς ψυχῆς
ἀνοίξαμε τὸν κόρφο μας
ἔλα νὰ μπεῖς ἔλα νὰ πιεῖς
ἀπὸ τὸν πόθο μας.

Κάτω ἀπ' τὴ γέρικη συκομουριὰ
ὁ ἀγέρας σκώθη κι' ἔφυγε
κατὰ τὰ κάστρα τοῦ βοριᾶ
καὶ δὲ μᾶς ἔγγιξε.

Θυμάρι μου καὶ δεντρολιβανιά,
δέσε γερὰ τὸ στῆθος σου
καὶ βρὲς σπηλιὰ καὶ βρὲς μονιὰ
κρύψε τὸ λύχνο σου.

Δὲν εἶναι ἀγέρας τοῦτος τοῦ Βαγιοῦ
δὲν εἶναι τῆς Ἀνάστασης
μὰ εἶν' τῆς φωτιᾶς καὶ τοῦ καπνοῦ

AGIANAPA II

Spring 1156*

Verses for music

Under the aging sycamore
madly the wind was playing
with the birds with the branches
but it never spoke to us.

Welcome and good luck O breath of the soul
we opened our hearts to you
do come in, do drink in
your fill of our desire.

Under the aging sycamore
the wind rose up and left
gone to the northern castles,
and never touched us even.

O my rosemary, O my thyme,
bind your breast tightly
and find a cave, find a lair
and hide away your light.

This is no Palm Sunday wind
no wind of the Resurrection
but a wind of fire, a wind of smoke,

τῆς ζωῆς τῆς ἄχαρης.

Κάτω ἀπ' τὴ γέρικη συκομουριὰ
στεγνὸς ὁ ἀγέρας γύρισε·
ὀσμίζουνταν παντοῦ φλουριὰ
καὶ μᾶς ἐπούλησε.

a wind of joyless life.

Under the aging sycamore
the wind returned dry,
reeking of florins everywhere,
and bartered us for gold.

ΣΤΑ ΠΕΡΙΧΩΡΑ ΤΗΣ ΚΕΡΎΝΕΙΑΣ

But I'm dying and done for
What on earth was all the fun for?
For God's sake keep that sunlight out of sight.

JOHN BETJEMAN

Homer's world, not ours.

W. H. AUDEN

Σχέδιο γιὰ ἕνα «εἰδύλλιο»

. . . .

—Τῆς τηλεγράφησα λουλούδια.
—Οὐίσκι ; Τζίν;
—Σήμερα οἱ ἀργυροί της γάμοι.
—Τὸ νοῦ σας μὴν
πηδήξει στὸ φουστάνι σας ὁ σκύλος·
θὰ τὸ λασπώσει· τὸν παραμελοῦν· γίνεται οἰκεῖος.
—Τζὶν παρακαλῶ. Μένει τώρα στὸ Κέντ. Πάντα
θὰ τὴ θυμοῦμαι στὴν ἐκκλησιά. Σὰ βγήκαμε ἔβρεχε· μιὰ μπάντα
ἔπαιζε στ' ἄλλο πεζοδρόμιο· θαρῶ Στρατὸς τῆς Σωτηρίας.
—Μέρες τοῦ Μάη, ὁ χρόνος τῆς Μεγάλης 'Απεργίας.
—Δὲν εἴχαμε οὔτε ἐφημερίδες.
—Δέστε τὸ βουνό·
ὅταν βυθίσει τέλος πάντων ὁ ἥλιος θά εἶναι μονόχρωμο καὶ εἰρηνικό.
Αὐτό εἶναι ὁ Ἅγιος Ἱλαρίων. Τὸ προτιμῶ μὲ τὸ φεγγάρι.

IN THE KYRENIA DISTRICT

But I'm dying and done for
What on earth was all the fun for?
For God's sake keep that sunlight out of sight.

JOHN BETJEMAN

Homer's world, not ours.

W. H. AUDEN

Sketch for an "idyll"

. . . .

—I wired her flowers.
—Whisky? Gin?
—Today's her silver wedding.
—Mind the dog
doesn't jump up against your skirt:
he'll muddy it. They neglect him, he's getting too familiar,
—Gin, please. She lives in Kent now. I'll
always remember her in the church. When we came out,
it was raining; a band
was playing on the pavement opposite, the Salvation
Army, I think
—Sometime in May, the year of the General Strike.
—We didn't even have papers.
—Look at the mountain:
when the sun finally sets it'll be one color all over, and
peaceful.
That's St. Hilarion. I prefer it by moonlight.

— Γράφει πὼς ἔχει κι' ἕνα φάντασμα ποὺ τριγυρνᾶ μ' ἕνα
σβηστὸ φανάρι.
—Ὁ Ἅγιος Ἱλαρίων ;
—Ὄχι, τὸ σπίτι της στὸ Κέντ.
—Ἐδῶ τὸ φάντασμα θὰ πήγαινε καλύτερα. Κάποτε — δὲν
μπορῶ νὰ τὸ ἐξηγήσω — ἡ μνήμη
σ' αὐτὸ τὸ φῶς γίνεται πιὸ σκληρή, μιὰ ζύμη
ποὺ τὴ στεγνώνει ὁ ἥλιος...
— Ζύμη ἀπὸ τί ;
Ἔχω κι' ἐγὼ πονοκεφάλους.
— Γνωρίσατε τὸν ποιητή,
ἢ κάτι τέτοιο, ποὺ ἔμενε τὸν περασμένο μήνα ἐδῶ ;
Τὸ αἴσθημα τ' ὀνομάζει παλίμψηστη λιβιδώ·
πάρα πολὺ ἀσυνήθιστος· τί θέλει
νὰ πεῖ, δὲν τὸ ξέρει κανείς· κυνικὸς καὶ φιλέλλην.
— Σώστροφος σνόμπ.
— Κάποτε ἀστεῖος· τώρα εἶναι στὰ λουτρά.
— Στὴν Ἰταλία καθὼς ἄκουσα.
— Ναί, κάποιο «σπά».
Λέει πὼς ὠφελοῦν τὴν ἀφροδίσια ρώμη.
Τοῦ ἔδωσα σύσταση γιὰ τὸν Ὁράτιο στὴ Ρώμη.
— Πολὺ ἀθυρόστομος, πῶς τοῦ ἐπιτρέπετε ;
—Ἀλήθεια, πῶς ;
Ἴσως στὴν ἡλικία μας νὰ γίνεται κανεὶς συγκαταβατικὸς
ἴσως ἀνάγκη νὰ ξεφύγω τὸν τρεχάμενο ἑαυτό μου
ἴσως αὐτὸ τὸ νησὶ ποὺ μὲ πλήττει σὰν ἀερόλιθος ἄλλου
κόσμου.
— Γινόσαστε μελαγχολική, Μαργαρίτα. Μὰ εἶναι τόσο ὡ-
ραῖα·

—She writes that it has a ghost who goes about with an
extinguished lamp.
—St. Hilarion?

—No, her house in Kent.

—The ghost would be more appropriate here. Sometimes—
I can't explain it—memory
grows harsher in this light, dough
dried by the sun . . .

—What kind of dough?

I get headaches too.

—Did you meet the poet,

or whatever he was, staying here last month?
He called feeling palimsestic libido:
most unusual; no one knows
what he means. A cynic and philhellene.
—An introverted snob.

—Amusing sometimes. Now he's
taking the baths.
—In Italy I heard.

—Yes, some "spa."

He says it encourages sexual vigor.
I gave him an introduction to Horace in Rome.
—How could you, he's so shocking.

—How, indeed?

Maybe at our age one makes allowances
maybe out of need to escape from my ordinary self
maybe it's this island that bores me like a meteor from
another world.
—You're becoming sad, Margaret. But it's so beautiful:

ὁ ἥλιος, ἡ θάλασσα· ἕνα παντοτινὸ καλοκαίρι...

—"Α! τούτη ἡ θέα

ποὺ ὅλο ρωτᾶ κι' ὅλο ρωτᾶ. Προσέχετε κάποτε τὸν καθρέφτη

πῶς κάνει ἐντάφιο τὸ πρόσωπό μας; Καὶ τὸν ἥλιο τὸν κλέφτη

πῶς παίρνει τὰ φτιασίδια μας κάθε πρωί; Θὰ προτιμούσα

τὴ ζεστασιὰ τοῦ ἥλιου χωρὶς τὸν ἥλιο· θ' ἀποζητούσα

μιὰ θάλασσα ποὺ δὲν ἀπογυμνώνει· ἕνα μαβὶ χωρὶς φωνή,

χωρὶς αὐτὴ τὴν ἀνάγωγη ἀνάκριση τὴν καθημερινή.

Θὰ μὲ ξεκούραζε τὸ σιωπηλὸ χάδι τῆς ὁμίχλης στὰ κρόσια τοῦ ὀνείρου·

αὐτὸς ὁ κόσμος δὲν εἶναι ὁ δικός μας, εἶναι τοῦ Ὁμήρου,

ἡ καλύτερη φράση ποὺ ἄκουσα γι' αὐτὸ τὸν τόπο.

"Ησυχα Ρέξ!

—Εὐχαριστῶ, μὴν κάνετε τὸν κόπο,

ξέρω τὸ δρόμο. Θὰ ἤθελα νὰ προλάβω ν' ἀγοράσω πανί,

σαράντα πῆχες δίμιτο, γιὰ τὸν περιβολάρη μας τὸν Παναγή·

ἀπίστευτο! τόσο λέει τοῦ χρειάζεται γιὰ μιὰ βράκα...

Καθὼς μιλούσατε θυμόμουν ἕνα Σάββατο, τὸν Μπίλλ, στὴ βάρκα

στὸν Τάμεση... Κοίταζα τὸ φουλάρι του ὅλο τὸ δείλι.

Σφύριζε καθὼς ἔλαμνε, «Πές της το μὲ τὸ γιουκαλίλι».

Τί νά 'γινε ἄραγε;...

—Σκοτώθηκε στὴν Κρήτη.

the sun, the sea, an everlasting summer.

—Ah, this view

that questions and questions. Have you ever noticed how the mirror sometimes
makes our faces death-like. Or how that thief the sun
takes our make-up off each morning? I'd prefer
the sun's warmth without the sun; I'd look for
a sea that doesn't strip one bare: a voiceless blue
without that ill-bred daily interrogation.
The silent caress of the mist in the tassels of dream would refresh me:
this world isn't ours, it's Homer's—
that's the best description I've heard of this place.
Quiet, Rex!

—No, please don't bother,

I know the way. I'd like to have time to buy some cloth:
thirty yards of woven stuff, for our gardener Panagi;
incredible, he says he needs that much for those old baggy trousers he wears . . .
As you were speaking I remembered Bill, one Saturday,
on the Thames . . . I gazed at his scarf all the evening.
As he rowed he was whistling, "say it with a ukulele."
What's become of him, I wonder?

—He was killed in Crete.

—Ὅμορφος, πολὺ ὅμορφος... Θὰ σᾶς περιμένω τὴν Τρίτη...
Ἥσυχα ποὺ κυλοῦσε ὁ Τάμεσης μέσα στοὺς ἴσκιους...
Καλὸν ὕπνο.
— Κρίμα ποὺ δὲν μπορέσατε νὰ μείνετε γιὰ τὸ δεῖπνο.

—He was handsome, so handsome . . . I'll expect you on
Tuesday . . .

How softly the Thames flowed among the shadows . . .
Sleep well.

—It's a pity you can't stay for dinner.

ΠΡΑΜΑΤΕΥΤΗΣ ΑΠΟ ΤΗ ΣΙΔΩΝΑ

Ἢ τάχα Κοῦρον
Κυπρίδος εὐκόλποιο καὶ Ἑρμάωνος ἐνίψεις.
ΧΡΙΣΤΟΔΩΡΟΥ ΕΚΦΡΑΣΙΣ

Ὁ νέος πραματευτὴς ἦρθε ἀπὸ τὴ Σιδώνα
χωρὶς νὰ φοβηθεῖ τὸ θυμωμένο Ποσειδώνα.

Κοράκου χρῶμα τὰ τσουλούφια του, ὁ χιτώνας του πορφύρα
καὶ τὸν κρατάει στὸν ὦμο του μιὰ χρυσὴ πόρπη· μύρα

ἀνασαίνει καὶ ψιμύθια κάθε πτυχὴ τοῦ σώματός του.
Μπῆκε στὴν Κύπρο ἀπ' τὴ θαλασσινὴ πόρτα τῆς 'Αμμο-
    χώστου

καὶ τώρα χαίρεται μὲς στὰ στενὰ τῆς Λευκωσίας τὴ λια-
    κάδα.
Μιὰ τουρκοπούλα στὴν αὐλή, καὶ σείστηκε ἡ περιπλοκάδα

ποὺ κορφολόγαε μὲ τὰ σιντεφένια δάχτυλά της.
'Εκεῖνος διάβηκε τοῦ ἥλιου τὸν ποταμὸ σὰν ἕνας θεῖος πε-
    ράτης,

σὰν ὄνειρο ψιθυριστὰ τραγουδώντας: «Ρόδα στὸ μαντήλι».
Λὲς γύρευαν τοῦ Δία τὰ πέδιλα τὰ βυσσινιά του χείλη.

PEDDLER FROM SIDON

At once you knew him for the son of a full-breasted
Aphrodite and of Hermes.

*CHRISTODOROS' DESCRIPTION**

The young peddler came from Sidon
unafraid of angry Poseidon.
His curls crow-colored, his chiton purple,
fastened at the shoulder by a golden clasp,
his body reeking of myrrh and make-up.
He entered Cyprus through Famagusta,
now indulges in the sunlight
of back lanes in Nicosia.
In the courtyard a young Turkish girl:
the creeper that she trims with ivory fingers
sways shyly to her touch.
The peddler crosses the sun's river
like a walking god, the song he sings
dream-soft: "Roses in a kerchief . . . ,"
as if his crimson lips
longed to kiss Zeus' sandals.

Ἔτσι προχώρεσε καὶ κάθησε πλάι σ' ἕνα γοτθικὸ παραστάτη
ὅπου τοῦ Μάρκου τὸ λιοντάρι κάρφωνε μ' ἀλαφιασμένο μάτι

ἕναν κοιμάμενο βοσκὸ πού μύριζε τραγὶ κι' ἱδρώτα.
Ἀκούμπησε, ἔβγαλε ἀπὸ τὸν κόρφο του καὶ κοίταξε μιὰ τερακότα·

ἕνα γυμνὸ πού γλιστροῦσε ἀβέβαιο στὴ σαλμακίδα κοίτη
ἀνάμεσα στὸν κοῖλο Ἑρμὴ καὶ τὴν κυρτὴ Ἀφροδίτη.

He walks on so, then stops
to sit beside a Gothic gate-post
that offers the wild-eyed lion of Mark
glaring down on a sleeping shepherd
who smells too much of goat and sweat.
The peddler leans back; his hand
feels inside his shirt, removes
a terracotta statuette.
He studies it: a naked youth that glides,
uncertain, on the effeminate couch
between concave Hermes and convex Aphrodite.

BIBLIOGRAPHICAL NOTE

In this note we do not attempt to cite all possible sources that would be relevant to a thorough study of Seferis's poetry, a purpose better served (for works before 1962) by G. K. Katsimbalis' Βιβλιογραφία Γιώργου Σεφέρη (Athens 1961), which also appeared in Γιὰ τὸν Σεφέρη (see below). We offer here only a list of the first Greek editions of the various volumes that constitute Seferis's collected poems, his own principal prose works and translations, and, in addition, the most important works devoted to his poetry in English, Greek, and other languages.

I. First editions of Seferis's poems (published as volumes)

Στροφή [*Turning Point*] (Athens, 1931)

Ἡ Στέρνα [*The Cistern*] (Athens, 1932)

Μυθιστόρημα [*Mythistorema*] (Athens, 1935)

Τετράδιο Γυμνασμάτων [*Book of Exercises*] (Athens, 1940)

Ἡμερολόγιο Καταστρώματος [*Logbook I*] (Athens, 1940)

Ἡμερολόγιο Καταστρώματος, Β [*Logbook II*] (Alexandria, 1944)

«Κίχλη» [*"Thrush"*] (Athens, 1947)

Ἡμερολόγιο Καταστρώματος, Γ [*Logbook III*] (Athens, 1955), originally published as . . . Κύπρον, οὗ μ'ἐθέσπισεν . . .

Τρία Κρυφὰ Ποιήματα [*Three Secret Poems*] (Athens, 1966).*

II. Seferis's principal prose works

Τρεῖς μέρες στὰ μοναστήρια τῆς Καππαδοκίας [Three Days at the Monasteries of Kappadokia] (Athens, 1953). Also in French: Institut Français, Athens, 1953.

Δοκιμές [Essays], 2nd ed. (Athens, 1962)

Delphi (Munich and Ahrback/Hanover, 1963). Reprint from the Greek text in Ὁ Ταχυδρόμος, Athens, 1962.

* This short volume appeared in December, 1966, too late to be included in this English edition.

Discours de Stockholm (Athens, 1964)

Ἡ Γλῶσσα στὴν Ποίησή μας (Thessaloniki, 1965)

III. Seferis's principal translations

Θ. Σ. Ἔλιοτ: Ἡ Ἔρημη Χώρα καὶ ἄλλα ποιήματα [The Waste Land and Other Poems], 3rd ed. (Athens, 1965)

Θ. Σ. Ἔλιοτ: Δολοφονία στὴν Ἐκκλησία [Murder in the Cathedral], 2nd ed. (Athens, 1965)

Ἀντιγραφές [Copies] (Athens, 1965)

Ἆσμα ἀσμάτων [The Song of Songs] (Athens, 1966)

Ἡ Ἀποκάλυψη τοῦ Ἰωάννη [The Apocalypse of St. John] (Athens, 1966)

IV. Selected translations of Seferis into English and other major languages

Robert Levesque, *Séféris* (Athens, 1945). French, with Introduction by the translator.

Bernard Spencer, Nanos Valaoritis, Lawrence Durrell, *The King of Asine* and *Other Poems* (London, 1948). Introduction by Rex Warner.

Edmund Keeley and Philip Sherrard, *Six Poets of Modern Greece* (London, 1960). Introduction and Notes by the translators. Also published in an American edition (New York, 1961).

Rex Warner, *Poems* (London, 1960). Introduction and Notes by the translator. Also published in an American edition (Boston, 1961).

Christian Enzensberger, *Poesie* (Frankfurt am Main, 1962)

Filippo Maria Pontani, *Poesie* (Milan, 1963). Introduction and Notes by translator, Greek text *en face*.

Filippo Maria Pontani, *Le Parole E I Marmi* (Milan, 1963). A collection of essays from *Dokimes*.

Börje Knös and Johannes Edfelt, *Dikter* (Stockholm, 1963)

Hjalmar Gullberg, *Stenarnas Dictare Tolkningar* (Stockholm, 1963)

Jacques Lacarrière, *Poèmes* (Paris, 1964). Introduction by Ives Bonnefoy; Preface by Gaetan Picon.

Sture Linner, *T. S. Eliot and C. P. Cavafy* (Stockholm, 1965). Accompanying a translation of Cavafy's poems. See also, by the same author, *Giorgos Seferis: en Introduktion* (Stockholm, 1963).

Lysandro Z. D. Galtier, *"El Zorzal" y ostros Poemas* [*"Thrush"* and other Poems] (Buenos Aires, 1966)

Rex Warner, *On the Greek Style* (Boston, 1966). Selected essays from Δοκιμές.

V. Critical books on Seferis

Andreas Karandonis, *Ὁ ποιητὴς Γιῶργος Σεφέρης* (Athens, 1957)

Γιὰ τὸν Σεφέρη, ed. G. P. Savidis (Athens, 1961). A collection of essays on Seferis in Greek by many hands, commemorating the thirtieth anniversary of the publication of Seferis's first volume, Στροφὴ [*Turning Point.*]

VI. Critical articles in English on Seferis

S. Baud-Bovy, "A Greek Poet (G. Seferis)," *The Link*, Oxford, June 1938, pp. 1-6.

Nicholas Bachtin, "English Poetry in Greek (Notes on a comparative study of poetic idioms)" Parts 1 and 2, *The Link*, Oxford, June 1938, pp. 77-84, and June 1939, pp. 49-63. Commentary on Seferis's translation of Eliot (see especially Part 1).

W. B. Stanford, *The Ulysses Theme*, Chapter XIV (Oxford, 1954), pp. 176-78.

Edmund Keeley, "T. S. Eliot and the Poetry of George Seferis," *Comparative Literature*, Summer 1956, pp. 214-26.

Edmund Keeley, "George Seferis and Stratis the Mariner," *Accent*, Summer 1956, pp. 153-57.

Philip Sherrard, "George Seferis" in *The Marble Threshing Floor: Studies in Modern Greek Poetry* (London, 1956), pp. 185-231.

Kimon Friar, "George Seferis: The Greek Poet Who Won the Nobel Prize," *Saturday Review*, Nov. 30, 1963, pp. 16-20.

G. Georgiades Arnakis, "The Tragedy of Man in the Poetry of George Seferis," *The Texas Quarterly*, Spring 1964, pp. 55-67.

Edmund Keeley, "Seferis's Elpenor: A Man of No Fortune," *The Kenyon Review*, Summer 1966, pp. 378-390.

NOTES

The following notes are intended to be factual rather than interpretive. Some derive from Seferis's own notes to the sixth edition of his Ποιήματα (Athens, 1965). A few are based upon George Savidis's detailed notes to Seferis's *Logbook III*, included in Γιὰ τὸν Σεφέρη, ed. G. P. Savidis (Athens, 1961), pp. 304-409, and published separately as Μιὰ Περιδιάβαση (Athens, 1962). The additional notes are included to assist the English-speaking reader generally, as well as the specialist in modern Greek literature.

Page

1 The colloquial meaning of the title is "novel," but it has other connotations also, as the poet indicates in the following note:

> MYTHISTOREMA—it is its two components that made me choose the title of this work: MYTHOS, because I have used, clearly enough, a certain mythology; ISTORIA [both "history" and "story"], because I have tried to express, with some coherence, circumstances that are as independent from myself as the characters in a novel.

1 *Poésies*, "Fêtes de la Faim," 11. 3-4.

5 The "poet" referred to is Dionysios Solomos, and the phrase cited is from his prose work, *The Woman of Zakynthos*, Chap. I.

7 Aeschylus, *The Libation Bearers*, 491. Orestes is speaking at Agamemnon's tomb, reminding his father of the bath where he was slain by Clytemnestra.

9 The quotation is from Plato, *Alcibiades*, 133 B. In a note on the poem, Seferis says that these words, spoken by Socrates to Alcibiades, once gave him a sensation akin to that evoked by the following lines from Baudelaire's "La mort des amants":

> Nos deux coeurs seront deux vastes flambeaux,
> Qui réfléchiront leurs doubles lumières
> Dans nos deux esprits, ces miroirs jumeaux.

11 See Homer, *Od.* xi. 75ff., where the shade of Elpenor, youngest of Odysseus' companions, asks that his oar be planted on his seashore grave to perpetuate his memory. See also the note to page 281 on Elpenor.

15 The initials are those of Maurice Ravel (1875-1937), the French composer.

25 In Homeric mythology the meadow of asphodels is the dwelling-place of the dead. See *Od.* xi and xxiv. 12ff.

27 During the wedding ceremony in the Orthodox Church, the bridal pair exchange both crowns and rings.

27 The Symplegades, through which Jason and the Argonauts had to pass, were dangerous clashing rocks at the juncture of the Bosphorus and the Black Sea (Pontus Euxinus).

31 See note to page 11.

33 Hydra, a rock island off the northeastern coast of the Peloponnese, contributed substantially to the naval forces that helped to win independence for Greece in the early nineteenth century. This contribution is celebrated annually with colorful festivities.

37 Pliny, *Letters,* 1, 3.

41 Sophocles, *Electra,* 694. From the passage which describes Orestes' participation in the chariot-races at Delphi.

45 Younger son of Hector and Andromache. At the fall of Troy he was either flung from the walls by Neoptolemus or killed by Odysseus. See also the *Iliad.* vi. 402-403.

51 Aeschylus, *Agamemnon,* 1. 958. The line is from the speech by Clytemnestra justifying Agamemnon's treading on the purple carpet leading into the palace.

59 See *Od.* x. 526ff. where Odysseus is instructed by Circe to sacrifice, on visiting the dead, a young lamb and a black ewe, turning their heads towards Erebus.

71 In a note to the first edition of *Book of Exercises,* the poet writes: "This book is made up either of various poems which have no place in any of the other selections that I've already published or might publish later, or of occasional pieces dedicated to friends, or of exercises, some more complete in form than others. Under the circumstances, the book has, I imagine, no other coherence than that provided by ten years of continuous effort towards poetic expression, and perhaps it is nothing more than a contribution to criticism."

75 Kifisia is a cool, well-watered residential district lying some eight miles north of central Athens.

75 Aedipsos, on the northwest coast of Euboea, has been a famous spa since Roman times.

79 George Theotokas (1905-1966) wrote a number of novels and plays, including *Argo,* a novel translated into English and published in London by Methuen and Co. Ltd. in 1951. Theotokas "discovered" Syngrou Avenue in his early work, Ἐλεύθερο Πνεῦμα (*Free Spirit*), published in 1929. The avenue, running from the Temple of Olympian Zeus to Faleron and the sea, was at that time the broadest in Athens, "one of the symbols

of the new era which it was our destiny to express," according to Theotokas (in Ἐποχές, Athens, February 1964, p. 14). In his Ἐλεύθερο Πνεῦμα, he writes: "Day and night, towards the Faleron shore, Syngrou Avenue carries the newly born and still unexpressed rhythms of a powerful lyricism that call for powerful poets." Cf. the second stanza of "A Word for Summer," p. 167.

83 Cf. Joachim Du Bellay, *Les Regrets.*

85 The *Erotokritos* is a Cretan epic of the seventeenth century written by Vitzentzos Kornaros, a work of 10,052 verses in the chivalrous genre, telling of the love of Aretousa, the daughter of a King, and the valiant Erotokritos. Seferis has written a critical study of this work, reprinted in Δοκιμές (see Bibliographical Note).

89 Book III, 1. 10 of his "Meditations."

101 See note to page 27.

103 D. I. Antoniou, a contemporary Greek poet (see Keeley and Sherrard, *Six Poets of Modern Greece* [London, 1960]), has served for a number of years as an officer in the Greek merchant marine. The title of the poem is a nautical term identifying the direction of the prevailing wind: between Sirocco and Levante, or ESE.

107 Pelion is a mountain range in Thessalian Magnesia. The centaur, Chiron, is said to have dwelt on its wooded slopes.

107 Santorini: see the epigraph to *Gymnopaidia,* p. 61.

107 Spetses, Poros, and Mykonos are popular Aegean islands.

109 Omonia ("harmony") and Syntagma ("constitution") are the two largest squares in central Athens. The dialogue here makes use of "katharevousa," the purist language.

109 Aeschylus, *Agamemnon,* 659.

117 Literally "Stratis the Mariner," a persona that appears frequently in Seferis's poetry (see Bibliographical Note).

125 Aeschylus, *Eumenides,* 143. The cries are uttered by the Furies after they have been aroused from their sleep in the temple of Apollo at Delphi by Clytemnestra's ghost and urged to continue their task of hunting down Orestes.

127 On the eve of the feast day of St. John (June 24), it was customary in Seferis's childhood village of Skala near the town of Vourla in Asia Minor—as in other Greek communities generally—for the children to light small fires in the streets after sunset and jump over them for good luck (see Nikos E. Milioris, Τὰ Βούρλα τῆς Μικρᾶς Ἀσίας, Athens, 1965, II, 236). Among the various divinatory rituals practiced by unmarried girls on this feast day are the two mentioned in the poem: 1) The girl drops molten lead into a container filled with

"silent" water (i.e., water brought secretly from a spring by a young girl or boy who is forbidden to speak to anyone on the way), and the shape that the lead takes on cooling indicates the trade or profession that the girl's future husband will follow; 2) The girl undresses at midnight and stands naked before a mirror, invoking St. John and asking him to reveal the man she will marry; the first name that she hears on waking the next morning is that of her future husband (see G. A. Megas, *Ἑλληνικαὶ Ἑορταὶ καὶ Ἔθιμα τῆς Λαϊκῆς Λατρείας*, Athens, 1963, pp. 217-18).

129 In 356 B.C. Herostratus burned down the famous Temple of Artemis at Ephesus in order to make his name immortal.

131 Nijinski: the famous Russian dancer.

153 Aeschylus, *Agamemnon*, 1,314; from Cassandra's speech just before she enters the palace to be murdered.

153 Aeschylus, *Agamemnon*, 958. See note to page 51.

167 See note to page 79.

197 "Bread and Wine," 7, ll. 11-14.

203 Ghegs and Tosks are the names of two Albanian tribes.

205 Vercingetorix was the son of a former king of the Gallic tribe, the Averni. He led the Gallic revolt against Caesar in 52 B.C., was defeated and put to death after Caesar's triumph.

205 Stéphane Mallarmé, "*Le Tombeau d'Edgar Poe*," l. 1.

207 The opening line of Marcel Proust's *A la Recherche du Temps Perdu* (*Du côté de chez Swann*).

207 Hylas was a page and companion of Heracles on the Argonaut voyage.

221 In Greek: *Ἡ Χώρα τοῦ Ἀχωρήτου*. This is one of the epithets applied to the Virgin as the Mother of the infinite, and therefore uncontainable, Deity. From it derives the name of the Church of the Saviour of the Chora (Kariye Camii) at Constantinople.

233 The allusion is to the *Iliad*. vi. 457: "Then in Argos . . . you shall bear water from Messeïs or Hypereia." The line is from Hector's speech to Andromache.

233 See Thucydides, VII, 87: "At first the Syracusans treated them terribly in the stone quarries. . . ." The relevant passage refers to the Athenians and their allies who were taken prisoner by the Syracusans after the destruction of the Athenian expedition to Sicily in 413 B.C.

249 *Louis Lambert*.

255 From *Mythistorema*, 7.

259 *Iliad*. ii. 560; from the catalogue of ships.

259 The citadel is the ruined acropolis of Asine, close to the modern village of Tolos on the coast of the Argolid. The

landscape has changed considerably since the poem was written.

269 One of two large gates of early Alexandria, Egypt, known as the Rosetta Gate in Arabic times. The other was called the Gate of the Moon.

279 Agapanthi (literally "love flowers") are African lilies. For "Stratis Thalassinos," see note to page 117.

279 See *Od.* xxiv. 12ff.

279 See *Od.* x.

281 Elpenor, to whom reference has been made in *Mythistorema* (Nos. 4 and 12), is a central figure in Seferis's poetry. In Homer's *Odyssey* he is described as a somewhat foolish and feeble-hearted companion who finally kills himself in a fall from Circe's palace while heavy with sleep and wine. Seferis has written of this figure as follows: "Perhaps you will ask why I write about them [the Elpenor-type] with sympathy. Because the men who belong to this category, among the heroes (in the Homeric sense, not, for God's sake, in the Carlylian) are the most sympathetic. Even the Homeric Odysseus, when he sees Elpenor, first among the dead, pities him and sheds tears. I do not say lovable or admirable, I say sympathetic, sentimental, mediocre, wasted. . . . He (Elpenor) symbolizes those to whom we refer in daily conversation with the expression: 'the poor devil.' However, let us not forget that these guileless men, exactly because they are 'easy,' are often the best carriers of an evil which has its source elsewhere" (see *Foreword,* fn. 5, same source, p. 502).

281 This line is from Solomos's "The Destruction of Psara" (1825). The island of Psara was razed and its people massacred during the Greek War of Independence (1821-1829). The complete poem, among the more famous in modern Greece, may be rendered as follows:

> On the blackened ridge of Psara
> Glory walking alone
> Recalls the gallant young men:
> On her head she wears a crown
> Made of what little grass
> Remained on that desolate earth.

289 For "Stratis Thalassinos" see note to page 117.

303 The phrase is from the Introduction to the *Memoirs* of General Makriyannis, one of the principal leaders of the Greek War of Independence. His *Memoirs* is, perhaps, the most important prose work in Greek literature of the nineteenth

century. See *The Memoirs of General Makriyannis 1797-1864*, edited and translated by H. A. Lidderdale (London, 1966).

305 Virgil, *Aeneid.* ii. 55.

305 Makriyannis, *Memoirs,* II, 258.

307 African lilies. See "Stratis Thalassinos among the Agapanthi," page 279.

309 Aeschylus, *Agamemnon,* 179-80.

311 *Thrush* was the name of a naval transport sunk off the island of Poros during the Second World War; see Section III of the poem, page 327.

311 Plutarch, *Consolatio ad Apollonium,* 115 D.

313 This house, at the sea's edge on the island of Poros, for a while a hotel, was called Γαλήνη (Serenity). In his "A Letter on 'Thrush'" (see *Foreword,* fn. 5, p. 501). Seferis says: ". . . that Victorian house in Pompeian red gave me, for the first time in many years [i.e., the autumn of 1946], the feeling of a solid building rather than of a temporary tent."

315 Elpenor (see note to page 281) appears at this point, followed by Circe; they become the protagonists of Section II of the poem.

325 The term "Soulmonger" was suggested to the poet by the *Agamemnon,* 438: "Ares, the bodymonger."

327 See *Od.* xi. The voices referred to in this passage are those of the dead in Hades. "The old man" of line 18 is not Teiresias, however, but Socrates, as is indicated by lines 21 ff., which are based on the *Apology* (cf. XXVII, and Socrates' concluding statement).

327 Cf. *Od.* xi.

331 The "old suppliant" mentioned here is Oedipus; the "invisible fields" are those referred to in *Oedipus at Colonus,* 1,681.

331 The allusion is to the star Antares of the constellation Scorpio: *cor Scorpionis.*

333 See Hesiod, *Theogony,* 270ff. The Nereids, daughters of Nereus and Doris, were nymphs living at the bottom of the sea, reputedly propitious to sailors—especially to the Argonauts. The Graeae, children of Phorcys and Ceto, were also reputed to be sea-nymphs: divinities of the white foam seen on waves, grey-haired from birth. The "rising goddess" of the following verse is, of course, Aphrodite.

333 The line recalls the refrain of the *Pervigilium Veneris*: "cras amet qui numquam amauit, quiqui amauit cras amet."

333 See the *Erotokritos,* Book I, 1,365.

335 With the exception of "Memory I" and "Memory II," the poems in this volume were written in Cyprus during the

poet's visit there in the fall of 1953. See the poet's note to the first edition.

335 The quotation is from Euripides' *Helen,* where Teucer speaks of "sea-girt Cyprus, where it was decreed by Apollo that I should live, giving the city the name of Salamis in memory of my island home" (ll. 148-50). The quotation appears again in the epigraph to "Helen," p. 349.

337 Agianapa (sometimes spelled Agia Napa) is a village near the sea to the south of Famagusta, Cyprus.

341 In a note, the poet says: "Gourds which are used as jugs. The decoration of these gourds is among the more interesting folk arts of Cyprus: ornamental designs, figures of heroes, either actual or satirical. Only old men were able to give me information about this dying art." In this instance, the ornamental figures are representations of the damned as they appear in church frescoes of the Second Coming (see Savidis, *Γιὰ τὸν Σεφέρη*).

341 "Alakatin" is the colloquial term for the well-wheel mentioned here.

345 See Herodotus, I, 199: "When a woman has once taken her place there, she does not go home before some stranger has thrown money into her lap and has had intercourse with her outside the temple; but as he throws the money, he must say: 'I summon you in the name of the goddess Mylitta' (that is, the Assyrian name for Aphrodite) . . . . There is a custom like this in some parts of Cyprus."

349 Euripides' play assumes that not Helen herself but a phantom of Helen went with Paris to Troy. Helen herself was carried by Hermes to the Egyptian court of Proteus, where she was eventually reunited with her husband Menelaus long after the end of the Trojan war.

349 Platres is a summer resort on the slopes of Mt. Troödos in Cyprus.

353 The phrase is taken from a fresco in a countryside church at Asinou in Cyprus.

357 Revelations, 21, 1.

361 *Paradiso,* XIX, 146-47. The allusion in Dante is to Henri II de Lusignan, king of Cyprus and Jerusalem from 1285 to 1324, regarded by Dante as one of the more lawless and perverse monarchs of Christendom. The poem has to do with Pierre I de Lusignan, king of Cyprus and Jerusalem from 1359-1369. See the note that follows.

361 The relevant historical background to this poem can be found in R. M. Dawkins' translation and edition of Leontios

Makhairas' *Recital concerning the Sweet Land of Cyprus entitled 'Chronicle'* (Oxford, 1932), I, 215-69 (pars. 234-81).

365 A "Turkopolier" was the commander of the "Turkopoles" (literally "descendants of the Turks"), indigenous troops of Turkish or Arabic origin employed by the crusaders as light cavalry. The "Turkopolier" was always a Frank.

367 The translation is by R. M. Dawkins, *op.cit.*, I, 445. This work is in large part the source for the various historical allusions that appear in the poem.

369 See Dawkins, *op.cit.*, I, 595ff. (pars. 599-611) and Savidis, Γιὰ τὸν Σεφέρη, p. 84. The specific reference is as follows: "And after he was crowned, King James sent to the castle [of Buffaneto near the village of Koutsovendi] and they cut off their heads [i.e., of Perot and Wilmot Montolif]; they put them into a chest and set them on a mule, and brought them to Cava: and the mule died, and there they buried them."

371 The Bacchae were women inspired to ecstatic frenzy by Dionysus. It was concerning them that Euripides wrote his play of that title.

373 See Heracleitos, Diels, *Die Fragmente der Vorsokratiker*, B 15.

377 Aeschylus, *The Persians*, 894-96. The lines are spoken by the chorus as they recall the extent and power of the Persian Empire under Darius, and lament the disaster inflicted by the Persian defeat at the battle of Salamis.

377 From Psalm XXVIII (Septuagint).

379 Aeschylus, *The Persians*, 447. From a speech in which the Messenger describes the destruction of the Persian fleet at Salamis.

381 In a note the poet refers to the wartime prayer of Commander Lord Hugh Beresford, R. N., who fell in the battle of Crete: "O God our loving Father . . . Help us to keep in mind the real causes of war: dishonesty, greed, selfishness, and lack of love, and to drive them out of this ship, so that she may be a pattern of the new world for which we are fighting. . . ."

383 Euripides is said to have been killed by hunting dogs while staying at the court of Archelaus, king of Macedonia.

385 Engomi is a village to the northwest of Famagusta, Cyprus.

387 Compare lines 21-37 of this poem with the following passage, relating to the Virgin's birth of Christ, in "The Book of James, or Protevangelium," XVIII, 2, of *The Apocryphal New Testament*, trans. Montague Rhodes James:

> Now I Joseph was walking, and I walked not. And I looked up to the air and saw the air in amazement. And I looked up unto the pole of the heaven and saw it standing still, and the fowls of the heaven without motion. And I looked

upon the earth and saw a dish set, and workmen lying *by it* and their hands were in the dish: and they that were chewing chewed not, and they that were lifting *the food* lifted it not, and they that put it to their mouth put it not thereto, but the faces of all of them were looking upward. And behold there were sheep being driven, and they went not forward but stood still; and the shepherd lifted his hand to smite them with his staff, and his hand remained up. And I looked upon the stream of the river and saw the mouths of the kids upon *the water* and they drank not. And of a sudden all things moved onward in their course.

The "ploughman" appeared as a shepherd in the 1st edn. of the poem.

391 This section includes all but three of Seferis's early rhymed poems and all but two of the eight rhymed poems that he published after *Mythistorema* (1935). These poems are tightly rhymed in the original; some make use of traditional forms and rhythms, including the "dekapentasyllavos" (see *Foreword,* p. v), while others (for example, *The Cistern*) contain intricate internal rhymes and verbal configurations. We have not aspired to any sort of close formal approximation of these poems in order to limit the distortion that such translation would involve; their inclusion in this appendix is, in any case, a tacit admission that our versions, compared to the originals, are little more than bones from which the flesh has disappeared. Indeed, we have omitted the three early poems ("Σχόλια," "Εἰς μνήμην," and "Δημοτικὸ τραγούδι") because they did not seem to us to come over into English adequately enough to justify their inclusion at all. We have omitted one late rhymed poem ("Νεόφυτος ὁ ἔγκλειστος μιλᾶ") for similar reasons, and we have kept another ("The Jasmin") in its original position since in this instance we have offered a formal equivalent.

395 Book III, 1,277-78. See note to p. 85.

397 The Hydra was a poisonous water snake with nine heads that merely grew in number when severed—unless cauterized, as Heracles proved in destroying it; also, a southern constellation represented as a snake on maps of the heavens.

407 Homer, *Od.* i. 8-9.

409 A phrase from a song popular in the 1920's.

413 From *A Narrative of A. Gordon Pym,* Chap. 10.

423 *Pythian Odes,* 3, 21-23.

427 The image is from the *Erotokritos* (see note to page 85), as are several others in the poem.

435 Domenikos Theotokopoulos, born in Crete probably in 1541, is better known as El Greco, painter, architect, and sculptor

He first studied in Venice, and later settled in Toledo, Spain, where he died in 1614. The inscription cited was written by El Greco himself on the plan of Toledo in his picture "View and Plan of Toledo" (painted *ca.* 1609 and now in the Greco Museum at Toledo).

443 In the ritual for Good Friday in the Orthodox Church, the entombment of Christ is re-enacted by carrying around the church, and the village or the district in which the church is situated, an image of Christ lying as though dead. This image is usually embroidered on a piece of material and the procession is known as the epitaphios procession.

459 In 1156 Renaud de Châtillon, a French adventurer who had married Constance, Princess of Antioch, in 1153, invaded Cyprus. After carrying off what gold, silver, and valuable vestments he could, he drove the inhabitants down to the shore, and they were set free only after they had paid a huge indemnity. Hostages taken from the leading clergy and lay people were held captive until the ransom was paid. See Steven Runciman, *A History of the Crusades* (Cambridge, 1952), II, 348.

471 Christodoros was a poet from Egyptian Thebes, living in the reign of the Byzantine emperor Anastasios I (A.D. 491-518). His *Description* (Ἔκφρασις) is an epic describing eighty statues in the gymnasium known as Zeuxippos in Constantinople. See the *Palatine Anthology*, Book II: the description of the statue of Hermaphroditus.

BIOGRAPHICAL DATA

The following data are based largely on G. P. Savidis, "*Σχεδίασμα Χρονολογίας τοῦ Γιώργου Σεφέρη*," *Ἐποχές*, Vol. VIII (December 1963).

1900. Born on February 29, in Smyrna.

1914. Moved with his family from Smyrna to Athens, where he received his secondary education.

1918-24. Studied in Paris, where he earned a degree in law.

1924-25. First visit to London.

1926. Appointed to the Greek Ministry of Foreign Affairs. Served in Athens until 1931.

1931-34. Served in the Greek Consulate in London.

1934-36. Resident in Athens.

1936-38. Consul in Koritsa, Albania.

1938. Appointed press officer to the Department of Press and Information.

1941. Married Maria Zannou. Accompanied the Greek government in exile to Crete, Egypt, and finally South Africa, where he served in the Greek Embassy at Pretoria until 1942.

1942-44. Press officer to the Greek government in Cairo.

1944. Accompanied the Greek government to Italy.

1945-46. Director of the Political Bureau of the Regent Archbishop Damaskinos.

1946-48. Ministry of Foreign Affairs, Athens.

1948-50. Counsellor of Embassy in Ankara, Turkey.

1951-52. Counsellor of Embassy in London.

1953-56. Served as Ambassador to Lebanon, Syria, Jordan, and Iraq. In 1953, 1954, and 1955, he visited Cyprus.

1956-57. Director of the Second Political Bureau of the Ministry of Foreign Affairs, Athens.

1957. Member of the Greek delegation to the United Nations, New York, during the discussion of the Cyprus question.

1957-62. Ambassador to Great Britain.

1960. Hon. D. Litt. (Cantab).

1962. Foyle Award.

1962. Retired from the diplomatic service, settled in Athens.

1963. Nobel Prize for Literature.
1964. Hon. D. Litt. (Oxon).
1964. Hon. D. Philosophy (Salonika).
1965. Hon. D. Litt. (Princeton).
1966. Elected Honorary Foreign Member, American Academy of Arts and Sciences.
1966. Appointed Honorary Fellow, Modern Language Association.